TEACHING
WRITING
Creatively

TEACHING WRITING
Creatively

Edited by David Starkey

Boynton/Cook Publishers
HEINEMANN
Portsmouth, NH

Boynton/Cook Publishers, Inc.
A subsidiary of Reed Elsevier Inc.
361 Hanover Street
Portsmouth, NH 03801–3912

Offices and agents throughout the world

The author and publisher wish to thank those who have generously given permission to reprint borrowed material:

" 'What's the Use of Stories that Aren't True?' A Composition Teacher Reads Creative Writing" by Kate Ronald was originally published in *Carolina English Teacher* (1995/1996). Reprinted by permission of the South Carolina Council of Teachers of English.

Excerpts from *The Triggering Town* by Richard Hugo. Copyright © 1979. Published by W. W. Norton & Company. Reprinted by permission of the Publisher.

Excerpt from "Baudelaire Series" by Michael Palmer. Copyright © 1987 by Michael Palmer. Reprinted by permission of the Author.

"Responding to Creative Writing: Students-as-Teachers and the Executive Summary" by Wendy Bishop was originally published in *Carolina English Teacher* (1995/1996). Reprinted by permission of the South Carolina Council of Teachers of English.

Library of Congress Cataloging-in-Publication Data
Teaching writing creatively / edited by David Starkey.
    p.   cm.
  Includes bibliographical references.
  ISBN 0-86709-432-X
    1. English language—Rhetoric—Study and teaching.   2. Creative writing—Study and teaching.   3. Report writing—Study and teaching.
  I. Starkey, David, 1962–   .
  PE1404.T399   1998
  808'.042'07—dc21   97-40635
                                                                        CIP

Editor: Peter R. Stillman
Production: Elizabeth Valway
Cover design: Joni Doherty
Manufacturing: Louise Richardson

Printed in the United States of America on acid-free paper

02 01 00 99 98   DA   1 2 3 4 5

For My Parents,
Betty and Frank Starkey

Contents

Acknowledgments

Like all editors, I have many people to thank. I'm especially grateful to my former colleagues at Francis Marion University. I spent many productive hours in conversation with Ken Autrey, Phil Gardner, Lynn Kostoff, Pamela Rooks, John Tassoni, Gail Tayko, and others. My department chair, Bob Parham, gave me the opportunity to find out firsthand what it means to try to teach writing creatively. Warren and Holly Westcott were kind enough to allow me to guest edit the 1995/96 special issue of *Carolina English Teacher,* in which Kate Ronald's and Wendy Bishop's articles first appeared; I'm obliged to the Westcotts and to the members of the South Carolina Council of Teachers of English. I'm also grateful to Wendy Bishop, my long-distance mentor and friend, who encouraged me to pursue publication of this book, and to Peter Stillman, who helped me resee and reshape the collection in important ways. Above all, I am indebted to my wife, Melodie; without her sound judgment, technical support, and friendship, *Teaching Writing Creatively* would never have been completed.

Introduction

A Polycultural Model for Teaching Writing

David Starkey

North Central College

Picture this: early evening, a cornfield in eastern Iowa at the end of August. A warm breeze whispers in from the west, thrumming the tassels and rustling the dark green leaves. A farmer, sitting in his pickup truck, wipes a hand across his soiled sweaty brow and looks out on his field, which follows a gentle upward slope until it vanishes at the horizon. Everywhere is corn: food for the country, food for the world.

This seems to be a quintessential American scene, yet environmentalists would tell us that something here is very wrong, for the farmer's cornfield is an extreme example of monoculture, a single crop planted over a vast area that disrupts a bioregion's natural ecology. As geneticist Wes Jackson (1994) points out, "Monoculture means that botanical and hence chemical diversity above ground is also absent. This invites epidemics of pathogens or epidemics of grazing by insect populations" (167). In response to the ecological and economic disasters that often accompany sustained monoculture, researchers such as Jackson have looked to an alternative they call *polyculture*. Basically, polyculture is the practice of growing several different crops in the same area, as opposed to vast stretches planted with a single species. Because of their deep and intricate root systems, which help collect nutrients and contribute to soil retention, native plants are allowed to live alongside those introduced by humans. Arguing that "species diversity breeds dependable chemistry," Jackson notes that insects and bacterial pathogens are better regulated if they are forced to spend their time and energy hunting for food

among the myriad forms of life in a polyculture (1994, 166). But the most
persuasive argument for polyculture is that—unlike our present system,
which relies on ever greater doses of fertilizers and pesticides—it is self-
sustaining. While the immediate payoff may be more modest, the long-term
gains of polyculture far exceed those of monoculture.

Any analogy is necessarily inexact, but for the reasons that follow, I
think it is fair to compare writing in the traditional composition classroom to
the monoculture of a large American farm. Likewise, there is a clear parallel between the sort of writing instruction discussed in *Teaching Writing
Creatively* and polyculture. While few college-level writing courses in the
1990s are likely to be as mechanistic, rule-bound, and hyperconscious of
genre as the "Current-Traditional" archetype held up to ridicule by James
Berlin, most composition classes are probably more conventional than those
who teach them might wish.

Monoculture does have certain advantages, of course. It wouldn't exist
otherwise. Crop output is predictable and productive. Harvesting can be
accomplished quickly and efficiently. Guesswork remains at a minimum.
Over the past century, monoculture has played an important role in making
America a world power. The history of Manifest Destiny is also the history
of "breaking" the prairie, of producing a harvest as abundant and reliable as
the natural world will allow. In the short term, monoculture still appears to
have clear advantages for agricultural interests intent on turning a profit.

Yet despite their apparent health, monocultures like the vast tract of corn
described earlier, as well as the far less fastidiously maintained single-crop
plantings in developing nations, are especially vulnerable to catastrophe. In
fact, the twentieth-century's reliance on monoculture has resulted in a loss of
genetic diversity that imperils food production around the world. *The New
York Times* reported that in a symposium sponsored by the Consultative
Group on International Agricultural Research, scientists agreed that "If the
erosion and deterioration of genetic resources continues . . . 'genetic options
for needed changes in agricultural production will be lost forever'" (Stevens
1991). The bounty, therefore, is temporary.

Writing teachers will have already noticed the similarities between
monoculture and the traditional composition classroom. Both are "safe," controlled environments where a clear goal is set: five hundred bushels an acre,
five essays in each of five predetermined "modes." Scheduled productivity
supersedes spontaneous growth. Boundaries are clearly marked and rigor-
ously enforced. The front forty acres grow only a genetically engineered
variety of winter wheat; the back forty is planted with a high-yield strain of
soybean. The analysis essay shall be no less than two thousand words with
ten critical sources and no personal narrative, due on April 30. All late papers
will receive an "F."

However, as farmers and teachers drawing on a monocultural model both
know, the appearance of endless, mathematically predictable productivity is

illusory. The crop bred for rapid growth and treated frequently with chemicals thrives in eastern Iowa but fails miserably elsewhere. Similarly, essays written only to meet the requirements of English 101 or 202 wither outside those environments. Writing that severely limits form and content and that blindly obeys artificially constructed boundaries is no more inevitable than an irrigation ditch or a county road. The five paragraph theme is the most notorious example of an artificial enclosure, but there are many others. Most instructors need only look at their latest stack of essays to confirm that the ordinary and predictable, alas, still reign in college English.

Granted, both monoculturalists and traditional composition teachers have developed sophisticated hybrids, and both routinely rotate their crops. But diversity is hardly the goal. The profit-minded agronomist and the traditional teacher are merely reacting to forces—plant diseases and swarming insects on the one hand, bored students and skeptical colleagues on the other—that have the potential for calamity. Traditional farmers and traditional teachers introduce the least amount of change that is viable, and the goal of each remains to produce a very specific, marketable commodity. "This is an era of specialists," Rachel Carson ([1962] 1987) lamented in the early 1960s, "each of whom sees his own problem and is unaware of or intolerant of the larger frame into which it fits" (349). The problem continues, in both environmental thinking and classroom pedagogy, today.

Certainly, from an economic standpoint the problems of polyculture are obvious. Because it is a complex system, polyculture makes for a troublesome harvest. Farming must be done on a smaller scale and may well take the form of modest patches of tillage alternating with uncultivated areas. Native plants and animals in a healthy ecosystem often require tracts of land that are larger than many farmers are willing to concede. Moreover, there is a kind of controlled anarchy inherent in polyculture that monoculturalists, raised with the belief that nature exists chiefly to be tamed, can't help but find repulsive.

Ultimately, however, the benefits of polyculture for the planet as a whole far outweigh the inconveniences. Polyculture is necessary for biodiversity, which in turn is necessary for the continuation of life. Polycultures are based on perennial plants, while monocultures are composed of annuals, which bloom only once, then die. Severe weather, fires, and insect or disease invasions will destroy a crop of annuals, but perennials, because of their well-established root systems, can bounce back from catastrophe with the coming of another spring. As Jackson notes, a "truly sustainable agriculture [must be] based on the polyculture of perennials. This would be an agriculture in which soil erosion is so small that it is detectable only by the most sophisticated equipment, an agriculture that is chemical-free or nearly so, and certainly an agriculture that is scarcely demanding of fossil fuel" (1994, 168). Monoculture benefits only itself (and the agri-business responsible for it), but each organism in a polyculture is likely to have symbiotic relationships with many other organisms in the ecosystem.

Again, instructors will be struck by the correspondence between this sort of farming and teaching writing creatively. Just as polyculture is finally the healthiest, most vigorous type of ecosystem, so teaching writing in innovative ways is inevitably healthier for students and teachers than approaching the activity from a traditional vantage. In polyculture, plants suited to a particular environment flourish; those that are unsuited perish. The ultimately detrimental chemical wizardry of monoculture is absent. In a class where writing is taught creatively, there is a similar value placed on what is native to a particular soil. Invasive exotics such as grammar drills and unimaginative prompts are kept in check by diverse writing assignments and by the diversity of students' own lives.

We know that plants in the wild don't really grow in evenly spaced rows on rectangular parcels of land. Neither, of course, does honest, thoughtful writing suddenly appear in neatly outlined themes. The traditional English 101 class—with its formulaic, tedious assignments—is like the monocultural crop of annuals: the writing done therein has its brief season, is harvested, then vanishes forever from the landscape. In contrast, a writing class that values complex, multi-modal writing is like a perennial polyculture: it blooms season after season and can withstand drought, flood, and periodic neglect. This is writing in touch with what Natalie Goldberg (1990) calls "wild mind." Since students who possess a range of invention and revision strategies can succeed in a variety of writing environments—both professional and academic—articles such as those included in this book will help teachers to inculcate skills that remain intact long after an expository writing class is over. If the root system is entrenched, what happens on any given day above ground is relatively unimportant.

Teaching Writing Creatively includes new work by a number of important polycultural teacher-theorists who, over the years, have actively cross-pollinated areas of writing that had once been isolated from each other. Yet the ideas of two extraordinary writers who are not contributors to the book—Donald Murray and Peter Elbow—should also be acknowledged. Both men have transgressed against conventional notions of style, voice, and genre. Both believe that in an important sense, as Murray (1995) argues, "all effective writing is autobiographical" (11). Both have dared to experiment.

Perhaps their influence will make some teachers nervous. After all, expressivists are generally out of favor in rhetoric and composition graduate programs, and the murky, still largely ill-defined world of creative writing may seem theoretically defective, even if many teachers secretly feel there is something important to be gained by traveling in its unsanctioned territory. Possibly the anxiety we feel about "creative" writing instruction stems from our knowledge that teaching composition in a departmentally or institutionally unapproved way may be, as Susan Hunter (1993) cautions, "hazardous to your academic health" (73). And in the minds of many compositionists, incorporating any form of creative writing into the curriculum of an expository writing course "softens" the class in unacceptable ways. Jane Tompkins (1988) indicates something of the conflict academic writers feel between the voice of the logical thinker and the voice that values affective discourse, which wants to "write about her feelings." The problem, as Tompkins sees it, is that "you can't talk about your private life in the course of doing your professional work" (169).

Contributors to *Teaching Writing Creatively* would disagree.

They are not alone, of course. Increasingly, composition teachers resist being characterized by their counterparts in literature as dull, inconsequential thinkers and writers—the drudges of the English department. Instead, they realize that teaching writing need not be a workaday pursuit. They are likely to share the conviction of contributors to this volume that students should have a stake in the writing they do, and that student and teacher writing problems are often very similar. Teachers like these value playful, passionate writing as much as writing that claims to be objective. They admire innovative form and alternate style. They cherish honesty.

Teaching Writing Creatively begins with articles that assert that all good writing must be, in some important sense, "creative." Kate Ronald's "'What's the Use of Stories That Aren't True?' A Composition Teacher Reads Creative Writing" describes the transformation of her upper-division Composition Theory and Practice class from a standard course in writing pedagogy to an environment that encourages poetry and fiction, where form is less important than students' interest in the forming power of their own ideas and language. John Tassoni recounts his own less successful attempts to "deconcise" college composition and creative writing, finding that the "Dia-Logs" that formed the centerpiece of his "course in crisis" were ultimately a productive way to discover just how he and his students go about the process of making meaning. In "Reclaiming 'Creativity' for Composition," George Karnezis describes the weight and placement of the word *creative* as encountered by a rhetor and writing program director; Karnezis contends that the institutional and ordinary public use of this term encourages an exclusive and narrow application, one that ignores the creative aspects of well-written nonfiction prose. Will Hochman's "The Legacy of Richard Hugo in the Composition Classroom" resees *The Triggering Town,* a collection of the poet's essays, as an unacknowledged yet seminal expressivist text, one that demonstrates that good student writing is only marginally about genre. And Hephzibah Roskelly's "Broken Circles and Curious Triangles: Rethinking the Writer's Workshop" draws on ideas by Ann Berthoff and Louise Rosenblatt to critique the creative writing workshop as a model for the composition class.

Section 2 includes a variety of ways to approach the teaching of writing as a creative endeavor, beginning with several articles that show how to help students better understand their own writing processes. Muriel Harris makes use of the Myers-Briggs Type Indicator (MBTI), a method of evaluating personality, to invite students to investigate their writing worlds and the commonalities among writers. Michael Steinberg's "Self-Discovery to Self-Examination: Teaching the Personal Essay as Inquiry" demonstrates that student essays can go beyond the narcissistic "I" to a deeper self-examination or self-reflection. Steinberg describes a number of guided writing exercises that use the narrative "I" as a wedge to delve into the self before moving outward to larger issues. In his chapter "The Degrees of the Lie," John Boe discusses eight common writing lies and concludes that "the first principle of just teaching and just writing is just telling the truth."

The next three chapters focus on alternative composing strategies and their possible classroom applications. Transforming what Winston Weathers calls "crots" into a related form he calls the "snapshot essay," Toby Fulwiler recommends how best to use these short prose stanzas, which are typically fifty to one hundred words and which each tell separate but related stories. Because they demand high reader engagement, Fulwiler contends, snapshots make readers forge their own transitions, generate their own inferences, and write their own conclusions. Sheryl Fontaine and Francie Quaas's chapter on collage essays describes a cousin of the snapshot essay, though one that relies on a multiplicity of authorial voices. According to Fontaine and Quaas, the collage essayist is like a photographer who combines photos taken over a long period of time and in various settings to create a startling new work. My own "'Habits of Opposite and Alcove': Language Poetry in the Composition Class" continues this inquiry into what might be called "postmodern" writing. I explore avant garde poetry, with its illogical semantics and "apocalyptic syntax," and consider how students might incorporate this discourse into what we normally consider successful college composition.

Art Young's "Beginnings: Voice, Creativity, and the Critical Essay" moves the discussion from twentieth-century to eighteenth-century literature and looks at the impact of using the entire range of the expressive-poetic-transactional continuum in developing students' writing abilities. Focusing on a composition class in which students read William Blake's "Songs of Innocence" and "Songs of Experience," Young discusses a unit that developed options for writing the critical essay—options that included choices in personal voice, in constructing an audience, and in mixing genres. The last chapter in Section 2, Alys Culhane's "One, Two, Three, Testing," takes a fresh look at taped response to student essays; Culhane explains the numerous ways she uses audiotapes to integrate written and verbal feedback on students' work in progress.

The book concludes with four chapters focusing on what we have traditionally called "creative writing," though composition teachers may well find that the ideas represented here can be applied successfully to expository writing courses. Patrick Bizarro's "Triadic Approach to Understanding the

Development of Literary Values in Students" uses Ann Berthoff's concept of "Triadicity" to help students reflect on their values as writers and readers of literature. Hans Ostrom's " 'Carom Shots': Reconceptualizing Imitation and Its Uses in Creative Writing Courses" considers experimental ways of using imitation, focusing on a technique called "carom shots" or "microstories," which complicate and enrich student reading and writing. In "My Other, My Self: Participants and Spectators in Introductory Fiction Writing Workshops," Lee Martin uses James Britton's distinction between the "participant" and "spectator" in communication acts to help his students identify significant autobiographical moments in their short fiction. His emphasis on critical thinking about the creative process allows students who are unlikely to become professional writers to nevertheless examine the choices they have made as both participants and spectators in their own lives. Finally, Wendy Bishop shows how she responds to and evaluates student poems to help students in her courses read and revise their own and others' work with more pleasure and insight. For Bishop, broadening response options through student-as-teacher and executive summary activities encourages writer autonomy, authority, and ownership of a text, while dismantling the notion of an "official" teacher who "invents" each student writer.

To return one last time to the vehicle of our dominant metaphor, let us imagine an alternative to the agri-business megafarm: an upland plover skims over a meadow of needlegrass, switchgrass, and big bluestem. A black-tailed prairie dog wriggles its nose and vanishes into its burrow. A farmer, sitting in his pickup truck, wipes a hand across his soiled sweaty brow and looks out on the prairie surrounding his twenty acres of creek bottomland, which is supporting oats, barley, rye, wheat, and corn. In a small movable pen next to the vegetable garden, a dozen feeder pigs are lounging in the early evening sun. The windmill creaks as it catches a warm western breeze.

And consider this alternative to the traditional writing classroom: students begin the course by addressing their own resistance and attraction to "creative" writing in the composition class. They are then given choices about what and how to write that at first seem unimaginably liberating: narrative, collage, imitation, collaboration, even fiction and poetry. Their teachers, themselves writers, participate in the creativity and experimentation. Writing assignments seem dangerously "fun," yet despite all this freedom, students are continually evaluating their own motivation for writing and questioning the honesty with which they write. When the term is over, writing remains a central part of their lives. Years afterward, perhaps, a former student tells her teacher how crucial the course was in her education. The teacher, naturally, smiles.

Is this vision of polyculture (drawn in part from Wes Jackson's (1980) *New Roots for Agriculture*) slightly utopian? Yes. Is it impossible? Not at all.

And, though at times it may strain against institutional and departmental restrictions—and in the process surprise and frustrate both teachers and students—teaching writing creatively holds the same promise of hearty sustainability. This volume, composed as it is of the varied opinions of seventeen writer-teachers, makes no claims for finality. It does, however, offer potential direction for those who want to make their classes environments where student writing, of all varieties, will flourish.

Works Cited

Berlin, James. 1982. "Contemporary Composition: The Major Pedagogical Theories." *College English* 44: 765–77.

Carson, Rachel. [1962] 1987. *Silent Spring*. Boston: Houghton Mifflin.

Goldberg, Natalie. 1990. *Wild Mind: Living the Writer's Life*. New York: Bantam.

Hunter, Susan. 1993. "The Dangers of Teaching Differently." In *Writing Ourselves into the Story: Unheard Voices from Composition Studies*, eds. Sheryl I. Fontaine and Susan Hunter, 70–85. Carbondale, IL: Southern Illinois University Press.

Jackson, Wes. 1980. *New Roots for Agriculture*. San Francisco: Friends of the Earth.

————. 1994. "Living Nets in a New Prairie Sea." In *Writing the Environment*, ed. Melissa Walker. 165–68. New York: Norton.

Jackson, Wes, and Marty Bender. 1984. "Investigations into Perennial Polyculture." In *Meeting the Expectations of the Land: Essays in Sustainable Agriculture and Stewardship*, eds. Wes Jackson, Wendell Berry, and Bruce Colman, 183–94. San Francisco: North Point.

Murray, Donald. 1995. *The Craft of Revision*. 1991. Fort Worth, TX: Harcourt.

Stevens, William K. 1991. "Loss of Genetic Diversity Imperils Crop Advances." *New York Times* 25 June: C1.

Tompkins, Jane. 1988. "Me and My Shadow." *New Literary History* 19: 169–78.

1

"What's the Use of Stories That Aren't True?"
A Composition Teacher Reads Creative Writing

Kate Ronald
Miami University

Writing a poem was one of my goals for the semester. I may not be a poet, but I won't be afraid to try this again.

—Margaret, final portfolio,
10 December 1994

I fear [Haroun] is too much like the folks of this foolish valley—crazy for make believe.

—Salman Rushdie, *Haroun and the Sea of Stories*

Salman Rushdie's first publication after *The Satanic Verses*—and the resulting death threat imposed on him by the ayatollah in Iran—was *Haroun and the Sea of Stories*, a fantasy novel centered around the question, "What's the use of stories that aren't true?" In this novel, a young boy journeys from his own land where "sadness was actually manufactured" in mighty factories, across the Ocean of the Streams of Stories in order to restore the gift of storytelling to his father. In the process, he saves the Streams of Stories, threatened with pollution by the Chupwallas (quiet ones); in fact, he saves the Chupwallas and his own people of Gup (the gossips), too. As in all good fairy tales, Haroun saves the whole day, the whole world. How? Through stories. Rushdie's latest novel becomes an answer to its initial question: the use of stories that aren't true is that they make things happen in the world and they keep people together in communities. In J. L. Austin's sense, stories that aren't true are "performative," changing both tellers and hearers as they are created, revised, retold, remembered. Rushdie's novel is, of course, an allegorical answer to the madmen who are so threatened by his earlier "stories"; it is also a defense and a celebration of the sanity of being "crazy for make believe."

In this article, I'd like to ask Rushdie's question in a different context. What's the use of stories that aren't true in a composition classroom, a class traditionally devoted to expository writing—to essays that argue, describe, explain, and sometimes, but not primarily, narrate? In composition classes, students traditionally read and write what's "true," using facts, observation, and details from "real life" or from texts to advance and support their meaning and their purposes. I would argue, however, that in composition classes we've always encouraged students if not to "lie" then certainly to stretch the "truth" in their expository writing; composition teachers, like all English teachers and the folks in Rushdie's valley, are also "crazy for make believe." But first, I want to talk about why, over the last several years, I've not worried so much about generic distinctions between expository writing and stories in the first place.

Perhaps I should begin also by saying that I am a composition specialist, trained in a composition (not a literature) Ph.D. program, working in a large and highly specialized English department. I do not, primarily, teach literature courses or literary texts, although reading good writing, including literature, is a part of every course I teach. Perhaps I should also admit that, except for the occasional verse in honor of my mother and children, I am not a creative writer. But I do write a lot, every day, every week. I would like to think that much of my work is "creative," that at least some of it provides the kind of pleasure I associate with reading stories, novels, and poems. And I came into this profession largely because I was also crazy for stories.

Besides, I don't want to get defensive here: although, as Joseph Moxley (1990) says, the "walls" between composition and "creative" writing are "not easily scaled," it's also commonplace for discussions like this one to begin with axiomatic statements about how "all writing is creative," and how distinctions between fiction and nonfiction, for example, are arbitrary. That's more true in some places than in others; in the middle and secondary school writing classes described by Lucy Calkins (1983), Nancie Atwell (1987), and Linda Rief (1992), students are encouraged to write, without regard to genre. The writing itself is the point. But higher up in the educational systems, the more specialized and categorized our thinking about writing becomes—and genres of reading, as well as genres of writing, are divided into separate areas of study—as Moxley says, the walls between creative, critical, and composition writing are high.

This article is about facing the walls between creative writing and composition, and rather than scaling them, taking the long way around, with a different destination in mind. I want to describe here how I came to learn that the generic distinctions among essay, poem, and story are indeed real, and useful, but also how I learned to blur, even ignore, those distinctions in order to help my students write more confidently and creatively, in whatever genre. This chapter is primarily about learning to respond to students' writing, to think and to read across boundaries, to adapt to my students' own reasons for writing rather than my own.

My goals as a writing teacher have shifted, to put it simply, from a focus on texts that my students write toward the students-as-writers. That does not mean that I ignore quality of student writing: but it does mean that I am least interested in the genre of that writing. It means more to me, for example, that Margaret, quoted in the first epigraph, will write another poem than if she had written ten well-organized essays that she would never return to again.

The Writing Workshop:
Students Choose Their Own Stories

I picked this story because it's the first thing that I started for me, not because I had to write it for a class.
—John, final portfolio

"Where do stories come from? [Haroun asked his father]. "From the great Story Sea," he'd reply. "I drink the warm Story Waters and then I feel full of steam. . . . It comes out of an invisible Tap installed by one of the Water Genies. You have to be a subscriber."
—Rushdie, 1990

John's excerpt, from a final portfolio of writing, reflects one of the most important principles of my teaching, that of choice. John "picked" the story he's referring to as part of his final portfolio section entitled "Best Edited Writing." This principle of choice, and its attendant responsibility for one's own writing, has become a central feature of all my writing classes. Several years ago, I changed my composition classes to composition workshops. I believe, with Berthoff (1981), that naming is a powerful act of mind, and the title "workshop" marks a tremendous change in focus for my students, their work, and mine.

Teachers like Lucy Calkins, Nancie Atwell, and Linda Rief have taught me the basic principles of writing workshops: (1) writers need time to write; (2) writers need to choose and be responsible for their own topics, forms, purposes for writing; (3) writers need responses to their writing in process; and (4) writers need opportunities to publish their writing for real readers. I won't dwell on each of these principles; the second one, about choice and responsibility, seems key to me, and it's resulted in this far-reaching change in my writing classes: I no longer assign topics, forms, or reasons for writing to my students. I do all that I can to help them figure out what they want and need to write about. Through many, many invention activities, and, through responses to drafts from me and other writers, students also have opportunities to discover and experiment with the forms of their ideas. Berthoff tells me that learning, first of all, is a "disposition to form structures," and that teaching composition

> by arbitrarily setting topics and then concentrating on the mechanics of expression does not guarantee that students will learn to write competently, and it certainly does not encourage the discovery of language either as an instrument of knowing or as our chief means of shaping and communicating ideas and experience. (19)

In my workshop, then, students start the process of discovery and knowing by choosing their own topics and forms for writing.

And given a choice, many of my students choose to write fiction or poetry, two genres I regularly banned from my composition classes for years, telling students that our department has courses and professors devoted exclusively to fiction and poetry and that's where they belonged if they wanted to write in those genres. *Mine* was a composition course in expository writing. However, as one decision leads to another, and as walls once cracked do come tumbling down, I began to realize how very silly, arbitrary, and controlling my prohibition on creative writing was. If I change my focus from the writing to the writer, from text to author, I find that genre does not matter as much as I once thought it did. If my goal in a composition course is to help students find reasons to write, to see the place of writing in their lives, both personally and professionally, then I find that genre becomes much less important. Instead of my having an Ideal Text in mind as students write, and measuring their papers against that standard, I now respond more like a reader, giving myself over to the writer's Ideal Text, letting the writer tell me what her goals are for a given draft at a given time in the course.

Changes lead to more changes, as any writer or teacher knows. When my students stopped writing according to my agendas, I realized that I could not read or respond to their texts in my old ways either.[1] Since I had not assigned the topic, the form, or the reason for writing, I did not have an easy, preset way into my students' drafts, a basis from which to respond, to tell them what I thought. I was reading in a vacuum and making vacuous comments. So now I insist that every draft be accompanied by an "author's note," in which students describe the genesis of the draft, their reasons for writing it, the effects they are aiming for, what they like best about the draft so far, what they like least, and what specific questions they would like a reader to answer or what specific parts they would like a reader to respond to, and why, and how. These authors' notes serve both writers and readers. For writers, they serve as a time and space from which to critically read, and reread, and plan; often I find that students figure out what's wrong, how to fix it, and where to go next in their author's note, making my job as responder one of simply reinforcing what they already know. For readers, authors' notes provide an entry to a draft, a way to begin to read, and a blueprint for response. Instead of responding to a student text as an exercise in meeting my standards, my notions of why they should be writing and what "college writing" should be, I must now respond to particular texts in terms of the particular questions the author has asked, in terms of the students' agendas. All of them are "subscribers" to the Streams of Stories; and my responsibility for reading locally mirrors my students' responsibility to tell me, in their authors' notes, what their stories mean to them, and what they want them to mean to a reader.

And yet, it's not always easy to respond to the variety of texts my students write each week. Sometimes I'm at a loss, and I admit I find myself mute more often in the front of poetry and fiction than essay, probably because I've been trained to read exposition critically and because I read fiction and poetry for pleasure. Sometimes I don't know what to say about a story that doesn't move me or a poem that I think is really pretty bad. Then I have to remember that the form is less important than the forming. The next section of this chapter will describe how I read and responded to three students in my 400-level composition theory and practice course last semester, a course in writing and writing theory for education majors in the semester before they begin their student teaching. My overall goal in this course is to create the kind of writing workshop I would like these future teachers to run in their own classrooms; therefore, our focus is on their own writing, and I'm less interested in what they write than in *that* they write; less interested in the form than that they recognize the forming power of their own ideas and language; less concerned that John, for example, write for an "academic," invisible audience than that he understand, find, and create his own readership.

Managing Responses: Does It Feel Like *Star Trek*?

> There is a little more pressure on myself, because this is getting into what I really want to write. So, I'm more worried about getting it right. Will it draw the reader in? Is the action effective, or does it drag? Does it feel like Star Trek?
>
> —John, author's note on draft

> Any story worth its salt can handle a little shaking up.
>
> —Rushdie, 1990

In his first journal entry to me, John told me that he wanted to be an author. A secondary education major, John loves to read but also wants to write, and write a lot:

I want to write, and feel compelled to do so. My goal is to become an author. However, so far, I haven't done much writing. I've read a few how-to books, and last semester I took a fiction writing class. My problem is motivational. I like to read and often do so when I could be writing. Staying current with what is being published is beneficial for an author wanna-be. (At least that sounds good; basically, I just like to read.) Then, again, I think part of the problem is time. It's hard to find the energy to be creative when one is: a husband, a student, working a part-time job, in the National Guard. I am planning to use the required writing assignments for this class as a good excuse to get some writing done. (John, Journal, 28 August 1994)

When John realized that the only "required writing assignments" were drafts due every other week, he immediately chose to write a *Star Trek* short story. ("I hope you are tolerant of science fiction," he told me in his next journal.) One of his goals is to write a *Star Trek* novel, and he wrote his story "To get used to writing in the Star Trek universe, as this is where my first novel will be set." (Journal, 28 September 1994). The first draft of this story began:

Captain's Log: Stardate 4419.5
    The U.S.S. Republic has arrived on station at the Klingon Neutral Zone. The Republic will spend the next month patrolling this area. All ship systems are functioning normally.
    Captain Willard R. Decker pressed the button that ended his log entry, and leaned back in the command chair. Things had been quiet along the Klingon Neutral Zone lately. However, Decker knew that was no reason to let his guard down. Command was a test, and the price of failure was all too often high.

Naturally, trouble soon surfaces in this quiet setting, and the story revolves around Captain Decker's command decisions as the *Republic* responds to a distress call inside the Neutral Zone, an attack by the Klingons, and Decker's decision to destroy his ship rather than be captured. At the end of the story, we find that this has been only a test, a simulation as part of Mr. Decker's training as a Star Fleet officer. Decker's "lesson" is that there's no fail-safe solution for real life.

In his author's note on the first draft, John told his readers that he "realizes this draft is very rough":

I know it needs a lot of work. In general, the story needs to be tightened up. I had originally planned to have Decker deal with his father's death, and the loss of his crew. After I finished this draft, I realized that these things don't happen to his father until six years after he graduates from the academy. So I am planning to change the emotional component of the story to Decker wanting to do well, so that his father will love him. But I haven't had time to add this element. I would appreciate any feedback about things that you thought work, and things you thought didn't. I plan to work on this part until I come to that mystical place where I decide that it's done. After that, I start work on my first book. (2 October 1994)

What struck me as I read this initial draft and author's note was the confidence John has both in his own story and in his ability to write. He was so sure of his character and the world in which this story is set. My initial response was encouraging. I told him that he had managed to capture the tone, setting, language, and action of *Star Trek* faithfully. (I watch *Star Trek*, and so I know this genre; another teacher would have had to ask more questions, I suspect.) I did tell him, though, that "given your new focus, should you back up in a few places early to let us see more of Decker, his life before this moment, especially his relationship with his father?" I also, on this first draft, cut a few words, an impulse I can rarely resist:

> Even though Decker knew that a constitution class starship was more powerful than a Klingon D-7 attack cruiser, three to one odds weren't good. ~~Still, it was their duty to try and rescue the damaged ship.~~ "Mr. Keller, target the lead ship. If they fire on us, I want you to make sure they regret it." Decker knew that their only hope of rescuing the Maru lay in ending this quickly, ~~before any more ships showed up.~~
>
> ~~"Aye, sir."~~
>
> Almost as if triggered by the captain's words, the Klingon ships fired on the *Republic*.

I wrote in the margin next to this paragraph: "I'm cutting the sentences that tell us what the details show us much more clearly." But mostly I responded as a reader, enjoying the action and John's ability to put me on the bridge of this Star Fleet vessel, in the middle of the action. I also asked for more background and details that would make John's stated theme clearer to me.

His next draft, now with the title "Final Exam" did not focus on Decker's relationship with his father, but more tightly on Decker's desire to succeed. In his author's note to this version, John asked about more technical aspects of storytelling: "Is the pacing effective? Is the ending satisfying—or to put it another way, are Decker's motives/actions believable?" I thought they were, given the limits of a short story and the universe of *Star Trek*, where everything is solved in less than an hour. There was one final line at the very end of the story that bothered me, that I didn't quite understand: after the "final exam," Decker's flight captain asks, "Do you want to retake the test?" and John writes, "For the first time Decker looked Pike in the eyes and said, 'That won't be necessary, sir.' They headed off towards the briefing room." Now, I knew what John was trying to convey here, that Decker has learned to accept his fallibility, but I just wasn't sure that these two lines were enough to show this change or why Pike would offer the option in the first place.

John never changed those lines, even though I wrote my questions about them next to every draft. That may seem stubborn, but it shows me quite a lot about John's reasons for writing, which extend beyond the class and my opinion, and his belief in his own sense of audience and purpose. I have to admit that I worried about the purposes of a *Star Trek* story in this class; at times I had trouble believing that working on this short story had much connection to the kind of writing that the academy values or to John's own classrooms down the road. However, John showed me the connection when he sent this draft off to several friends, also "trekkies," for the kind of specific feedback he needed. Here was a student, working as a writer, finding real readers and real purposes for writing; I realize that his *Star Trek* fiction and his insight into writing, and the teaching of writing, were indeed connected in ways that I would not have seen if I had remained focused on and fretful over genre.

Margaret showed me these connections perhaps more clearly than any other student last semester. She had been writing a variety of drafts—from an essay about teaching her nephew to write his name; a description of her grandfather sleeping that was really an argument about respect for old people and the pain of loss; and "The Valedictory Speech I Never Delivered," a scathing attack on the small-mindedness in her high school. But, on the last day of class, Margaret brought her favorite finished piece to class to show me and her small group. We ended up passing it around for everyone to see. It was a poem titled "Daddy's Girl," and she was giving it to her father as a Christmas present. In her cover letter to her final portfolio, Margaret described this poem:

> I have chosen to include in my "best pages" section my poem titled "Daddy's Girl." I have worked extremely hard on this poem to create my final product. My effort is evident when looking at the many drafts I have composed. Some of these drafts saw many significant changes, like line breaks. On other drafts, I changed only a few words. I do not consider myself an expert on poetry, but I do like this poem. (10 December 1994)

"Daddy's Girl" had begun as an essay, or at least as a prose poem. When I first saw this piece, it was a series of separate sentences, images of Margaret's father working on the car. It began: "Dad curved his hand around the plate of chrome and snapped the spring that released the hood." And on a separate line: "He looked over the mass of hoses and coils, which were covered with a layer of dust." The last "paragraph" read: "Finally he reached the hood again. He looked at me and said, 'Be good to my girl.' With that I pushed the silver door handle and left for school." Margaret's author's note on this first draft said:

This is a piece (I'm not sure it's a poem although I think I want it to be) I
wrote for my Dad. I got the idea for it when I went home and watched my
Dad check over my old school car. It was Dad's first car and mine, too, and
he treats it like it's a Rolls Royce. This is the piece I would like to put in
the class book. I have good, strong feelings about this one. I think the
reader can get a vivid picture of the car. Can you "see" the meaning here?
(18 October 1994)

Of course, I was thrilled by the "double meaning," the poignancy of "daddy's girl" as the car this man so lovingly touches and cares for as his daughter leaves for school. My first response on this draft was to tell Margaret that
she had a "great start," and that "I can see why this has such power for you."
My advice at this point was to "play around with the line breaks, making the
lines shorter and seeing what happens."

Over the next weeks, Margaret indeed played around with this poem,
making both subtle and substantive changes by rearranging the lines and
putting them together in different ways. Her "sentences" became stanzas:

Finally,
he reaches the hood again.
he looks at me and says,
"Be good to my girl."

I nod
and turn the key.
School starts
in ten minutes. (11 November 1994)

By the time she brought the finished poem to class, Margaret described her
work this way:

I think I have captured a few moments with my father before school well.
The line breaks seem to make these moments even more realistic for the
reader. As you and Lara [her group member] suggested, I experimented
with them to see what I liked and what I didn't. While I was experimenting, I discovered how the poem changed and formed with each break. I
think this was probably the most challenging piece I created this semester.
As I stated, earlier, I know little about poetry writing. However, I feel writing my own poem allowed me to learn about the art of writing poetry. I also
learned that, in writing poetry, all of the words must be carefully selected.
While it is also true in composing other drafts, poetry seems to have a more
delicate nature where each word is necessary and important.

Again, I'm pleased with Margaret's insights into the power of form here,
and especially the connections she makes between form in poetry and prose.
Because she chose this topic, and because she chose to write about her father

in a poem, a poem *to* her father, she learned much more about working as a writer, with a real audience and a real purpose, and her choices mattered to her.

My doubts about the propriety and the place of short stories and poetry in a composition class are partly resolved by what students like John and Margaret tell me about their learning. But I don't have only success stories to report, as my readers must suspect by now. I never knew quite what to say about rhymed, bouncy poems that "worked" but that seemed finished the minute they were written. I felt at a loss to help one writer of short stories who seemed so caught up in the world she was creating that she couldn't explain it to me, or to any reader. And a few times during this course, I steered writers away from short stories they were trying to write about people and issues very close to them; the distance, I felt, was masking their reasons for writing in the first place. Some of these students took my advice; some didn't. And the overall point is that perhaps my agenda as a reader isn't that important in the first place. "Shaking stories up" was the real work of this class, looking at them in different forms, for different purposes and audiences. Ted Lardner agues that "the languages of poetry and letters offer students avenues to make real sense of their experience" (101). I would agree, but I would add that it's the choice of form that offers the sense-making, more than the form itself.

What's the Use of Stories That Aren't True?

What's the use of stories that aren't true?

—Rushdie, 1990

I've wanted to do something on my Grampa because he's really special to me, but also because he makes a great story.

—Angie, author's note on draft,
20 October 1994

In this class of future teachers, two students, who were practicing fiction writers, wrote only stories all semester; and three students never ventured beyond the essay. But all the rest of the students in this class, and each of the writers whose work I've discussed so far, wrote a range of pieces, in a number of forms, over the course of the semester. I believe that part of the reason was the variety of work they were hearing from the other writers in the class, all a result of my requiring students to choose their own topics, forms, and purposes for their own writing. Angie was a poet, a real poet, who had published her work and who wrote every day. Her poetry was a true pleasure to read, but I felt quite superfluous at times as her reader; I behaved more as a fan than a critic. And although I did not encourage her to write anything besides the poetry I was enjoying so much, right after midterm she handed in a draft called "Grampa's Water," a descriptive essay, familiar to me as a composition teacher but a new step for Angie. In her author's note, she explained:

> I've had the idea for this piece for a few years now, although I wasn't quite sure how I'd string it together until recently. I want this to be a sincere but humorous piece about my Grampa and the way a fishing trip we had gave me lot to think about. Most of the story is true, though the situation is presented in a somewhat altered context. Some characters and time periods have been left out, for example, in order to keep it short and tight. What I'd like to know from you is simply, what do you think? Does it pull you in? The part I like best is the first section where I've been able to tighten it up a bit. I think the details are coming along pretty well here. The part I like the least is the second section. I like what I want to do, but not what I've done. The way this part is now I'm telling not showing. What suggestions do you have? Any ideas here would be great. I'm never quite sure how well I do with prose. (26 October 1994)

Angie had worked the first part of this essay like a poet, going over it word for word, tightening and condensing and making her grandfather live on the page. As usual, I simply raved. But in the second section, there was actually work for me to do as a reader: I said things like "You're moving too fast here," "This sentence is hard to get through." I crossed out phrases and said "This seems more stilted and wordy than you usually are." Through six drafts of "Grampa's Water," Angie and I wrote back and forth, examining the impact of specific words, moving scenes around, asking and answering questions of each other and the text, until she was satisfied enough to "publish" this essay in the class book. For example, next to "Fishing hadn't shown a better evening, though nothing had tugged our lines but the sun's reflection swimming on the water," I wrote, "'Shown' isn't the right word? Not very strong?" Angie's next version read, "We fished intently, though nothing tugged on our lines but the sun's reflection swimming on the water." We examined all her images of water, trying to connect and intensify their effect, from the lake itself, to the water jug the old man always carried, including images of rain, reflection, ripples, and the relentlessness of age. Her author's note on the last draft I read says:

> This is a polished version of "Grampa's Water." I'm glad that I've finally completed a piece that's been in my head for so long. While you're reading, I'd like for you to notice if the prose is engaging. Are there any parts left that lose you? contradict one another? weak spots? Did you like it enough to read it again? Does this give you what it promises at the beginning? Most important, does my intended theme come through strongly? It's hard for me to evaluate my prose because sometimes it seems to me like

poetry, and good poetry and prose are not the same things. (22 November 1994)

Writing a piece of prose nonfiction, then, was a major step for Angie. And this reversal, the idea of writing an essay as a stretch in a composition class, underscores my point about genre being perhaps the least important thing for teachers to consider in setting up writing courses. Yet she talks about this essay in language we usually reserve for fiction: the question "Did you like it enough to read it again?" reveals Angie's belief in the literary, aesthetic nature of this expository essay, and, I would argue, argues strongly for the effect of choice on a writer's confidence and belief in her own work. The question itself is an amazing act in a composition class in school. In the cover letter to her final portfolio, Angie described why writing an essay was, indeed, a creative act for her:

> At the beginning of the semester, I mentioned my intent to write different kinds of *pieces* on different kinds of *topics*. At first, I have to admit that I thought this was a very high goal to set, especially because I'm really pretty focused on writing poetry. Being around so many different kinds of people and their writing, though, helped me stay out of ruts and try new things. (10 December 1994)

The variety of writing that results from students choosing their own forms and topics, and the public reading and responding that are part of a writing workshop, then, often lead students to try forms that are new to them. The community of writers in a workshop challenges and sustains this kind of risk taking.

In the end, I'm not sure that the generic difference between creative and expository writing has ever mattered that much in terms of the way English teachers respond to student writing. Given our own love of reading literature, I suspect that we've always asked students to write the kinds of prose that give us pleasure in the first place. Our advice about "adding detail" and making ideas "more specific" seems tied more to our literary preferences than to any outside "standards" for expository writing.[2] Angie's "story" about her grandfather, for example, was "true," but through her own metaphoric language she made the story both more and less, as she heightened and condensed according to her own imagination, her own memory, and her own purposes. Her grandfather did, indeed, "make a good story," a story that became more real as the result of its telling.

And truth is not the issue anyway. Berthoff says:

> The emphasis on differentiating critical and creative writing, as if they were symptoms of different brain functions, has meant that we've lost the advantages that are there to be enjoyed if we concentrate instead on what they

have in common. . . . If we are to conceive of literacy as a facility in making meaning in reading and writing, we will need to understand the heuristic power of language itself. . . . Imagination must be rescued from the creativity corner and returned to the center of all that we do. (29)

If we think of the imagination in this way, then "true" and "untrue" stories blur into one another. The uses of stories that aren't true are many, and it's time we acknowledge their uses more fully in composition classes, especially if our purposes are to help writers develop and understand the uses of writing in their lives, rather than helping texts develop according to some predetermined notion of what they should look and sound like.

In *Haroun*, the story of the Ocean of the Streams of Stories in fact saves stories for the world. Haroun's father regains the Gift of Gab, everyone is reunited, and, we expect, lives happily ever after, all as a result of the telling of the story that is the novel. I'm sure that's an ending Rushdie would wish for, that stories would be free to roam the world, saving lives. However, Haroun learns at the end of his adventure that "Happy Endings are much rarer in stories, and also in life, than most people think" (201). Yet, the Walrus, the head guy of the Ocean of the Streams of Stories, announces that he's "learned how to synthesize them artificially. In plain language, *we can make them up*" (202). Like many articles in which teachers explore their own teaching, this article has built to a happy ending too, a vision of my students happily choosing and learning about the implications of those choices. I didn't make this up; I swear every word is true. And even if it's not, I hope it's useful to think about the place of stories and the imagination in composition classes.

Notes

1. One of the other name changes I've made as a result is that as I leave the building at the end of the day I no longer say of the stack of papers in my arms, "I have to grade/mark/correct these papers tonight"; now I say, "I have to read/respond to these papers tonight." I cannot emphasize enough the pleasure that this change has brought to my life.

2. I have explored this question of English teachers' stylistic preferences in "Style: The Hidden Agenda in Composition Classes," in *The Subject Is Writing*, edited by Wendy Bishop and published in 1993 by Heinemann (Portsmouth, NH).

Works Cited

Atwell, Nancie. 1989. *In the Middle: Writing, Reading, and Learning with Adolescents.* Portsmouth, NH: Boynton/Cook.

Austin, J. L. 1962. *How to Do Things with Words.* Eds. J. O. Urmsom and Marina Sbisa. Cambridge: Harvard University Press.

14   Kate Ronald

Berthoff, Ann E. 1981. *The Making of Meaning: Metaphors, Models, and Maxims for Writing Teachers*. Portsmouth, NH: Boynton/Cook.

Calkins, Lucy. 1983. *Lessons from a Child: On the Teaching and Learning of Writing*. Portsmouth, NH: Heinemann.

Lardner, Ted. 1990. "Voices Seldom Heard: Poetry and Letters in the English Classroom." *English Journal* 79: 100–101.

Moxley, Joseph. 1990. "Creative Writing and Composition: Bridging the Gap." *AWP Chronicle* 23: 1, 7–12.

Rief, Linda. 1992. *Seeking Diversity: Language Arts with Adolescents*. Portsmouth, NH: Heinemann.

Rushdie, Salman. 1990. *Haroun and the Sea of Stories*. London: Granta Books.

2

A Course in Crisis
Deconcising
"College Composition"
and "Creative Writing"

John Paul Tassoni
Miami University-Middletown

1: Initial Crisis

Juxtapositioning of Passages from Published Works

We have too often subordinated one system to another and forgotten all together the individual view, the poetic view, which is as close to the truth as the consensus. Or it can be as distant. (Lopez [1976] 1996, 277)

[Critics] want to make fiction safe; [creative writers] try to keep it disturbing, dangerous, misunderstood. (Camoin 1994, 4)

As I moved as a teacher between these worlds of composition classes and creative writing classes, my pedagogy in each became more similar. (Bishop 1994, 183)

The strange idea that reality has an idiom in which it prefers to be described ... leads on to the even stranger idea that, if literalism is lost, so is fact. (Geertz 1988, 140)

Every distance must be drawn to scale / and an inch off means someone absent. (Bateman 1994, 24)

15

Introduction to an Essay

In Spring 1996, creative writing drove my composition course crazy—or at least drove its teacher crazy, anyway. I'm speaking particularly about English 112: Composition and Literature, the second course in Miami University's freshman writing sequence. Recently, our department has made efforts to move the course away from the traditional, New Critical introduction to literature class that requires students to write explications of texts in the areas of poetry, drama, and fiction. As part of the effort to focus the course on students' own reading and writing strategies, I asked class members to experiment in their writing. Rather than compile portfolios full of conventional academic essays, they could engage issues raised in class through a variety of genres: through writing sequels to assigned readings, for instance; or juxtaposing a series of passages from critical articles, from short stories, and from their own writing; or writing dramatic versions of the poetry we had read; or rewriting published texts in ways that radically revised the race, class, or gender of lead characters; or composing a series of found poems based on words and phrases lifted from textbooks, popular magazines, or bathroom walls; or writing pieces that were part essay, part cartoon, part parable, part video, part anything.

This kind of experimentation seemed to me a perfect way for students to explore means of expression beyond conventional thesis-and-support essays and a logical follow-up to the first course in our freshman sequence, in which I ask students to take a critical look at academic discourse. Reading and writing alternative means of expression in English 112, students could not only strengthen their critical perspectives on academic discourse but actually challenge the status quo through new and startling means of response.

I spent a great deal of time thinking through the implications of this approach, designing projects such as the ones just mentioned for students who might have trouble getting started on their own, and selecting texts that would facilitate our discussion of pertinent issues, such as the situation of readers in culture, the impact of multiculturalism and feminism on literature classrooms, the role of literature in relation to social change, or any other issues that students might identify as significant. And as I do in all my classes, I arranged ample time for small-group and full-class writing workshops, for student-teacher conferences, and for students to revise their writing.

I had decided to go full throttle with "creative writing," but I have to admit I didn't know (nor do I know now) how many gears should constitute a full throttle, especially when it comes to doing "creative writing" in a "college composition" classroom. When workshop discussions about students' papers didn't seem to be reaching the level of sophistication they had in previous college writing courses I had taught, when students seemed to be using their creative writing to iron over and even sidestep issues we'd encountered through the literature, and when many students seemed to reject the existence of issues altogether, I figured I just didn't know enough about creative writing pedagogy to conduct the course in the manner I had initially planned. A month into the spring semester, I was experiencing crisis.

I guess part of the crisis stemmed from the fact that I didn't consider myself a "creative writer," at least as that term is commonly and too concisely used. When I was in college I wrote stories and poems and even had a one-act drama of mine produced on campus; however, in the last decade I've written and published academic essays almost exclusively—essays *about* literature, essays *about* teaching, and even essays *about* essays about teaching literature. I think the writing that I do is very creative, but it is quite different from the kinds of works you find in literary anthologies. And, as a writing teacher, I had, until my experiments in English 112, taught "college composition" (as that term is commonly and too concisely used) only; I had not been anywhere near a poetry or fiction or drama writing seminar since my undergraduate days. In other words (as you may have already guessed), I am writing this paper as a composition teacher who is just beginning to ask students to use poetry, drama, and other forms of "creative writing" to help them understand the intricacies of "college composition" and their own roles as readers and writers of culture; and my initial experiences with "creative writing" in "college composition" were anything but unproblematic.

2: The Crisis

Section of Formal Essay

Let me first start out by emphasizing that the crisis I experienced was my crisis, not my students'. I want to point this out because the crisis I describe involves a great deal of generalizing about students. Indeed, my generalizing about students was yet another contributing factor to my crisis.[1] At times I was reading mass failure into my curriculum when actually a number of students were conducting insightful projects, having meaningful workshops, and compiling excellent portfolios. The quality of many students' final portfolios, in fact, was what started me thinking about what went right with my course instead of focusing on what went wrong. But for several months, wrong was just about all I was seeing.

Responses to Responses, Etc.

Cheryl: John, I just want to let you know how great I think it is that you're letting us write about what we want and to write it how we want.

Me: Where do you think this leaves me, Cheryl? Should I have a say in what you're doing at all? Does this mean you needn't listen to my suggestions? Why are you writing the way you are? Why is this writing what you want? Why is it good to write this way?

Essay, Continued

My crisis began as soon as I began reading the creative works that students handed in as part of their initial portfolios, which I call "Dia-Logs" and which I will explain in more detail below. I didn't expect to see masterpieces—whatever they might be—in these Dia-Logs, but I had hoped to see some in-depth reflection on some of the issues we had discussed in regard to specific works.

At least two of my students' dominant assumptions about reading and writing, however, seemed to impede in-depth discussion of their works: (1) critical reading imposes "deep meanings" on texts for which no such meanings were ever intended; and (2) the writers of texts have no responsibility toward the meanings that readers might derive from their texts. Used in tandem (I've encountered students who will hold both positions, adopting the one that will accommodate them the most at any given moment), these positions make dialogue impossible: (1) we shouldn't read critically because we end up thinking about stuff that writers never intended us to think; and (2) we can say anything we want in texts we write regardless of the effect it has on readers, regardless of their protests, confusions, indifference, interests.

With the first position, we can't think about anything but what writers want us to think. On the one hand this turns us all into passive recipients of someone else's knowledge; on the other hand, it assumes we can actually, totally understand another's message without contextualizing that message in terms of our own interests and concerns, our own knowledge base. In other words, there's just one meaning we need to get out of a piece of writing; that meaning is there within the text; and if we look too far, we just start finding things that aren't even there. With the second position ("We can say anything we want"), anything goes. Writers aren't really trying to convey information to readers, but are only "expressing themselves." I am against the kind of static pluralism this position supports. I'm not opposed to self-expression, but I think that self-expression needs to be attended by critical scrutiny, on the part of readers and on the part of the self doing the expressing, and particularly on the part of student readers/writers in a liberal arts program. With this "anything goes" positioning, the imagined, intended, complete reading (assumed by the "you're-reading-too-much-into-this" position) is not only immune to criticism, it is immune to being read at all since being read is not its purpose.

Responses to Responses, Etc.

Cheryl: I don't understand why you asked all those questions about my poems. I think they're all right to the point and say what they need to say. They say I like sports, and they say Deion Sanders is a great athlete.

Me: Cheryl, I liked your poems but think you might be selling them a bit short in your explanation of them. I'd like to know how switching genres (moving the words from newspaper into a poem) affects meaning, if at all. If it doesn't affect the meaning, why make a found poem? I'd also like to know what meanings you think others might find in these poems. After reading your work, I'm particularly interested in the role of sports in society and what kinds of values you think the figures in your poems represent.

Essay, Continued

Since my course is geared toward discussions of how best to shape knowledge in a democratic and dialogic fashion, these two assumptions are well worth challenging. I like for my students to engage discourses vital to their roles as citizens in a democratic society, and I like for them to engage these discourses dialogically, that is, with a willingness to learn from others and to teach others in ways that challenge and extend knowledge, rather than merely transport, absorb, or ignore it.

A great number of the students in my Spring 1996 class, though, seemed determined to reinforce assumptions that limited their abilities and desires to read and write critically and creatively. Perhaps the most common project students attempted over the course's first unit involved writing a sequel to Antonio Moravia's "The Chase." In Moravia's short story, a man disappointed in his wife's lack of vitality notices one day that her "wildness" has suddenly reappeared. He follows her downtown only to discover that the source of her rejuvenation is a lover, whom she embraces passionately in the street. Rather than confront the lovers, however, the husband/narrator decides to return home. He bases his decision on a childhood experience in which his father had shot and killed a bird that the narrator had been admiring. Years later, he leaves his wife's beauty intact rather than sap her of her "wildness" in the manner that his father had sapped the bird of its beauty.

I like this story because it surfaces attitudes about marriage that students bring with them to the text. In my Spring 1996 class, we ended up talking about the antagonism many students felt toward the wife in the piece and their disappointment over the husband's lack of intervention. A good number of students, simply, felt that the husband had every right to pummel both his wife and her lover. By the end of the class, though, I think a few other class members and I helped to raise significant questions about the appropriateness of such a violent reaction, about the husband's possible role in instigating his wife's infidelity, and about marriage as a patriarchal institution. At the end of the session, I suggested to class members that they try to remember a significant event in their past that might have shaped their reading of Moravia's story or one that shapes their reading of life in general. In short, I felt we had had a productive session, one that teased out the intricacies of issues brought forth through the text, and one that directed discussion of those issues toward broader cultural issues and students' own lives.

Many students decided to write a sequel to "The Chase" as part of their portfolio projects. And student after student, it seemed, followed Moravia's narrator home, described his preparations for his wife's return, and then had him blow her away with a shotgun, or chop her to pieces with a hatchet, or mash her to pulp with a hammer. Sequels to other stories took similar routes, what I (to myself, in my own private Hell) began to call the "Tuesday-Night-Movie-of-the-Week Route." Students resolved conflicts with single acts of violence, with little concern for the complexities we had explored in the initial tales and little added to those initial tales but swift and bloody resolution. In my responses to early drafts of this nature, I raised questions about students' choices: Why, after his memory of his father shooting the bird and the discussion of his wife's beauty, would the man shoot his wife? What other possible endings did you consider, and why did you choose this one? Do you agree with the man's choice to kill his wife, or did you have him mash her to pulp to show something else? Is there a message you are trying to send through your sequel, something you hope readers will get out of it?

I was sitting in workshops and marking up papers in my office, listening to and reading my students' initial attempts at poetry, fiction, drama, etc., and I was asking these questions again and again, and the reply I was hearing most—in workshops and through subsequent memos they would write back to me—was that it was their work and that's how they wanted their works to go. They were not trying to explore any deep meanings; they just wanted to tell good stories and write poems about things that they liked; I was trying to read way too much into what they were trying to do.

Fueling the fires of my discontent, my students were enjoying themselves. Occasionally, class members expressed to me their uncertainties about how to respond to particular pieces of student writing in workshops, but more than a few wrote journal entries expressing the pleasure they had found in their "creative pieces." For some reason, I studied their happy, contented faces, listened to the genuine, unsolicited questions they had about effective response, and started to blame myself for what seemed a failed curriculum.

Draft Note

It occurs to me now that my students were alternately adopting these two positions based on notions of reader and writer that were, unlike mine, distinguishable. As writers they could say whatever they wanted. As readers they had to attend to whatever the writer intended. I needed to help them problematize these roles, to see that a reader has the power to open up multiple meanings in a text and that the power to see texts differently can be of value to them. And I needed to show them that as writers they have responsibilities to their readers, that there are times when they might need to be concise, other times when they shouldn't be, and that each instance carries some ethical consequence.

Knowing this now, knowing how students might distinguish between reading and writing, I'll know to interrupt our dialogues in order to discuss the assumptions students and I bring to the terms *reading* and *writing*.

Response to a Letter Submitted with a Final Portfolio

Me: I still have problems with your "Sex, Drugs, and Rock-n-Roll" poem, James. I'm glad you've included your interpretation of the piece, which allows me to write to you about some specific things. I've circled phrases in your explanation like "just there because I like it," "basically, just a way to end the poem," "really didn't mean anything by it." This is where I'm confused: Why spend the time excerpting lines from your favorite rock songs if you're not trying to convey anything or even discover anything about your own interests and concerns?

This is especially confusing to me because I think rock is a strong cultural force, and I think there is definitely an attitude toward women and sex expressed in your poem that could be attended to. Or is the effort to not make meaning something significant I need to understand? You certainly involve yourself in some strong meaning-making in your other story, "TV Wasteland," where you destabilize notions of reality and fantasy, especially in your use of the window as tv screen, so I wonder why you'd want to write something that's "just there."

Formal Essay, Continued

For each creative writing project that I had constructed and offered to students in the form of a suggestion, I had requested that students submit as well an explanation of their work. But following some of their requests, I let the class know as they began working on their creative pieces that the explanatory section of their project was not a necessity. My feeling—in spite of my opposition to simplified valuations of writers' self-expressions—*was* that "actual" writers of poetry, drama, and fiction are not required to explain their works to others, so why should my students, many of whom would rather devote time to developing and polishing their own works.

Passage from Research

Jan Ramjerdi (1994) says, "Most of what is said in [creative writing] workshops is a reflection of pretty elementary reader responses, responses you'd submit to a bit more scrutiny if you were contributing them in an academic class, and unfortunately the level of discussion often stays there, a series of unexamined first-level reader responses" (Garber and Ramjerdi, 15).

Teacher's Journal

Today I heard Nancy's story in a workshop group. She is writing a story about a white male college student who brings a black female student, whom he is in love with, home to meet his parents. He sets his parents up by not mentioning beforehand that it is a black woman he's bringing home, and Nancy does a good job of withholding this information as well, setting the reader up to examine his or her own surprise and bias. I liked the story but for the ending. The male student starts saying things like, "Look at her eyes, mom, look how beautiful and intelligent she is. Look at her skin; it's skin just like ours, only a different color . . ." In the end they walk in all happy together. I told Nancy the end bothered me because I became aware of the fact that the woman had become sort of a sociological experiment to the man, who was trying to shock his parents and who started treating his girl-friend like an object throughout the final scene, in which she says very little. Nancy said she hadn't thought about this. I told her it doesn't make her story wrong, but that she should consider whether or not she wanted to send out this kind of message or have her character considered in this light. She said she would think about this some more.

I liked this small-group workshop, but now I'm wondering how the other workshops went. At the end of class when I was talking to other students and asking them about their workshops, they mostly said they liked each other's works and just needed to touch up a few spots or make some things clear. I didn't get the sense that any of them had had a workshop like my group had.

Draft Note

I'm thinking that maybe I spend too much time just talking about politics in my composition class, that there's got to be more time spent on some of the small-fish issues, issues of style, etc., which aren't necessarily small fish. If we're going to be talking about alternative means of presentation, the forms of those presentations are going to be important. Should I make a point of discussing symbolism and imagery a little more? The idea is that maybe some things we need to say have to be said through the symbolic. Do I have time to talk about symbolism, about character, and plot, alongside all the talk I do of gender, class, race, interpellation, oppression, and liberation? What do I need to talk about for my students to become good creative and critical writers?

3: Nut Case Power

Teacher's Journal

My favorite part of *Manufacturing Consent,* the video we watched today, was when Noam Chomsky spoke about why he's never on television. He said it was the demands of concision that kept him off TV. To be on shows like "Oprah" or "Nightline" you need to be able to say something between two commercials. This is easy to do if what you are saying is in line with the status quo: "America in the greatest country on Earth"; "Anybody can make it if they try." When Americans hear lines like this, they tend not to question them, and the speaker never has to explain what he or she means. However, if you say things like Chomsky does—"Education is really a system of imposed ignorance"; "There's been no greater bloodletting regime in the history of civilization than that currently being run out of Washington"—people want you to explain yourself. This takes time, time to present evidence, time to sift through other people's perceptions, time to adjust what you have to say to meet the concerns, interests, discourse of those you're trying to convince. You can't do this in twenty or ten minutes. If you try, you come off sounding like you're from Neptune, trying to cram too much into too small a space, talking over or under people's heads.

I think you can look at the traditional English class this way. These classes typically put a lot of stake in concision, as students are taught to say something about a subject in five hundred or one thousand words, eliminating all tangents. By demanding concision on the part of our students, we could be depriving them and us of a real learning experience. We need to set up classrooms and writing assignments so that students can go off on tangents, change their minds, adjust their discourse for different audiences and situations, reflect more on what they are saying as well as on what others are saying about their writing. We need a genre to reflect this, and it occurs to me this is what Dia-Logs are all about. I'm not saying concision is altogether bad. I think essay writing, writing concise essays, is a good way to organize one's thinking, to develop a critical understanding on a subject. But essays could be too akin to closure, to concision, to allow students to explore certain topics fairly, to work through contradictions in their thinking and extend their knowledge on a subject. My Dia-Log approach challenges the demands of concision—it's a deconcise, a deconcisionist genre.

Formal Essay, Continued

Unbeknownst to myself I had, at least in part, prepared my course for crisis through my experiences with dialogic pedagogies, through which certain crises can be read as signs of a course's vitality. Crises, in other words, can be good things: they take us out of our routines and help us to reflect on our

situations in critical and creative ways; crises might also indicate that something new is happening, that we are, indeed, encountering and formulating
new forms of knowledge and communication. Apparently, I had been so
taken aback at what "creative writing" was doing to my classroom that I did
not realize how valuable my preparation in dialogic pedagogy might be
toward not only handling, but also perpetuating crises, nor did I consider
what else I might do to encourage students to share my crisis. I did not consider these things until I started to write this chapter—which has been a bit
of a crisis in itself. When I proposed this chapter to the editor of this collection, I intended to merely warn others in my position about the difficulties
they might face when they introduced "creative writing" into their "college
composition" courses, and in great part, that is still one of my objectives. But
as I started to reread my students' portfolios, reflect on what had transpired
over the semester, and think about what I might do differently the next time
around, it occurred to me that the crisis I experienced could be used to an
advantage, and in many respects, I had already used it to an advantage.

Responses to Responses, Etc.

Cheryl: By putting the story into a poem I was able to focus on the
things I like best about Deion: things like "jewelry," "smile,"
"speed," "28 million dollars." That is all. I think you're looking too
deep into my poems.

Me: What does it mean that you would like things like "28 million dol-
lar" and "jewelry" in a professional athlete? Do your likes and dis-
likes say anything about sports in America? About your own prior-
ities?

Essay, Continued

Having come through my initial panic, I feel confident in saying that a composition course in crisis can help students and teachers kick loose the sedi-
ment of academic discourse, look at ingrained patterns of learning and
instruction, and invent better, more dialogic and democratic ways of
approaching reading and writing. With Gerald Graff (1992), I believe that

> the most neglected fact about the culture war is that its issues are clearer
> and more meaningful to the contending parties than they are to [the] stu-
> dent. It is not the conflicts dividing the university that should worry us but
> the fact that students are not playing a more active role in them. (11)

Unconsciously, class members were playing a role in exploring the conflicts
between traditional conceptions of academic discourse and "creative writing," between aesthetic and political approaches to literature, and between

passive, "banking methods" of education and active, dialogic and democratic ones (see Freire [1970] 1990, 58): they were playing important roles, only I needed to find ways to make the issues clearer and more meaningful to them, and clearer and more meaningful to me.

These roles were being played out in my students' Dia-Logs. Usually, I break my courses into three units, and at the end of each unit, students submit a Dia-Log. A Dia-Log generally consists of all the responses students have written to assigned texts (which other students and I respond to throughout the unit), their responses to other people's responses to their responses, any journal entries they might compose in relation to class discussion, any creative pieces they might attempt as a way of engaging unit issues, and their multiple drafts of a single "main project"—an essay, a story, etc. I think of the Dia-Log as a genre unto itself, a genre representing both centrifugal and centripetal forces. The Dia-Log is centrifugal in that students do a lot of freewriting that takes them out onto many different planes of discussion, and it is centripetal in that they focus one of these planes into a concise, polished piece of writing. In other words, the Dia-Log is at once a concise and deconcise genre.

In good Dia-Logs, I can see students grapple with the various ideas and issues broached in class. Another class member or I have raised a question about an assertion in a response statement, and the student writer responds in detail to the question and any subsequent questions raised about entries in his or her Dia-Log. Students develop their thinking on these subjects; change their minds; challenge others' responses; do independent research; support previously unexamined assumptions; draft, redraft, and revise papers; and all along speak with me and with peers in workshops and one-to-one conferences. I grade Dia-Logs by virtue of students' engagement with topics relevant to the class. The "A" Dia-Loggers tend not only to do the most writing, but also to tackle the most heady issues. And when I respond to the Dia-Logs, I look for points of intersection and conflict in the various entries, asking students to reflect on these points or to consider the impact of some of these entries on points they might be trying to make in their main project. It usually takes five to six weeks for students to compose a Dia-Log, and it usually takes me two weeks to respond to a batch of forty. They are cumbersome, messy, deconcise packets of writing, but they give me much more time to study students' thinking and writing, and to intervene in that thinking and writing, than do the five-hundred-word themes I used to, and many teachers still do, assign to students in composition classes.

It was because my students were composing these cumbersome, messy, deconcise packets of writing that I had a chance to individually address students' assumptions about writing and reading and to address those assumptions in the context of their own writing, at the level at which they were perceiving reality. And because Dia-Logs helped me to engage and literalize these discussions, I do not think my course was a failure. I suspected it wasn't a complete failure when I read a series of found poems by a student named Mary (who wasn't mentioned before, because she wasn't part of my crisis) on environmental issues, when I saw the way she had reread/rewritten food labels, hunting magazines, and school syllabi to show our culture's pervasive hatred of nature. But I know now it was not a failure when I think about my final exchange with James, because I could point out the varying degrees of meaning he was making in his work and because he was concerned enough about his writing to want feedback even after the course had ended; and when I think about the workshop discussion I had with Nancy, because we could talk about the meanings I had found in her work and because she could reflect on these meanings as she revised her story (maybe she wanted the white man's objectification of his black girlfriend to be an issue, after all); and even when I think about the response-to-response series I had with Cheryl, because I could at least turn her resistance to meaning making into an issue. The deconcisionist nature of the Dia-Log approach is just what I needed to develop my own sense of crisis and to let it play out in dialogue with my students.

All I needed was a better way to make that crisis more apparent to my students, more the main topic of discussion, more a part of the day-to-day talk in the class. I'm now making plans to approach my English 112 course as a crisis in itself, a crisis in genre.

4: A Course in Crisis

List of Things I Am Thinking About After "Creative Writing" Drove My "Composition Class" Crazy

I should conduct full-class workshops with samples of student writings, workshops that contain both creative papers and composition papers, and have discussions about the differences and the similarities in both genre and response. I can also arrange for more post-workshop discussions to address oddities in texts students might encounter and problems/successes they might have with response.

I can encourage students to write standard responses and creative responses for single readings, ask other students to respond to the different responses, and then I can ask the student authors to write about the comparisons and contrasts they find in the ways people responded to their work.

For specific responses and for main papers I should require student writers and readers to answer the type of response protocol sheet that Wendy Bishop describes in *Released into Language: Options for Teaching Creative Writing* (1990), where she includes various response questions for various genres. Perhaps even more useful would be the list of questions she described in her 1996 CCCC presentation, "Alternative Styles Doesn't Mean 'Anything Goes': Responding to, Evaluating, and Grading Alternate Style" in which she offered questions and comments writers could ask themselves about their writings ("Can I describe why this writing requires this style/format?" and "Have I done everything I can to 'teach' the reader how to read my piece while still maintaining the integrity of my writing goals and ideas?") and questions/comments that classmates and teachers might ask in one-to-one conferences and peer workshops ("Can you tell us what effects you were hoping for, where you achieved them and where you think you may have fallen short?" and "Here's how I read your text. Here's where I had trouble reading your text and why."). In addition, I could offer students questions/ comments pertinent to political issues we discuss in class: "How does your work relate to dominant notions of gender, race, and class?"; "Are the questions I've offered you as part of this response protocol relevant to your work? Are they impeding your work? Are there other questions you or your readers should be asking about your writing?" The questions I have in mind would help students to investigate their own purposes for writing (both "creative writing" and "college composition") as they are writing, to scrutinize what their writings might say about themselves and their culture, and to consider what it might say to others.

In subsequent discussions, we can examine the function of response protocols themselves. I'm curious to see if these questions might shape students' writings, and if so, if they shape their writing in beneficial ways. In these discussions with students, I can examine whether I need to respect my assumption about creative writers not needing to write analyses of their own work. I can wonder out loud, with my students, whether the freshman composition class, or any college class for that matter, should be considered a situation unto itself, demanding a genre unto itself, a genre in which students should indeed explain the intentions governing their works.

Before students submit their first Dia-Logs, I can give them this chapter as a way of suggesting to them the various issues with which I'm concerned (the anything-goes approach, the you're-reading-too-much-into-this position, the Tuesday-Night-Movie-of-the-Week Route, political versus formalistic reading/writing, the demands of concision, etc.) and then ask them to locate themselves in this article among the issues that concern them. I can ask them to indicate points of interest, points of contradiction, and points in need of more consideration in my Dia-Log, and I can ask them to write their own classroom narratives, their own stories of crisis.

Note

1. Throughout this piece, student comments and my responses to those comments are paraphrased, based on my impressions of the interactions I had with students over the course of my crisis.

Works Cited

Bateman, Claire. 1991. "Map." In *The Bicycle Slow Race*, 24. Hanover, NH: University Press of New England.

Bishop, Wendy. 1990. *Released into Language: Options for Teaching Creative Writing*. Urbana, IL: NCTE.

———. "Crossing the Lines: On Creative Composition and Composing Creative Writing." In Bishop and Ostrom, 181–197.

———. 1996. "Alternative Styles Doesn't Mean 'Anything Goes': Responding to, Evaluating, and Grading Alternate Style." (29 March,) Workshop presentation at the College Composition and Communication Conference. Milwaukee, WI.

Bishop, Wendy, and Hans Ostrom. 1994. *Colors of a Different Horse: Rethinking Creative Writing Theory and Pedagogy*. Urbana, IL: NCTE.

Camoin, Francois. 1994. "The Workshop and Its Discontents." In Bishop and Ostrom, 3–7.

Freire, Paulo. [1970] 1990. *Pedagogy of the Oppressed*. Trans. M. B. Ramos. New York: Continuum.

Garber, Eugene, and Jan Ramjerdi. "Reflections on the Teaching of Creative Writing: A Correspondence." In Bishop and Ostrom, 8–26.

Geertz, Clifford. 1988. *Works and Lives: The Anthropologist as Author*. Stanford, CA: Stanford University Press.

Graff, Gerald. 1992. *Beyond the Culture Wars: How Teaching the Conflicts Can Revitalize American Education*. New York: Norton.

Lopez, Barry Holstun. [1976] 1996. "Winter Count 1973: Geese, They Flew Over in a Storm." In *Literature: The Human Experience*, 6th ed., eds. Richard Abcarian and Marvin Klotz, 274–78. New York: St. Martin's.

Manufacturing Consent: Noam Chomsky and the Media. 1992. (Videorecording). Montreal, Quebec, Canada: Necessary Illusions.

Moravia, Antonio. 1990. "The Chase." In *Literature: The Human Experience,* 5th ed., eds. Richard Abcarian and Marvin Klotz, 746–49. New York: St. Martin's.

3

Reclaiming "Creativity" for Composition

George T. Karnezis
North Central College

You all know what happens when you tell a new acquaintance that you teach English. Suddenly you become the high priest(ess) of commas and usage, and your companion becomes an embarrassed potential victim ("Oh, I'd better watch my language," or "I've always been a lousy speller"). The experience, startling when we first enter teaching, quickly curdles into a cliché, perhaps forcing us to change our reply to "I teach literature," a response that may elicit some embarrassment about not reading enough, but hardly ever an "Oh, gosh, I've just never been a very good reader." Cordial conversation may then follow. You are asked to recommend some good books (almost always fiction, and never poetry), and happily escape the role (cue another metaphor) of grammar/usage parole officer checking up on someone's progress in basic literacy.

I've tested various responses to such queries about what I do, but am still experimenting. My latest is: "English, mainly writing courses, especially for first-year students." Still, eight years after moving to my current job, I come home one day to some news.

Scene 1

My wife has been talking to a neighbor on whom I'd used this response eight years ago, though maybe I had left out that part about first-year students.

"I was talking to Kate today and she was really surprised to learn you taught composition. All these years she's had the impression you taught creative writing."

"Where did she get that idea?"

"Well, she just assumed that when you said you taught *writing*, it must have been *creative* writing."

"Ouch, " I say, "Kate teaches art in elementary school, but when you told her I taught *composition* that probably sounded to her like I was teaching something like industrial arts instead of ART."

My wife nods, knows what's coming, and accepts my now familiar and still fervently delivered minilecture on how the presumption of creativity falls to fiction or poetry while other school-taught "writing" consists of vaguely defined, uncreative, prose nonfiction entities called *papers, themes,* or *compositions*. Outside the Creative Writing Oasis there stretches a curricular Wasteland littered with an unimaginative language in uniform conscripted for various assigned duties. While there may be exceptions, composition courses find it hard not to distinguish themselves by the absence of the word *creative* in their titles. Except for their occasional nod to the narrative-descriptive essay, used as icebreakers early on, such courses may even warn students against looking into their hearts and writing. Its writing assignments are driven by necessity rather than inspiration. They are intended to prepare students for writing challenges posed, as is often said, by "future academic or career work." To speak or even think of the imagination as an element in these courses is to invite bewildered stares from students well-tutored by pedagogical and curricular cues to isolate "creativity" in writing.

Quick Cut

While drafting the above, I attend an evening session for parents at my daughter's elementary school on how to encourage positive attitudes toward writing. The visiting presenter (as usual, from a distant place to lend him authority) is a happy fellow with a good routine, including a guitar. He talks about the awful constraints of formulaic writing and about how he's learned so much out of school about *real writing*. He shows us samples of his own writing from the bad old days when he was in elementary and junior high school and wrote dull prose book reports and the like. He takes a few swipes at topic sentences and tells us about the pleasures of the imagination. We are invited to write some poems, and to think about how we can make writing fun and enjoyable for any child whose inner writing soul cries for expression. ("People worry too much about their children writing complete sentences. Not to worry. Students will naturally learn to do that.") When he refers to student writing, he usually calls it stories, and he gives us some useful tips on how to ask our children questions that will get them to add detail to their work. We agree this is preferable to teachers writing *awk* and *elaborate* in the margins. As he winds things up, I realize again how such presentations make it easy for anyone to choose sides, and I sense the gratitude of the few parents in attendance. Still, I wonder whether I will ultimately see their children in my classroom, quite adept at narration and description, but relatively crippled and hostile when it comes to writing of a different and, probably to them, uncreative sort.

Back to Scene 1

If my wife or other sympathetic audience continues to indulge me, the beat goes on. I'll begin weaving in questions about the dissing of rhetoric, protesting once again the "palsied" reputation it's gained since being "pockmarked by a century in which it has been . . . associated merely with sophistication (in the less positive sense of *that* word), cant and emptiness" (Andrews 1992, 2). I'll insist that we need to refine our notions of language forms and use so that we resist those crudely suspect polarities embedded in curricular and student language that serves only to perpetuate the ghettoization of *creative* writing as a specialty that defines itself as what it is not. We need (my voice rises) to question our practices, discursive, pedagogical, and institutional, which place "composition," however unintentionally, near the bottom of a hierarchy whose pinnacle is the world of creative writing.

Pause. A deep breath before a conclusion that explores some broader implications of my theme: this is, I say, no mere academic quarrel over "words" and their respective cachets. The issue relates not only to how the teaching of writing is conceived within English departments, and to how such conceptions influence relationships among writing teachers; it also influences how we compartmentalize our experience generally. What, I ask, are the larger effects of our habitually separating the creative, the personal, and the imaginative *from* the allegedly more prosaic and public forms of writing? If we assume such a separation, have we not also resigned ourselves to the notion that little creative fulfillment is derived from our "work," or from the broader public (or curricular) realm where writing serves more immediate "practical" and even political (academic? career?) purposes? Such pleasures and rewards are then consigned to "creative" writing courses where, in the relative solitude of your own curricular garret you can, how to put it, "be yourself," "find yourself," and rediscover or invent your authentic existence largely independent of that getting and spending world that forces its impersonal writing assignments on us.

In the Garret

My speech finished, I retire to my own garret, already worried that I've been too quick to polarize and even caricaturize such matters. Surely teachers of composition, especially those tuned into the traditional rhetorical canon of invention, and sufficiently sensitive to qualities of grace and style, seek to impart to their students a sense of the "creative" dimension of all writing.

And surely many composition teachers, schooled as most are in literature, recognize the flexibility of the essay form, its ability to wield elements of narration, description, and dialogue when appropriate.

Even if this picture is a partial corrective, I suspect many students and teachers still experience composition as a comparatively uncreative industrial art. Following curricular signals as well as what's communicated to them by the division of labor in most institutions, students understandably locate creativity in the designated courses (or genres) and resign themselves to the relatively grim necessity of those other kinds of writing demanded by school and, ultimately, work. Is this, I wonder again, preparing them for a life in which their daily worklife is seen as a grind, for which the weekend is their reward?

This privileging of the "creative" can begin quite early, as illustrated again by my admittedly indirect contact with an elementary school experience. Daily my fifth grader leaves her regular classroom for her more "advanced" reading class. There, students read exclusively fiction, learn about figurative language, and are asked to write their own fantasies and to create posters or three-dimensional models of the scene from a novel. They read no nonfiction and are hardly ever required to create in any nonfiction forms. The message here is clear: if you are an advanced reader, you get to read a variety of narrative fiction. In the regular class, you read textbooks. Thus, early on the world divides into prosaic and poetic, the constrained regular classroom and the playfully creative one reserved for the smart kids.

In its way, this division mirrors the chasm in the English discipline familiar enough to most since those like Maxine Hairston and Wayne Booth asked us to acknowledge the split between those who study literature or lit crit, and those who have developed an interest in rhetoric and composition. While ideally these interests should complement one another, the truth is, despite the purported growth in the esteem given to composition studies, an interest in them often dooms one to considerably lower status and employment conditions in most departments. Any young aspirants to the field of English must recognize these tensions and try to deal with them as elements of their future professional identity. If they seek some sense of how these interests can complement one another, if they refuse to view the teaching of composition as the necessary purgatory that precedes their arrival at the special haven of teaching literature, and if they can avoid the pressure to choose up sides, they will do so despite the still prevailing pecking order. Any success they achieve in trying to balance these interests will be measured by their ability to embody a professional model that does not merely tolerate the need for teaching composition, but sees that need as an opportunity to help students form themselves as readers and writers sensitive to powers and limitations of various kinds of discourse. In short, they will see themselves as true rhetoricians engaged in the creative play of language, whether they are producers or construers of texts. Despite linguistic and institutional prejudices, they will teach composition as the creative writing it must be if its position in the curriculum is to exceed the constrained versions of literacy traditionally associated with (especially) first-year writing courses.[1]

My garret musings (now frankly evolving into an essay) finally lead me to some suggestions about how to challenge prevailing prejudices against any claim composition might make to being a species of creative writing. I believe a case needs to be made so that we and our students will become more suspicious of invidious curricular labels that make it too convenient for us to see the teaching of composition and creative writing as radically discontinuous projects. The trick, of course, is, without excessive appeals to modern critical and discourse theory, to help ourselves and our students to expanded notions of what's creative, while still acknowledging that, yes, the formulaic pressures of some forms of writing exist as genre proprieties or what classical rhetoricians called *decorum*. But admitting such constraints does not mean that students should see the academic essay, for instance, as limited to the dull exfoliation of wooden thesis-evidence models manufactured by those who have mastered a paint-by-number technique, any more than they should see creative writing as the reckless disregard for anything resembling form. There are, I believe, things we can do (which I'm sure many of us are already doing) to reduce these divisions and encourage our students to see forms of language as genuine creations that require choices involving the interplay of imagination and judgment.[2]

As a case in point, consider even this specimen of a potentially dull assignment given to my fifth-grade daughter:

FAMOUS AMERICAN REPORT

PARAGRAPH 1: Family information
    The first paragraph is to be about your famous American's family. Include information about his/her parents, brothers and sisters, wife or husband, and children. If there are other relatives of importance, mention them too.

PARAGRAPH 2: Childhood and Education
    The second paragraph contains information about the date and place of birth of the person and his/her early schooling and education. If he or she was college educated, discuss this also.

PARAGRAPH 3: Important Events in the Person's Life
    Include at least three important events in the person's life. Include descriptive details.

PARAGRAPH 4: Contributions
    Include information about what this individual did for his/her profession or his/her contribution to society.

PARAGRAPH 5: Your Evaluation
   Tell what you learned about this individual, how you feel about him/
her, and why you feel this way.

This assignment is an easy target, especially for our friendly writing consultant who would doubtless become considerably exercised over its view of
writing as a fairly dutiful dumping of data into appropriately labeled recy-
cling bins. Rather than follow his suit, I prefer to grant the elementary teacher's need to provide needed "guidelines," especially at an early age, to teach
students that writing is something composed rather than tossed together. But
that goal might be reached more effectively if students are given a bunch of
facts about a famous American and then asked to invent ways of grouping
these facts. ("Joey Smith put these facts on cards and had them all arranged,
but they fell out of his school bag and got mixed up; can you help him organize his information for a paper?") In this scenario, students are invited into
a problem-solving role that casts them less as gatherers than as arrangers of
information and composers of a larger piece. Depending on the grade level,
higher-order questions of sequencing and arrangement can be considered.
For instance, if the American was controversial, why not start with a story
dramatizing a conflict? Let's hear about King in Birmingham or about the
insistence of my daughter's subject, Eleanor Roosevelt that Marian Anderson
be allowed to sing at the Washington Monument. These stories might very
well *begin* this "report" and thus teach students that narrative needn't be
reserved for a particular place.
   Further fiddling with this assignment would help students appreciate the
choices it presents them. As written, of course, these directions seem to
channel the writer's moves rather than invoke any sense of writing as a
choosing of options. Certainly young writers, like any writers, may be invited
to incorporate the voice of their subject to capture something about an important event, or about the subject's education or childhood, just as they might
use the words of others to capture their subject's contributions to a profession. And is there a place amidst these paragraphs for some physical description that might further reveal character?
   My point is that even potentially dreary assignments like this needn't
hamstring the imagination nor reduce the writer's freedom to explore various
ways of presenting "information" that breathe some energy and life into
potentially inert facts. Further tweaking of this assignment might invite the
student to project a particular audience for this "report." What would happen,
for instance, if the student knew that his paper was intended for students of the
same age in another country? Invoking any number of rhetorical situations
even in the early grades could teach students that writing is always situated in
circumstances that needn't be limited to the implicit audience of the teacher-
grader monitoring students' capacity for merely following directions.[3] At

higher levels of education, our being able to fold such invitations to "handle" the assignment in various ways can do much to eliminate that glibly dictatorial tone that writing prompts may fall into. We can, I think, generally pay more attention to whether the rhetoric of our own prompts constructs apprentice writers more creatively as choice makers, experimenters, and even risk takers. As Wallace Stevens (1951) noted:

> The deepening need for words that express our thoughts and feelings . . . makes us listen to words when we hear them, loving them and feeling them, makes us search the sound of them.

"What does it mean," remarks philosopher Hans-Georg Gadamer, "that in all of antiquity no silent reading was done, and what does it mean that we no longer hear a real voice when reading?" (1992, 65). Gadamer may be putting the case too strongly, but his point about the potential losses in reading exclusively with the eye to the exclusion of the ear is worth noting. Those of us with experience in writing centers can appreciate the power of students' voices to reveal a certain fluency their writing has been unable to capture. My own training of tutors insists that they have students read their work aloud. While this technique is not an infallible corrective to student error, often a large percentage of miscues are caught. But the value of voicing what one has written can often extend further, helping not merely to correct miscues, but to improve upon even correctly written sentences and generate new material as well. In general, I believe our regular classroom teaching can do more to remind our students of the potentially voiced quality of much printed expression, and that to speak of prose rhythms in sentences means that the force of poetry is not owned by the explicitly poetic form, but earned also by prose writers like Wendell Berry who can capture a thought or a meaning by the cadences, not just the semantics of their prose:

> Moreover, if standards are to be upheld, they cannot be specialized, professionalized, or departmented. Only common standards can be upheld–standards that are held and upheld in common by the whole community. When, in a university, for instance, English composition is made the responsibility exclusively of the English department, or of the subdepartment of freshman English, then the quality of the work in composition courses declines and the standards decline. This happens necessarily and for an obvious reason: If students' writing is graded according to form and quality in composition class but according only to "content" in, say, history class and if in other classes students are not required to write at all, then the message to the students is clear: namely, that the form and quality of their writing matters only in composition class, which is to say that it matters very little indeed. High standards of composition can be upheld only if they are upheld everywhere in the university. (Berry 1987, 89)

   How many of us routinely ask students to orally interpret, not merely
read aloud, their own passages or ones like these? Our pedagogy might do
well to encourage such oral performances so that students can understand the
oral-aural dimension of language, becoming attuned to the special cadences
that all writers depend upon—not merely to embellish meaning, but to
achieve it. We would ask them not only to notice and analyze the shape and
rhythm of Berry's prose, but to try to enact its voiced quality in order to
experience its language as performable, that is, orally interpretable.[4] Classroom practices that listen to writing will testify to how much prose like Berry's depends on the arrangement of word groups, the accumulation of linked
clauses, and the sudden pauses created by the two uses of the colon. By
reading with their lips and ears, students will sense the rise and fall of Berry's prose, its anticipation and partial suspension of meaning by the accumulation of conditional clauses, so that his writing creates not merely thought,
but the experience or contours of a mind *thinking*. If we approach language
this way, we can also help students talk more concretely about "style" and
"voice" once we ask them to consider how to sound out the first two sentences of this passage, catching the contempt in the staccato polysyllabic
"specialized, professionalized, or departmented," as opposed to the relatively
smoother, gentler cadences and effective repetitions in the second sentence,
where Berry invites us to see that standards are not merely "common," but
to hear its phonetic as well as to see its visual connection with "community."
Perhaps most important, such exercises will also take the study of punctuation out of the hands of testmakers, who see it as merely a proofreading
rather than more properly as a rhetorical and compositional skill integral to
the creation of meaning.[5]
   What holds true for prose rhythms and tone also applies to the attention
we might pay to imagery as part of the writer's general repertoire. Here is
Hannah Arendt's prose working to impart to us the impulse behind her collection of essays, *Men In Dark Times*. We want our students to understand
that Arendt's prose finds fresh language for talking about the enlightenment
her profiles might offer us:

> That even in the darkest of times we have the right to expect some illumi-
> nation may well come less from theories and concepts than from the uncer-
> tain flickering, and often weak light that some men and women, in their
> lives and works will kindle under almost all circumstances and shed over
> the time span that was given them on earth—this conviction is the inartic-
> ulate background against which these profiles were drawn. Eyes so used to
> darkness as ours will hardly be able to tell whether their light was the light
> of the candle or that of the blazing sun. But such objective evaluation seems
> to me a matter of secondary importance which can safely be left to poster-
> ity. (ix–x)

The presence of this light imagery is no mere adornment to Arendt's thought in this preface, but integral to it. To understand her meaning will involve, quite literally, using it, or thinking in it, much as a poet invites readers to name the world in language crafted to disclose fresh possibilities. In Arendt's case, we have a nuanced imagery of light and darkness that, recalling the savagery of the modern era and the holocaust in particular, distinguishes a time made dark by a public relations discourse of "highly efficient talk and double talk of nearly all official representatives who . . . explained away unpleasant facts and justified concerns" (viii). In Arendt's view, that public realm that once provided "a space of appearances" for human affairs where people could "show in deed and word, for better and worse, who they are and what they can do," no longer contains the necessary light for making such appearances visible to us. As a result, the light we need has been extinguished by what some typically call (her preface is dated 1968) credibility gaps or an invisible government wielding "speech that does not disclose what is but sweeps it under the carpet . . ." (viii). Arendt adds to this critique Heidegger's dismay over the leveling effects of the sheer quantity of public talk as having the effect of *obscuring* everything—for where so *much* talk is present, publicity is cheap and, because so *much* is being brought to light, everything and nothing is distinguishable or valued.

Thus it is against this harsh light, which really keeps us in the dark, that Arendt offers us her portraits as "some illumination" or modestly "flickering and often weak light" given off by those whose lives and works provide not only us, but their own time with illumination. In such a paraphrase, we find ourselves on the edge of a stale metaphor. Certainly she wishes these portraits to be *illuminating*, but what her imagery strives for is a freshening of the light imagery nested in this term, a reminder, if you will, of the visual dimension of the effect of those lives and works on an age like ours where a harsher light of publicity does not enlighten but obscures as a result of its very intensity. There is, I think, some bitter irony mixed with hope in Arendt's penultimate sentence: the degree of illumination ("light of a candle or that of a blazing sun") is, it seems, less important to her than the fact that some discernment, some illumination, occurs at all.

To regard imagery and metaphor, as I am here, as instruments of thought, not merely skills of expression, should be familiar enough to any student of language, especially if they've read Suzanne Langer, I. A. Richards, or, more recently, Johnson and Lakoff; but for many students, this perspective remains unrealized and figures of speech are esteemed purely for their emotional or visual "effect." If so, these creative uses of language are again housed comfortably in particular genres meant to appeal to an imagination unstained by thought or intellect. As a result, another creative element in the reading and writing of prose is given insufficient scope and publicity, leaving "figures of speech" inadequately appreciated for the work they do so often as "figures of thought." [6]

Similar attention can be extended to narrative as a rich resource for nonfiction prose writers in various professions and disciplines. My experience with most students reveals they associate narrative almost exclusively with fiction, though they may give a brief nod to the "personal" or "narrative" essay that's enough like a short story to be respectable. As I noted earlier, the narrative/descriptive mode is often used as an icebreaker in composition courses, giving students the idea that it's a kind of limbering-up exercise before the more serious tasks of "analysis and synthesis" required in academic work. While they may hear that narrative is "useful" for clarifying or illustrating "a point," they still treat it as a skill to be nurtured in creative writing classes and used sparingly, if at all, for those "other" sorts of papers.

Such a prejudice might be best challenged by having students read and study the use of narrative as something more than an embellishment or anecdotal accompaniment to an otherwise expository or analytical piece. The idea is to complicate and perhaps even confuse the distinction between narrative and analysis, story and thought, so that we can appreciate what drives certain writers to insist on narrative as an instrument for inquiry and analysis. It is as if writers are using narrative not merely as a vehicle, but depending on it as a form absolutely necessary for communicating the substance of their knowledge.[7]

A recent example comes from Paul Farmer, a medical anthropologist who has studied medical practices, particularly in Haiti. Writing in a special issue of *Daedalus* entitled "Social Suffering," he notes that he, like other anthropologists, studies personal distress or disease as the translation of "large-scale social forces," always asking how such "forces ranging from poverty to racism become *embodied* as individual experience" (261–62). After two paragraphs offering some evidence of the vulnerablity of much of Haiti's rural population to suffering, he insists "the experience of suffering . . . is not effectively conveyed by statistics or graphs. The 'texture' of dire affliction is perhaps best felt in the gritty details of biography . . ." (262–63). Farmer insists that the two stories he will recount "are anything but 'anecdotal'"—as if to claim for his writing a kind of weight and density. He needs to tell these stories, he says, because they capture, in their form, an analysis that is both historically deep and geographically broad (74). As such, these biographies are embedded "in the larger matrix of culture, history, and political economy" (272). For Farmer, it is that matrix that must be understood if we are interested in not only making sense of extreme suffering but also explaining it. His writing mixes biographical details with an analytical acumen that makes it hard for us to think about the causes of suffering in Haiti independently of a dense network of historical forces that created the life and death of both of his biographical subjects. Reading Farmer's accounts leaves one feeling that individual suffering is not interpretable, not really knowable outside this larger context. Consequently, he must situate his "protagonists" in space and time (that is, present the scene in which their lives are played out) so that his narrative can reveal their lives as "plotted" events.

As both a practicing doctor and medical anthropologist, Farmer must write about suffering in Haiti not solely from the point of view of the individual caretaker focused on a particular patient. Such a view could be captured in a case study, which, in a sense, is anecdotal. But to do justice to his dual role, and to understand individual suffering as linked to larger forces, he needs a narrative to tell the larger story. To treat individual patients without trying to explain what forces brought them to their fate is to practice medicine that places human suffering exclusively on the back of the sufferer, making every patient special or unique, rather than part of a broader matrix that is complicit in that suffering.[8]

For students of writing, pieces like Farmer's reveal the blurred lines between exposition, narrative, and analysis. If we study such writing carefully, we will obtain a deeper sense of how narrative schema inhabit worlds outside the fictional, worlds that can become objects of both imaginative and intellectual apprehension. Just as we attended to the oral and figurative dimension of prose, we can also help our students experience the creative use of narrative in disciplines that we might have thought escaped the habit of storytelling. Examples of this narrative impulse appear in the work of writers such as Derrick Bell (1987) and Patricia Williams (1991), who use narrative to explore issues in the law. While Bell implies that his use of fantasy in *And We Are Not Saved* admits tools of "unreason" into legal discourse, he applauds a fellow legal thinker's claim that "allegory offers a method of discourse that allows us to critique legal norms in an ironically contextualized way. Through the allegory we can critique legal doctrine in a way that does not replicate the abstractions of legal discourse" (6–7). Similarly, Williams's *The Alchemy of Race and Rights* candidly admits that her writing is an "intentional departure" from the conventions of legal writing, and that it invokes a "model of inductive empiricism, borrowed from—and parodying— systems analysis, in order to enliven thought about complex social problems" (7). Looking for discourse "that forces the reader both to participate in the construction of meaning and to be conscious of the process," Williams mines "all sorts of literary devices, including parody, parable, and poetry."[9]

While one way to resist the isolation of creativity in creative writing courses is through pedagogical practices such as I've sketched, I can't help the feeling that larger curricular issues are involved here. If students in English continue to experience nonfiction prose almost exclusively in first-year composition courses, or perhaps in some advanced composition courses, the curriculum may still be sending them the wrong messages. As an alternative, imagine survey courses in "literature" that take as one of their goals the historical development of the essay, or the development of English prose. A curriculum that showed nonfiction prose writers in the company of poets, novelists, and playwrights would help discourage students from seeing certain literary forms as rejects from a main stage reserved for those creative actors who enact the drama of *creative* human expression. Students may then come to appreciate the extent to which a broader range of discourse, in a surprising variety of disciplines, deserves to be called creative writing.

Notes

1. Wayne Booth's essay "Litcomp" in Winifred Horner's *Composition & Literature: Bridging the Gap* (Chicago: University of Chicago Press, 1983), 57–80, remains a useful reminder on this point, as are some pieces in his *The Vocation of a Teacher: Rhetorical Occasions 1967–1988* (Chicago: University of Chicago Press, 1988), especially 86 ff. A particularly cogent defense of the broader sense of purpose and vocation worthy of writing teachers is Marshall Gregory's "The Process of Writing, the Formation of Character, and the (Re)formation of Society," *Perspectives* (Winter 1993), 28–42.

2. While working on this essay, I rediscovered S. M. Halloran and Annette Bradford's "Figures of Speech in the Rhetoric of Science and Technology" in *Essays on Classical Rhetoric and Modern Discourse,* eds. Robert J. Connors and Andrea Lunsford (Carbondale, IL: Southern Illinois Press, 1984), 179–92. The writers explore the rhetorical and creative dimension of technical and scientific prose, forms of writing usually regarded as so constrained by convention that tact and judgment are not called for in their composition.

3. See Erika Lindeman's valuable discussion in Chapter 13 of her *A Rhetoric for Writing Teachers,* 2d. ed. (New York: Oxford University Press, 1987).

4. In his *A History of Reading* (New York: Viking, 1996), Alberto Manguel notes the habits of early readers: "Faced with a written text, the reader had a duty to lend voice to the silent letters, the *scripta,* and to allow them to become, in the delicate biblical distinction, *verba,* spoken words—spirit. The primordial languages of the Bible—Aramaic and Hebrew—do not differentiate between the act of reading and the act of speaking; they name both with the same word" (45).

5. Some treatments of style encourage the attention I'm promoting here, especially Chris Anderson's, *Free/Style* (New York: Houghton Mifflin, 1992). See also Richard Lanham's, *Analyzing Prose* (New York: Scribner's, 1983), especially Chapter 5, and, to some extent, Martha Kolln's, *Rhetorical Grammar: Grammatical Choices, Rhetorical Effects* (New York: Macmillan, 1991). Chapter 4 of E. P. J. Corbett's *Classical Rhetoric for the Modern Student,* 3d. ed. (New York: Oxford University Press, 1990) covers style and reminds us that students often lack the necessary tools for talking very precisely about stylistic features (404ff.). This deficiency further reduces their chances of seeing or hearing the creative dimension in much nonfiction prose.

6. On this broader use of metaphor, see S. M. Halloran and Annette Bradford, "Figures of Speech in the Rhetoric of Science and Technology," *Essays on Classical*

Rhetoric and Modern Discourse, eds. Robert J. Connors and Andrea Lunsford (Carbondale, IL: Southern Illinois Press, 1984) 179–92, as well as I. A. Richards's *The Philosophy of Rhetoric* (New York: Oxford University Press, 1971), George Lakoff and Mark Johnson's, *Metaphors We Live By* (Chicago: University of Chicago Press, 1980), and http://metaphor.uoregon.edu/metaphor.html.

      7. Some valuable insights about narrative's function appear in Jerome Bruner's *The Culture of Education* (Cambridge: Harvard University Press, 1996).

      8. On medical narrative see Katherine Hunter's, *Doctor's Stories: The Narrative Structure of Medical Knowledge* (Princeton: Princeton University Press, 1991), and http://web.lemoyne.edu/~hevern/narpsych.html.

      9. Other sources on legal narrative include Norval Morris's, *The Brothel Boy and Other Parables of the Law* (New York: Oxford University Press, 1992), James Boyd White's, *Heracles' Bow* (Madison: University of Wisconsin Press, 1985), the issue of *Michigan Law Review* devoted to "Legal Storytelling," (August 1989), and http://web.lemoyne.edu/~hevernlnr_law.html. Of particular interest is Bernard J. Hibbits's, "Making Sense of Metaphors: Visuality, Aurality and the Reconfiguration of American Legal Discourse," *Cardozo Law Review* 16:2 (1994): 229–356.

Works Cited

Anderson, Chris. 1992. *Free/Style: A Direct Approach to Writing.* Boston: Houghton Mifflin.

Andrews, Richard, ed. 1992. *Rebirth of Rhetoric: Essays in Language, Culture, Education.* London: Routledge.

Arendt, Hannah. 1968. *Men in Dark Times.* New York: Harcourt.

Bell, Derrick. 1987. *And We Are Not Saved: The Elusive Quest for Racial Justice.* New York: Basic Books.

Berry, Wendell. 1987. *Home Economics.* San Francisco: North Point Press.

Booth, Wayne C. 1983. "Litcomp." In *Composition & Literature: Bridging the Gap,* ed. Winifred B. Horner, 57–80. Chicago: University of Chicago Press.

Corbett, E. P. J. 1990. *Classical Rhetoric for the Modern Student.* 3d ed. New York: Oxford University Press.

Farmer, Paul. 1996. "On Suffering and Structural Violence," *Daedalus* 125 (1): 261–83.

Gadamer, Hans-Georg. 1992. "Interview: Writing and the Living Voice." In *Hans-Georg Gadamer on Education, Poetry, and History: Applied Hermeneutics,* eds. Dieter Misgeld and Graeme Nicholson, 63–71. Albany: State University of New York Press.

Gregory, Marshall. 1993. "The Process of Writing, the Formation of Character, and the (Re)formation of Society." *Perspectives* 23 (2): 28–42.

Halloran, S. Michael, and Annette Bradford. 1984. "Figures of Speech in the Rhetoric of Science and Technology." In *Classical Rhetoric and Modern Discourse,* eds. Robert J. Connors, Lisa Ede, and Andrea Lunsford, 179–92. Carbondale, IL: Southern Illinois Press.

Hibbitts, Bernard J. 1994. "Making Sense of Metaphors: Visuality, Aurality, and the Reconfiguration of American Legal Discourse." *Cardozo Law Review* 16 (2): 229–356.

Hunter, Katherine. 1991. *Doctor's Stories: the Narrative Structure of Medical Knowledge.* Princeton, NJ: Princeton University Press.

Kolln, Martha. 1991. *Rhetorical Grammar: Grammatical Choices, Rhetorical Effects.* New York: Macmillan.

Lakoff, George, and Mark Johnson. 1980. *Metaphors We Live By.* Chicago: University of Chicago Press.

Lanham, Richard. 1993. *Analyzing Prose.* New York: Scribners.

Manguel, Alberto. 1996. *A History of Reading.* New York: Viking.

Michigan Law Review. 1989. Issue devoted to "Legal Storytelling." 87 (8).

Morris, Norval. 1992. *The Brothel Boy and Other Parables of the Law.* New York: Oxford University Press.

Stevens, Wallace. 1951. *The Necessary Angel: Essays on Reality and the Imagination.* New York: Vintage.

White, James B. 1985. *Heracles' Bow: Essays and Rhetoric and Poetics of the Law.* Madison: University of Wisconsin Press.

4

The Legacy of Richard Hugo in the Composition Classroom

Will Hochman

University of Southern Colorado

A survey of America's "best" essays shows that today's most widely anthologized essay writers frequently blend such creative writing as poetry, narrative, and memoir with their expository prose. Almost all of Houghton Mifflin's *Best Essays* for the last five years prove the point. Academic discourse in our composition classes seems to be following a similar pattern. How can composition teachers utilize creative writing assumptions and techniques? How can we use more human approaches to writing that emphasize trial and error and deemphasize talent? How can we use our *own* writing? How can we use metawriting? And how can we encourage students to better understand their own thinking and emotional writing resources?

Answers to these questions may be found, in part, in the work of poet and professor Richard Hugo. In a number of his essays, Hugo's creative writing pedagogy emerges as pedagogy that can also enhance the composition classroom. The differing "disciplines" of creative and expository writing have much to exchange with each other, particularly when we can be clear about their common elements. Richard Hugo's creative writing pedagogy is directed at the most common of elements in all writers—their humanity and their relationships to language, ideas, and feelings. Hugo offers both practical pointers about writing and advice about self-discovery in the context of creative writing.

The Triggering Town, which offers some of Hugo's best essays on Creative Writing, was originally published by Norton in 1979 as a collection of a poet's literary essays.[1] It soon became a popular text in creative writing classes because it was useful for both students and teachers. Hugo describes various methods he used to find and develop his poems, yet he is not didactic and makes it clear that "his way" need not be the reader's way of writing. *The Triggering Town* is a very human text—it can encourage students to *want* to think and learn more about their own writing processes while it is a text that also teaches teachers about humility and flexibility.

Although focused on poetry, Hugo's writing legacy, as it is mapped out in *The Triggering Town,* can help to define issues and practices in today's composition classroom. Whether you are a teacher of creative writing or composition, or both, is not important. Many of Hugo's ideas are common to most writing acts. His predilection was undoubtedly writing poetry, but his most basic beliefs about writing helped shape his (and many of his friends' and students') successful nonfiction and fiction.

Before I detail some of Hugo's pedagogy, let me tell you a story about him. I'm remembering one particular class that was taught by Richard Hugo at the University of Montana in 1975. Hugo had an arthritic hip and wasn't able to move around very easily. It was a beginning creative writing class and I thought I was pretty hot because I was Hugo's TA. The class "lesson" had less to do with writing and was more about humility; at least that's what I can recall (with the help of fellow TA, Ed Meek) today. Hugo was talking about a picture and how he used it as a writing landscape. During his explanation, a young freshman dropped her notebook and all of her papers spilled onto the floor. We were sitting in a circle and when the notebook fell, none of us knew what to do. Hugo got up and then, with difficulty, kneeled down on one knee to pick up the papers. That one act made me stop feeling "hot" as a TA and realize the need for genuine humility and grace in the creative writing classroom.

At the foundation of Hugo's humility was his belief that all students could write at least one great poem or story. "Great," as it's used here, should be understood as relative to each writer's abilities and personal experiences. I'd like to push this point about possible student greatness into the world of composition. What if our attitude about teaching freshmen to write included the prospect that students might well produce great writing? If not great in a literary sense, great in a human sense. What if we learned to believe that some students might create the greatest writing of their lives—in *our* classes? This isn't so farfetched. Though it's always our hope that students will progress beyond the "term" that limits our classes, perhaps some don't. Some students may never again write an extended essay that includes who they are as centrally as they might in our classes. What if it's exactly that human ingredient that allows students to express their thinking and feeling more cogently through one of our assignments? Maybe that human point combined with some artificial assignment constraints and some weird or lucky timing will synthesize into a truly fine text. Composition teachers sometimes approach reading a batch of student essays as drudgery—and for good, underpaid reasons. But what if we approach that batch of papers as possibly containing a writer's best piece of writing? Richard Hugo knew what even the hope of that one great text could do for both student writers *and* their teachers.

Good student writing is only marginally about genre. It has more to do with intelligence, creativity, and language skills. Hugo wanted to help writers learn how to tap their own imaginations. One of his best methods was explaining how "triggering" thinking could enable a writer to find what he or she really needs to say.

> The initiating subject should trigger the imagination as well as the poem. If it doesn't, it may not be a valid subject but only something you feel you should write a poem about . . . The point is, the triggering subject should not carry with it moral or social obligations to feel or claim you feel certain ways. (1979, 5)

All writing teachers want to create assignments like these. If we don't engage our students' imaginations with the writing challenges or "triggers" that we give them, then we can depend only on that sense of obligation "to hand *something* in" to motivate our students to write. Hugo made it clear that the "triggering assignment" should not be burdened with a sense of obligation. Instead, the freedom to change was an essential part of Hugo's concept of triggering—and it's essential in composition classes too. Multiple drafts demonstrate the flexibility of how initial reception of our assignments can change if we really encourage students to drop a sense of "the assignment" and to find what it is they really need to say. Hugo professed that the "triggering town" of a poem was not what the poem is about. It was a place for a writer to begin, but implicit in his thinking is the challenge for the writer to find his or her own "town."

In *The Triggering Town*, Richard Hugo developed an approach to writing that assumes a poem can be said to have two subjects, the initiating or triggering subject which starts the poem or 'causes' the poem to be written, and the real or generated subject, which the poem comes to say or mean, and which is generated or discovered in the poem during the writing (4). Hugo believed that the real triggering in writing happens when "physical details correspond to attitudes the poet has toward the world and himself" (5). This approach to writing parallels the way composition classes may "trigger" writing with discussions, assignments, readings, etc. A number of composition classes today depend on students thinking about their own experiences to discover the content of their writing. Triggering in a broad sense emphasizes thinking about individual writing processes, which is the real subject of most composition and creative writing classes anyway. Hugo knew that a large part of teaching writing meant encouraging students to discover and generate their own thinking and feelings about the worlds they were living in. Hugo's notion of triggering gave his students and readers the ability to intuitively understand a method of writing that challenged them to reach beyond the surfaces of what they initially wrote.

An essential part of what made Hugo confident that student writers could progress beyond the triggering town was his belief that thinking about language was always as important as anything a writer was writing about. He stressed the idea that "The subject should serve the words" (6). Many composition teachers might think that's fine for a poet, but in a class of freshman essay writers, stressing subjects is often more interesting and stimulating than stressing language. Today's composition theory typically emphasizes ideation over concerns about sentence rhythm, word choice, grammar, spelling, and punctuation. However, most of us probably don't think writing is ever an either-or process when it comes to ideas and language. I think what Hugo meant was that writers can "follow" their language into ideas—in other words, that consciousness about *what* a writer's words were actually doing helped writers develop clearer and more creative conceptions about what their writing could mean.

I've found one way to ease the constant tension between ideas and language handling is to listen to my students. Recently, while they were working on rewriting an assignment, I asked my students to read several essays from *On Writing Well* (Zinsser 1990) that deal with sentence- and word-level rewriting concerns. I noticed that their metawriting for this essay assignment frequently mentioned a relationship between focusing on Zinsser's language-handling advice and being surprised at how this focus increased rewriting energy at all levels. In Hugo's terms, the triggering challenge of word or sentence rewriting helped writers move beyond that particular trigger to find out more about their own ideas and feelings.

I think Hugo focused on language because he sensed that so many of his students had not experienced enough language-centered concentration in their lives, but he was not dogmatic. In fact, he believed that "Once you have a certain amount of accumulated technique, you can forget it in the act of writing" (1979, 17). Hugo believed strongly in the humanity of student writers and knew enough about psychology to understand that when students could feel confident in their accumulated skills, they would be freer to find ideas. In other words, he knew that good language skills created more possibilities for individual thinking and feeling.

One of my favorite chapters in *The Triggering Town* is "Stray Thoughts on Roethke and Teaching." Hugo uses Roethke to illustrate the point that integrity is the real source of a teacher's authority. "Emotional honesty is a rare thing in the academic world or anywhere else for that matter, and nothing is more prized by good students" (1979, 29). I doubt there are many writing teachers who have never had to confront the difference between what we might feel about particular student writers, and what we may say or write on their papers. All of us would probably like to think we are consistently fair and not biased by our emotions, but the truth of this is, we can probably only *try* to construct a sense of emotional honesty.

Personally, the technique that most helps me to believe in my own emotional honesty as a writing teacher is doing my own assignments. It shows my students that I am not so far beyond them as a writer myself. And it teaches me about my own assignments. I also maintain that we teachers who do our own assignments are much better readers of writers who are trying to answer the same writing problems that we ourselves have experienced. However, this pedagogical support is secondary to the point that we can at least be honest about our own assignments because we've actually done them *with* our students. The preposition is important here. Our assignments aren't "for" or "at" or "to" our students. Instead of the typical opposition between students and teachers, there's a real basis for collaboration among writers and readers.

In other words, if you teach writing, write![2] It strikes me as hypocritical when I meet a writing teacher who isn't writing or is afraid to show a stranger his or her writing. I simply don't see any integrity to the idea that teaching writing does not mean doing writing. If we ask our students to write, to read and constantly to subject their thinking, feelings, and writing to the scrutiny of others, why should we ask less of ourselves?

Hugo believed that the writer's quest for self is an essential part of poetry, and he knew that finding that self was not a matter of inspired talent so much as hard work and a willingness to experiment. "Real experimentation is involved in every good poem because the poet searches for ways to unlock his imagination through trial and error" (1979, 33). This notion is not limited to poetry. As freshman composition teachers, it's essential for us to teach students that our classes are not about seeing who has talent and who doesn't, but are about developing processes that can enable thinkers to better express themselves. Or to put it more simply, experimentation and drafting give student writers more opportunities to discover and improve themselves, as well as their texts.

One of *The Triggering Town's* most unusual chapters is "Nuts and Bolts"—it's a very personal list of writing rules. Hugo describes many of his notions about writing, as well as detailing his actual practices. He qualifies them as suggestions, saying, "If they work for you, good." Of course in a chapter that says don't use semicolons and write only with number 2 pencils, we can quickly assume that some of his points are arbitrary and personal. In showing us his personal writing rules as an *illustration* of how a writer guides himself through the act of writing, Hugo is really suggesting that each writer must develop his or her own "nuts and bolts" and that it's appropriate for each writer to include the personal elements that enhance one's writing process.

How does awareness of writing processes translate into student essays? One technique that does this is easily described in our composition jargon as "metawriting." I define metawriting for my students as simply telling the story of how their texts were written. I think I know when I'm a success as a teacher in a class of freshman composition, and it's not when I read an "A" paper. Instead, when I read metawritings that describe the sincere rewriting efforts that have enabled students to learn more about their thinking than they first thought, I know they're constructing the real foundation of a writing process. Doesn't that sound rosy? The fact is, that most metawriting is about the struggle to write, as Hugo himself demonstrated in essays such as "Ci Vediamo" in *The Triggering Town.*

I'd like to conclude with a point Hugo made in his chapter defending creative writing classes. Hugo believed creative writing classes were the most humane classes in the university. He knew that most of the content classes spent too little time recognizing who was in them and that creative writing classes were probably the one academic place a student really had to think about who he or she was—or wanted to be—as a writer. In *The Triggering Town,* Hugo told the story of a student reading an autobiographical story out loud to a creative writing class in 1940. The story was about a fourteen-year-old boy going to a whorehouse with some older boys. The student was candid about his failed attempts to seem confident and the story ended with him panicking and running away. Hugo claimed that that story would have gotten the student thrown out of most classes in his school. However, the teacher in Hugo's class

> raved approval, and we realized we had just heard a special moment in a person's life, offered in honesty and generosity, and we better damn well appreciate it. It may have been the most important lesson one can teach. You are someone and you have a right to your life. Too simple? Already covered in the Constitution? Try to find someone who teaches it. Try to find a student who knows it so well he or she doesn't need it confirmed. (65)

I maintain that Hugo's point about the ability of creative writing classes to affirm each student's humanity is true of all writing classes.[3]

Notes

1. Hugo's other essays on writing can be found in his posthumously published autobiography, *The Real West Marginal Way.*

2. See "When Writing Teachers Don't Write: Speculations About Probable Causes and Cures" by Maxine Hairston for a very good discussion of the pedagogical necessity for writing teachers to write. Also see "Being a Writer vs. Being an Academic: A Conflict in Goals" by Peter Elbow and "Writing Teachers Writing and the Politics of Dissent" by Frank D. Walters for some good updates on Hairston's thinking.

3. Hugo wrote a number of poems that address issues of affirming humanity and humility. In *Making Certain It Goes On,* see for example: "Degrees of Gray in Philipsburg" (216), "What Thou Lovest Well Remains American" (235), "Letter to Levertov from Butte" (307), and "Villager" (415).

Works Cited

Elbow, Peter. 1995. "Being a Writer vs. Being an Academic: A Conflict in Goals." *College Composition and Communication* 46 (1): 72–83.

Hairston, Maxine. 1986. "When Writing Teachers Don't Write: Speculations About Probable Causes and Cures." *Rhetoric Review* 5: 62–70.

Hugo, Richard. 1984. *Making Certain It Goes On*. New York: Norton.

——— . *The Real West Marginal Way*. 1986. Eds. Hugo, Ripley S., Welch, Lois, and Welch, James. New York: Norton.

——— . 1979. *The Triggering Town*. New York: Norton.

Meek, Ed. 1988. "What Thou Lovest Well Remains American." *The North American Review,* June: 58–59.

Walters, Frank D. 1995. "Writing Teachers Writing and the Politics of Dissent." *College English* 57 (7): 822–39.

Zinsser, William. 1990. *On Writing Well*. 4th ed. New York: HarperCollins.

5

Broken Circles and Curious Triangles
Rethinking the Writers' Workshop

Hephzibah Roskelly

University of North Carolina-Greensboro

Scene 1: A group of twelve students, seven women, five men, sit in a classroom. They are in one large circle. They are quietly reading, looking over notes on a page. One, slightly outside the circle, says, "Would someone like to begin?" A brief hesitation, and one does, a male who sits across from the questioner. "The writer does a great job with . . . ," he begins. The discussion that ensues has many in the circle contributing, commenting on the text in front of them all. The one who asks the first question, the teacher, nods and occasionally makes a statement to redirect or to help the group move on. It is the fiction workshop in action.

Scene 2: A group of twenty-two students, fourteen women, eight men, sit in the same classroom earlier in the day. They are arranged in four circles. They are quietly reading, studying notes on a page. One slightly outside the circles, near the front of the room, asks a question. "What do you think of what you read?" A brief hesitation, and students begin to talk in each circle. "I really liked it when you . . . ," from one woman. "I wondered why you . . . ," from another. The discussion ensues, many in the circles contributing, commenting on the texts in front of them. The one who asks the first question, the teacher, nods to groups and moves among them, occasionally making a statement that redirects attention or pushes the groups to move on. It is the composition classroom in action.

These two groups of circles seem much the same to the casual observer, and even to the not-so-casual student who may be a part of both classes. Both circles emphasize writing from the group—and the discussion of that writing. The two groups both pay attention not only to the texts but to the writers, who sit in the circle and hear the reactions from their classmates and whose presence helps shape the reaction the group gives. Both classrooms locate the focus of the discussion in the responses of readers to the piece of writing, the class members who have read and prepared to comment on their readings. In short, the workshop in both creative writing and in composition seems to bring to life Aristotle's triangle within their circles—the relationships among speaker (writer), audience (readers), and subject (texts) that composition students are in the process of becoming familiar with through their textbooks and classroom discussions of communication and effect.

Of all the ideas and strategies that composition has learned from the creative writing classroom, it is the workshop that has been most universally accepted and most successfully translated. With good reason. The writing workshop recreates the dynamic that teachers of writing, no matter what their individual persuasions, want most to achieve. With the elements of rhetoric present in the actions of their students, teachers can confront directly issues of intention and revision, relationship between readers and writers, the emergence of purpose, considerations of appropriateness and style. This interplay comes naturally when students themselves have a hand in creating it, when it is they who ask the questions about intention: "Did it mean that she would never leave him when she wrote the note about Japan?"; about revision: "If she changed the first paragraph, would you get into the scene better?"; about voice: "Should he sound mad when he's trying to get somebody to change their mind?"

The fact that much recent composition theory reinforces the idea of the writer's workshop makes this staple of the creative writing classroom even more appealing to composition teachers. Karen Burke Lefevre's work on invention (1987) suggests that ideas occur to writers and thinkers in social ways as much or more so than in isolation and that to value the methods for achieving such social interaction is to enhance students' abilities to compose effectively in writing and in speaking. "Rhetorical invention becomes an act that may involve speaking and writing, and that at times involves more than one person; it is furthermore an act initiated by writers and completed by readers, extending over time . . ." (1). LeFevre's research grounds itself in the work of social psychologist Lev Vygotsky, whose experiments with young children establish the social nature of problem solving, and the social roots of individuation in language and thought. Reading their work, and that of others—Freire, Britton, Bruner, Bruffee—a teacher finds a mandate for the writing classroom to become a space where the social group has primacy, where the circle is the geometrical shape of choice.

Yet a problem begins to emerge. Theories from compositionists, philosophers, psychologists, educators, and anthropologists have been embedded in the claims that composition makes for its activities: social construction theory for group work; theories of learning and development for process instruction in writing; theories of literacy for canon expansion. But creative writing as a course, which is the genesis of the writers' circle, has itself avoided—often with great force—the claims of theory, and the need of theory in the classroom. In the introduction to *Colors of a Different Horse,* a book he coedits with Wendy Bishop on creative writing and composition, Hans Ostrom (1994) characterizes the continuing distaste for theory among creative writing teachers: "They may think, 'It's damned hard to write, damned hard to publish, win fellowships, earn a living through writing. I can't afford time to theorize about teaching, even if I wanted to. What I need is some luck, some time to write, and the courage to keep writing, none of which "theory" can give me.'" Ostrom calls the writing teacher's outlook "besieged," manifesting itself in hostility for critical and pedagogical theory (xvi–xx).

Creative writing courses are still dominated, as Ostrom and others have pointed out, by an incredibly resilient New Critical model, with the text as "verbal icon" and readers and writers the searchers after the tenor and vehicle of its expression. Consequently, these teachers resist attempts at challenges to the sanctity of the text. Often vehemently. As Eugene Garber (1994) puts it in an ironically exaggerated comment in Bishop's and Ostrom's book: "Creative writing workshops glory in the idiosyncrasies and particularities that escape the nets of critical paradigms and thereby keep us human and individuated. Workshops are piratical, eclectic, pragmatic, care nothing for theoretical consistency, create camaraderie and support, help people and WORK LIKE NO OTHER ACADEMIC ENTERPRISE WORKS [writer's caps]" (13).

The belief that practice works BECAUSE theory is not involved is widespread among teachers who dislike or distrust theory's explanations. This aversion to theory, expressed by this teacher and many others, is really, I would argue, an aversion to considering the messy effects of allowing readers and writers to invade the texts students study. Theory itself can be seen as an explosion of ideas about change—the way things alter when reader and writer and experience become part of the text produced and interpreted. And the deep resistance among creative writing teachers to theory—its benefit, even its existence—should strike the first warning that a writers' workshop circle may in fact not perform some of the operations that composition teachers hope for in their classes.

The clearest instance of theory's lack of force in the workshop—and the clearest way in which the writer's circle perverts the aim of composition courses—can be found in the rules of the workshop itself. Describing the workshop in an essay in Bishop's and Ostrom's collection, Francois Camoin (1994) writes of these rules: "Imagine a class in which the teacher is, for the most part, silent. Imagine texts which deny their own authority. (For it is the Law of the Workshop, as powerful as the law of incest is in the culture at large, that *the author must not speak.* This fundamental Law shapes the workshop, makes it what it is)" (4). The silence of the writer is the primary rule of the workshop, one that was true in my workshop days at the University of Louisville, one that remains true on my campus, and, as Camoin attests, at many others as well.

This silence extends beyond the writer. Several years ago, a graduate student in my university, an M.F.A. student and first-year composition instructor, came to talk to me about the fiction workshop he was a student in. Repeating a comment from one of his classmates, he said, "And so Joe said, 'If I were your reader, I would not understand why Hallie leaves in such a huff.'" He went on to talk about the story and his intentions before I stopped him. "Wait a minute," I said. "Who does Joe *think* he is?" The student stared at me a minute. "I don't know," he said. "Somebody else. Not my reader." The reader, like the writer in the workshop, is silent. The workshop group members who speak in that classroom are not real readers, but stand-ins. The classroom responder becomes something like an editor, or arbiter of taste, appropriateness, or expedient notions of "what the market will bear," not a reader at all. As a former workshop participant says, "The workshop response to stories like mine that claim the master narrative, that aim to expand its range of vocalizers, is to silence them with disapproval couched in technical terms. I have seen this in every workshop I have attended." And she concludes with a parenthesis "(and here is a place for some enlightened pedagogy)" (Garber, 18).

This role of the classroom responder as false reader is reinforced in recent research by Mara Holt and Wendell Mayo on collaborative groups and workshops. Significantly, these teachers note, students relished the role of responder rather than writer. They were positive in the roles as "critical readers." "They felt connected to the group when they played the role of the Institution themselves. As one student wrote, 'the only time I did not feel displaced . . . was when I was reviewing someone else's work'" (10). In a classroom of writers and readers where neither talks, what happens to the triangle of communication? What kind of community circle is it where the main law is silence?

The writers' workshop is often a perversion of the kind of dynamic movement among writer, subject, purpose, and reader that rhetoric creates, and the writers' circle needs to be broken up enough to consider the real readers, real texts, real writers who form it. As Ann Berthoff (1982) pointedly argues, teachers of writing need to keep in mind that "meaning is dynamic and dialectical, that it depends on context and perspective, the setting in which it is seen and the angle from which it is seen" (43). She proposes a new triangle to amend Aristotle's, a curious one she calls it, with broken lines to indicate the mediated, unfinished quality of communication in the interpretive process.

This new triangle in our workshop circles would allow students to be conscious of their roles as meaning makers, finding out "how being conscious of what we are doing is the way to find out how to do it" (44).

Composition has certainly not escaped the perversion of communication in its triangles and circles even though it attempts to use rather than ignore theory when it sets up its own circles in the classroom. In my first year composition class this semester, students are writing on Harriet Ann Jacobs's use of rhetoric in *Incidents in the Life of a Slave Girl*. We have as a class talked about the power of voice and of experience and begun to derive some generalizations about how arguments get made effectively. I have written openings on the board that seem especially promising. When students bring drafts to the workshop the next class meeting, I sit in on one group and listen to students read. Two of the five students have written as first sentences, "Harriet Ann Jacobs uses emotional appeals to make the reader have to sympathize with her condition." I recognize this sentence. It's one I have written on the board in the last class. Students defend themselves when I question. "You didn't say we couldn't use it." "Are you interested in this kind of rhetorical strategy to write about?" I say. They both shrug. Other group members say, "If I didn't know Ms. Roskelly had written it on the board, it wouldn't affect me when I read." Later, when I read drafts, I see students who are desperately trying to fill in the blanks of the assignment I've made, with little of their own interest evident in their prose (despite the fact that they were interested in Jacobs and in rhetoric in class discussion).

In spite of our best efforts, composition teachers who use the workshop, the circle of the group to talk about texts, fail to find ways to help their students' prose have what Peter Elbow calls "real voice," the kind of authenticity that comes from seeing themselves as real readers and real writers in their groups. The institutional authority of the teacher and the teacher as representative of "how it's done" remains central to students' writing more often than we would like to admit. Far from being a "zone of proximal development," or the negotiated, dialogic space Berthoff calls for, the composition peer group is often a place where, like in the creative writing circle, the real reader becomes simply the stand-in, the real writer becomes silent in the face of what really matters, which is "what will sell" in the market of the writing classroom.

How do both of our professional circles of writing teachers—creative writing teachers and composition teachers—themselves learn to foster in the groups they create the authenticity of experience that both theory and our own practice tells us we need? First, we might consider what difference it might make to say, as Berthoff does with assurance, that all writing classes "are creative writing classes" (95). Teachers must change their ideas of what creativity might be and how it might be discussed. Hans Ostrom notes that one fear creative writers have about composition and rhetoric teachers is the desire of rhetoricians to explore deeply the creative process. "Those who study 'writing' without adjectives (just plain writing processes, not 'creative' or 'imaginative' or 'art' writing) are eager to study creative writers—in part to determine whether 'creative' is a useful adjective. With their very attitude toward the writing they wish to study, they thereby threaten to demystify an entire domain, or at least to demystify that crucial adjective, 'creative'" (xvi). It's clear from Ostrom's comment that writers fear this demystification, as if there's something shameful about the hard process of writing, or as if smoke and mirrors is part of the act of writing itself. One difference that making all writing classes "creative" would have is to demystify the process of composing, at least in part, and release it into language.

The first step toward making our circles real then is to find ways to break the composition/creative writing boundary. Wendy Bishop (1993) has argued eloquently for a way to see beyond the categories that drive much of the writing instruction with departments: "We need to be crossing the line between composition and creative writing far more often than we do. In fact, we may want to eliminate the line entirely" (117). Her own courses, as she describes them, have attempted to cross the line using creative thinking to compose in a variety of genres in both courses labeled "composition" and "creative writing." "My writing courses—no matter what they're called in the college catalog are now emphasizing writing commonalities, process instruction, genre experimentation for comparisons, if not just for a break, and obviously, I'm teaching more similarly in all these courses than I would have expected to when I started teaching 17 years ago and read the descriptions for courses I was then being assigned" (117).

We need to understand how arbitrary those divisions are and work against them in the name of the kind of creativity that produces good writing no matter what the genre. Graduate students in my teaching seminar this semester used a poem as a tool for talking about composing theory, and the class began an intense discussion of how they might confront a student response to an analytical assignment written in poetry. They were not at all resolved to "accept" the poem since that was a genre they didn't teach. Composition teachers would have to bring genres, forms, and styles into their writing workshops that many now diminish or proscribe. Students in these new composition classes would be writing stories and arguments; a story about identity and courage perhaps and an argument that explores Jacobs's voice in *Incidents in the Life of a Slave Girl.* They would both read and write poems and conduct research projects—a study of children's learning and rhyme, for example. In these possible assignments students would see all their work as instances of the forms of their own imagination, and as demonstrations of how language helps shape experience and evidence. More radically and much less practiced already, new creative writing classes would ask for written critical analysis as well as fictional narrative, or use journals and nonfiction as a part of creative writing work and workshop discussions.

But the "philosophic laboratory" of creative thinking and writing that Berthoff has advocated for writing classes can't be fostered by redesigning assignments or by changing titles alone. The primary step toward forming an authentic circle of interpreters in our classrooms is to investigate the strategies that work toward the end of making powerful interpreters of our students. Louise Rosenblatt's (1978) work describes the transactional process of interpretation as one in which readers bring experience to the text in a collaborative moment that she calls the event of interpretation, or the poem. *The Reader, The Text, The Poem* is her exploration of the dynamic of that interpretive event, and teachers of writing can find in her discussion a blueprint for reenvisioning the activity in their own classrooms.

Rosenblatt shows the reader as active, not a blank slate for a prefabricated message. The reader builds a response from what she knows already of life and texts and what she learns from the reading experience. The poem, the interpretation of the text, "is not an object or an ideal entity. It happens during a coming-together, a compenetration, of a reader and a text" (12). Writing teachers must recognize readers' creativity, as well as writers', in making their circles, and in this way they can establish the conditions for the circle to be composed not of ideal representatives of texts, writers and readers, but of real readers and real writers engaged in a process of negotiation.

Writing teachers need to find ways to rethink the method of conducting the workshop so that it reflects the kind of dynamic interchange that Rosenblatt describes in her investigation of interpretation. Teachers who use the writers' circle as real transaction rethink their traditional roles as guardians of authority and power who have final say on not only genres available but also—and especially in creative writing—on the conditions under which they happen most effectively. It's this authority that undercuts the uses of theory in the creative writing classroom. Despite the fact that the teacher in the workshop may not speak much, the authority of the teacher/writer as a symbol of how writing works speaks more loudly than any other voice in the circle. As one creative writing teacher describes the workshop dynamic, "We assess publishability in terms of poorly articulated, but nonetheless prevalent, standards of 'good writing.' We promote the idea that these standards reflect universal and enduring aesthetic values that exist somehow outside their cultural construction. We proceed as if writing is somehow a "natural activity," firmly rooted in talent, which cannot really be taught, but only nurtured" (Haake 1994, 80). And it's true in the composition class as well, where teacherly authority is signaled by the controls placed on groups' responses or on the forms of discourse. Institutional authority, with the teacher its representative and guardian, maintains its own mystification by talking *around* processes, effects, and connections rather than *of* them.

As Rosenblatt and Berthoff have attempted to remind us for more than two decades, meaning is made in the real transaction between readers and texts, in the action of negotiating meaning as they make the poem. The circle is a fine place for this negotiation, where writers talk, readers talk, and teachers talk as readers and writers. Where texts speak too, of the forms of their construction, of the processes of their invention. The observer enters this writing classroom and sees new kinds of circles, hears new kinds of conversation. One begins: "Tell me why you . . . ," and is answered: "I was trying to. . . ." And is brought into connection: "You see how you're looking for a way to decide. . . ." The observer listens to participants move back and forth in their talk, not just around the circle, but through it, making the conversation real, rather than predetermined, the forms created rather than replicated. There's a reason the space in the middle of the workshop circle stands empty. It's not dead air. That's where the poem happens, where the curious triangle fits just right.

Works Cited

Berthoff, Ann. 1982. *The Making of Meaning.* Portsmouth, NH: Boynton/Cook.

Bishop, Wendy. 1993. "Crossing the Lines: On Creative Composition and Composing Creative Writing." *Writing on the Edge.* 4 (Spring): 117–30.

Bishop, Wendy, and Hans Ostrom, eds. 1994. *Colors of a Different Horse: Rethinking Creative Writing Theory and Pedagogy.* Urbana, IL: NCTE.

Camoin, Francois. 1994. "The Workshop and Its Discontents." In Bishop and Ostrom, 3–7.

Elbow, Peter. 1981. *Writing with Power.* New York: Oxford University Press.

Garber, Eugene, and Jan Ramjerdi. 1994. "Reflections on the Teaching of Creative Writing: A Correspondence." In Bishop and Ostrom, 8–26.

Haake, Katherine. 1994. "Teaching Creative Writing if the Shoe Fits." In Bishop and Ostrom, 77–99.

Holt, Mara, and Wendell Mayo. Nov. 1990. "Negotiated Course Design: Hybrid Applications of Pedagogy in Writing Courses." Paper presented at MMLA. Kansas City, MO.

Jacobs, Harriet Ann. 1990. *Incidents in the Life of a Slave Girl.* New York: Oxford University Press.

Lefevre, Karen Burke. 1987. *Invention as a Social Act.* Carbondale, IL: Southern Illinois University Press.

Ostrom, Hans. 1994. "Introduction." In Bishop and Ostrom, xi–xxiii.

Rosenblatt, Louise. 1978. *The Reader, The Text, The Poem.* Carbondale, IL: Southern Illinois University Press.

6

When Writers Write About Writing

Muriel Harris
Purdue University

As a tutor in our writing lab for many years, I've observed at close range how much some students enjoy narrating their own stories on paper. I also know how expressive narrative stymies other writers and how uncomfortable they can be moving out of the realm of what they perceive as objective reporting of information. When assigned to write personal accounts, they compose chronologically appropriate prose that reads like a videotape script: first this happened, then that happened, and then afterward, that happened. The writing tends to be flat, lacking any spark of creativity, and the student composing such discourse often seems as bored by it as the potential reader might be. Such students compose limp, lifeless prose because they are assigned to write personal essays and cannot find a way into overcoming their reluctance to explore their lives publicly or becoming invested in the topic they've chosen. Personal writing is difficult for them, though other students come to any form of expressive writing ready to engage with their thoughts, emotions, and stories. But even artful storytellers and writers of journals and personal essays often struggle to find tales they want to tell or events or personal insights to explore in writing.

One response to this and a way into helping students engage with personal writing and also assisting them to grow as writers is an assignment unit that invites students to investigate their own writing processes and compare their writing habits and preferences with those of other writers. This permits a kind of personal storytelling and analysis that can often create—even in writers who are usually unsuccessful in this mode—compelling stories about themselves and their friends as writers. They are given an opportunity to look inward as well as outward from a perspective most writers have not considered before. Good writers are usually fascinated by probing through various aspects of how they write; less successful writers become interested in giving words to what causes them problems and what they dislike, and they are often surprised by similar accounts of composing difficulties told by good writers. Since students have been writing throughout their school career, they can explore familiar territory with fresh perspectives and often wind up knowing more about how they write and/or how they might write in a more productive manner.

I first launched into classroom attention to how writers write in my tutor training courses, which enroll students preparing to become peer tutors. Here the purpose is to help the group understand how composing processes can differ from writer to writer, an important set of insights for tutoring because of its emphasis on individual differences, but also of great value to any writer. By the time writers are enrolled in postsecondary institutions, they have been given a great deal of advice and instruction on how to write. But they have rarely had the opportunity to think about how they as individuals write and how writing practices can vary from writer to writer. Acquiring a metalanguage to talk about their writing habits permits students not only to investigate their writing processes and preferences but also to think about whether they are composing in ways that are or are not productive for them. Writing center theory and practice focus on individualizing writing assistance, and tutors commonly report the improvement students can experience when they recognize better ways to approach writing tasks. Not better in any absolute way—but better because some approach is more appropriate for that particular person. Much of this awareness of difference among writers as well as self-diagnosis can be achieved in the classroom. Thus, although the sequence of activities described here has been used in tutor training courses, the outcome is clearly beneficial for any writer, and I offer this series of assignments as a unit for use in composition classrooms as well as activities that can include class discussions, journals, interviews, and writing assignments.

A particularly useful way to initiate the topic of individual variation in writing processes is to launch into a discussion of human differences. This can be done in terms of how we conduct our daily lives, beginning with an informal analysis of one of the spectrums of human cognition, such as a learning style inventory or a personality preference test. Particularly useful in a writing classroom is the Myers-Briggs Type Indicator (MBTI) because it has provided a number of very useful insights into composing processes. *Personality and the Teaching of Composition*, by George H. Jensen and John DiTiberio (1984), and Thomas Thompson's collection of essays, *Most Excellent Differences: Essays on Using Type Theory in the English Classroom*, are book-length discussions of the MBTI and composition. A useful bibliography of other works, as well as a helpful brief introduction to the MBTI and its uses in the composition classroom, is offered in Sharon Cramer and Tom

Reigstad's "Using Personality to Teach Writing (1994)." In its comprehensive form, administered by professionals, the MBTI offers consistent and highly reliable information that students can use in career counseling and other areas. But in the composition classroom, where the purpose is only to raise awareness of differences among people, one of the short forms of the test can suffice—though it is important to remind students that a brief, informal version serves only as an introduction to ways that people differ and does not offer the consistency of the complete form (as administered by professionals) and should not be taken as accurate analysis. Various short forms are available on World Wide Web sites[1] and in books such as Kiersey's and Bates's *Please Understand Me: Character & Temperament Type,* and they usually consist of about thirty-five to fifty questions that ask for preferences between two alternatives, such as the following:

I prefer:

_____ a. quiet, thoughtful time alone.

　　　　　(or)

_____ b. active, energetic time with people.

_____ a. making decisions after finding out what others think.

　　　　　(or)

_____ b. making decisions without consulting others.

_____ a. avoiding deadlines.

　　　　　(or)

_____ b. setting a schedule and sticking to it.

_____ a. the abstract or theoretical.

　　　　　(or)

_____ b. the concrete or real.

_____ a. being free to do things on the spur of the moment.

　　　　　(or)

_____ b. knowing well in advance what I am expected to do.

The results of the Myers-Briggs are tallied along four dimensions indicating how individuals respond to the world around them:

extravert (E)	-or-	introvert (I)
sensing (S)	-or-	intuitive (N)
thinking (T)	-or-	feeling (F)
judging (J)	-or-	perceiving (P)

Each of the four dimensions is a continuum along which individuals fall, some with a strong preference at one end or the other and others with less pronounced preferences. These are, moreover, preferences and not static pigeonholes, and people generally move back and forth along the spectrum, inclining toward one end or the other of the spectrum in different situations. Even the boundaries between the four dimensions tend to blur, and the dimensions are affirming for all in that they describe preferences at both ends in terms of strengths and weaknesses of each type. For example, the first dimension identifies extraverts (the Jungian spelling is maintained here) as those who focus their energy outward toward interaction with people and things while introverts are more drawn to inner experience, their own reflections, and plans for future action. Extraverts, who prefer activity and active experience, tend to leap into tasks with little planning while introverts think best alone and prefer to plan first before acting. The sensing (S)–intuition (N) dimension identifies "sensers," those who prefer (and value more highly) sensory perception—what they see, hear, touch, smell, and taste—and are the practical and realistic types, as differentiated from "intuitors," who prefer intuitive perception and are attracted to abstract, theoretical ideas. The thinking (T)–feeling (F) dimension distinguishes between "thinkers," who value objectivity in decision making and base judgments on logic and facts, and "feelers," who use subjective bases of valuing and give more weight to "people issues" and values in decision making. The fourth set looks at how people approach a task and separates the spontaneous and flexible types ("perceivers") from those who prefer closure and do not like leaving decisions unmade ("judgers"). This is only a very brief summary of the characteristics of these types; literature on the MBTI offers extensive analyses of characteristics typical of each preference type.

Class discussion of the MBTI preferences focuses not on test scores or labels but on comparing and talking about the differences they suggest. There are the list-makers of the world (J's), those who prefer to begin with general principles and/or the grand plan of the paper (N's), and those who prefer to get the details down first ("I have to collect notecards for days beforehand") (S's). Some students like to work quietly by themselves (I's), while others prefer studying in coffee shops or other places where there are people around (E's). One type needs to weigh all the facts (T's), though another type would rather bring harmony to a group rather than deciding who's right (F's). This is intensely interesting stuff, and students are always delighted to find soulmates in the class who also can't work well alone in a library carrel or who make up lists for the pleasure of crossing off items as they are accomplished or who think other people's feelings are more important than the facts when deciding something. Stories are told, crazy roommates and siblings are described, and unarticulated habits get put into words ("every semester I buy a daily planner and then forget to use it"; "I used to have this favorite tree stump where I sat and got my ideas") and given a perspective.

All of this sharing of preferences and personal quirks opens up the discussion to chatting about who needs to write with outlines, who plans for awhile in her head, and who just sits down and writes in order to figure out what he's going to write about, who prefers writing about personal experience and emotion and who prefers writing that focuses on factual information. The importance of this initial sharing and recognition of differences is that it opens the door to deeper understandings of how writers differ when they write and when they choose what they write about; and the discussions give students a vocabulary to start articulating aspects of writing processes that they recognize but had no terminology for. The metalanguage they acquire will begin to show up in the papers written for this assignment and the journals kept during this period. Later, when the whole unit is coming to a close, it is particularly useful to return to and summarize again such discussions as new insights will occur to the writers. Human curiosity about ourselves and how the people around us cope is the driving force in all these discussions and the writing, and I have yet to find any student in any class who finds any of this to be unexciting. Class discussions can go on endlessly as students compare where they have to sit when writing, what music they want to listen to, what they do when they're stuck and can't write any more, who was (and wasn't) a defining influence on their writing. Nontraditional students are especially relieved to hear that others have writing problems they thought were unique to themselves, and some writers—those who suddenly find that it's OK to admit that they don't start with that dreaded outline as they've been told to for years—are equally relieved to air their secret guilt. Students are encouraged to keep writing about all this in their journals, especially to observe and record more details about their writing. If time permits, mini–research projects can be launched as students become observer-recorders, watching other students in study halls and residence hall lounges and taking notes about various behaviors that were mentioned in class discussions or collaborative groups. Short reports from collaborative groups can be presented to the class for further discussion.

The major writing assignment that grows out of all this is an extensive research project that asks writers to engage in a series of interviews with someone else, preferably a person who probably writes differently than they do, and to compare that person's writing processes with their own. The other person might be a teacher whom they admire, a professional in a field in which writing is an integral part of the day's work, a parent or other relative, or a roommate or friend. The class preparation for these interviews focuses on discussions of what to ask, how to ask it, and what to look for. The focus is not on the other person's theories about writing but on that person's writing habits and attitudes. Class discussion usually generates a long list of interview questions that can be asked, such as the following:

Tell me about important writing times or incidents in your life.

Show me something you wrote and tell me the story of how it got written. Was that representative of how you write?

Tell me about where and when you usually write and what you usually use: paper, pencil, or computer. Do you think any of this makes a difference in your writing?

What is the purpose of most of your writing: to inform? entertain? persuade? present experience? earn money? help you feel fulfilled? get a good grade? help you think? get emotions out so that you can go on? complete an assignment?

Tell me a story about a time when you were really pleased or disappointed with what you wrote.

Tell me about someone who was a major influence on your writing.

What happens in the days and hours before you write? What are your first words on paper? notes? an outline? random jottings?

Do you show your work to others as you are working on it? What kind of feedback do you like?

The papers that result are a potpourri of insights and stories. Some students report on what they learned about their own writing processes and describe ways they have found that might improve those processes. Cherie, for example, concluded that

> I discovered my writing habits are bad habits. I need to change them if I want to improve my writing. I need to revise and reread my papers. Procrastinating seems to be the root of my problem. I also learned, by interviewing my roommate, that using a computer can be very helpful. Overall, this assignment made me take a closer look at my writing and helped me to see what I need to do to try and improve my skills.

Suzanne reported the following:

> Describing my approach to writing is, in a clichéd sense, like trying to put method to madness. I do not consciously follow a plan each time I write a paper. In fact, my papers seem to just materialize, leaving me with no clear conception of the process which I follow. Talking with Amy about her methods of composing a paper has revealed to me exactly how lax my writing process is. Amy has provided me with an example of how she writes so I may better analyze my own writing. . . . If I briefly glance at my writing process, I see no order. But small characteristics, such as my list-making, and writing of my first draft, do pervade my writing. This introspective approach to writing has helped me discover how I write. By talking with Amy, I have found new ideas to help aid in composing papers.

What Suzanne is recording in the excerpt quoted here is of particular interest because earlier in the semester she was somewhat mystified by how writing—including her own—gets done. Initially, Suzanne was a competent but anxious writer, concerned that she needed to improve but unable to think

about how that might happen. She tended to shrug off discussions of composing, dismissing the process as mysterious and not available to analysis.
Thus, the last sentence in the paragraph quoted above indicates Suzanne's
new awareness of her ability to think about her own writing processes and
how she might improve them. Cliff, a physics major for whom writing was
"getting your grammar right," started making connections from the MBTI
discussions to his writing: "I feel that when I began to understand how I
learn and what my personality was like, I began to use that information to
enhance my writing." For some students, such as Amy, class discussions
were more productive than the papers that resulted: "It is difficult to grasp
the various ways [that people write] without hearing people discuss them. I
appreciate the class discussions more than anything else in the class because
it is the easiest way to learn about other ways of writing."

The investigations of various writing habits generally turn up several
factors that are both important in contributing to good writing and that vary
from writer to writer. Time of day and background noise or music (or lack
of it) are frequently topics of interest, as in Tony's description of the editor
of the weekly newspaper in his home town:

> She says that her ability to write seems to peak in the afternoon hours espe-
> cially when she has been able to sleep until 10 or 11 o'clock. Mary says
> there is no chance of her writing anything sensible before 10 A.M. or like-
> wise late at night. . . . In contrast to Mary's habits listed, my ability to write
> is anchored in the early morning or late night hours. I tend to be more cre-
> ative when I have less sleep than normal, but I make more mechanical
> errors. . . . Music is very important to my writing and I know that I often
> think of outlines for entire papers while spacing out to music. And it
> doesn't seem to matter what type of music I listen to, Rap, Top 40, old
> Rock, and even some Country, they all seem to entice me to write.

Holly, however, reports different environmental preferences:

> Coffee houses are Nicki's favorite place to write. She has to be among peo-
> ple. Anytime day or night armed with her favorite pencil, one part of her
> mind stays preoccupied with her surroundings while another is totally
> focused on her writing. I don't know how she does it! I have to write in
> almost absolute silence, and I find that words tend to flow more easily from
> me early in the morning.

Class discussion of such factors might relate them back to personality
preferences (as, for example, the likelihood that Nicki would score highly as
an extravert on the MBTI scale), might focus on the need to locate other factors in the environment that can hinder or help writers, or might address the
problem of having to write under less than ideal conditions.

Another common thread of investigation centers on utensils used when writing. Roger describes the strong impact of the pencil:

> I cannot write with pens, at least not if I want to be able to decipher what is written. An old fashioned number two pencil is what I like. It gives me the freedom to erase easily. It also has a good smell to it. I like to see lead dust on my hands and wood shavings in the air; it makes me feel like I am working. It is also sort of romantic, like the way Hemingway or Fitzgerald may have done it.

Rachel prefers pens and makes correlations to the color of the ink:

> I prefer to write everything out on paper, preferably old scrap paper. I like to use blue ink but will write with a pencil or black ink if I'm in the mood. As I reflect over my writing experiences, it seems that those papers that were most formal, e.g., a term paper, were usually written in black ink first and then typed out. Regardless of the writing utensil, it must be a smooth writer and no fine point pens!

Erin offers a lengthy analysis of her use of pen and computer:

> I write just about every way I can—on paper, on the computer, on church bulletins, on restaurant napkins if the mood hits me. My writing tends to be more descriptive and real when I write it out on paper (then I usually transfer it to the computer). My writing on the computer tends to be more analytical and thought provoking (i.e., term papers, research, etc.). I prefer the convenience of the computer because my fingers can keep up better than when I write on paper and I can do spell check, move things around, and not worry about losing my stories! I prefer the convenience of the pen because I can write whenever and wherever I choose, as the mood strikes me (providing I have a pen). My writing on paper tends to be more introspective and mushy, but I don't necessarily think that that is a bad thing. I like the difference that each medium brings to my writing—it gives it more character, styles, and depth. . . . I tend to get too nerdy and intellectual when I sit in front of the computer, and I get a little too emotional on the written page, so they create a perfect balance between the two of them.

The influence of the computer on writing habits and the types of writers who use computers are both good topics for discussion in class and useful questions in the interviews. As a topic for class discussion, the use of computers in writing can include hints on how to use the computer effectively and how to incorporate it into writing processes. For some students, this can be an opportunity to examine their reluctance to use computers and to consider whether that reluctance is valid, given their writing preferences, or whether they might be able to use computers more productively. Roger, for example, expresses a strong disinclination to move to a computer before the last draft and compares his writing to his roommate's, who writes exclusively on computers:

> Bert is a Computer Technology student part-time and a full-time worker for SOA [Subaru of America]. Most of his writing consists of reports for his employer. Bert is very much a member of the computer age and that is why he heads for the seat in front of the computer screen to begin writing. He turns it on, clicks on Word, and just starts typing. He seems to think that the computer leads him to the words he wants to use. He will type for awhile and then go back over the first few paragraphs to make whatever corrections are needed. This philosophy comes from the way his mind works on a mechanical wavelength. He sees the paper as individual parts integrated to make one idea. This is from the present mind set that the sum of the parts equals the whole. . . . His exact opposite is me. I . . . cannot help but think that writing must have rituals. I believe the best thing about computers is that they produce a nice looking paper, and should be used only for the finished product.

The papers that result from these writing process studies can roam through a variety of topics as writers follow threads suggested by their findings and musings. Some writers start with a focus on writing habits that leads to contemplation of what a "writer" is. Steve realized, "I have to release sentiment in my writing and allow it to just flow. I also realized that a writer is only a writer when he writes, meaning I had to write even when there wasn't an assignment." Marla starts out assuming that "a writer is one who writes, just as a swimmer is one who swims," but then, contemplating a challenge from the friend whom she chose to study, she found herself asking more basic questions about what defines a writer and whom she writes for. Her engineering friend, she finds, "wrote when necessary and as little as possible and without much pre-thought. I asked if he considered himself a writer, because indeed he does write, and he only asked in return if I thought I was an engineer because indeed I do solve problems. He got me." As for herself, Marla wrote, "First of all, I write sometimes for classes, and often for myself. Actually, even when I write for classes it is still for myself, for the most part. Besides the professor, I don't like when other people read my writing. It is a very personal thing to me."

These last two sentences from one of Marla's papers open up an important topic—that for some writers, their writing is so personal and private they become uncomfortable when it becomes public. This acknowledgment can be a key to unlocking a number of antipathies to writing or to general feelings of reluctance to write. For some, being unwilling to share their writing with others may stem from the feeling of having their personal thoughts invaded, and for others, it may be a fear of evaluation. Until these deeper causes are articulated and worked through, some writers remain hesitant to write anything, not realizing that they are also cutting themselves off from attempting many kinds of writing that are neither personal nor private. Yet the preference for nonpersonal dominates the writing of other students such as Cliff, who explains rather adamantly that he writes "to express my ideas and facts that I gather, like experimental results or descriptions for a design of something. . . . I do not typically write things for myself, such as a personal journal, nor do I write radical, persuasive material. I feel that it is a waste of my time." Yet, later in the same paper, Cliff admits "that it took a lot to overcome my fear of writing."

The influences that shape student writing also weave their way into these discussions. For Rachel and the other writer, Amber, whom she wrote about, teacher influence varies:

> When Amber writes for teachers, she likes to include some elements of humor. She said she will sometimes conform to the professor's demands so her papers will get good grades but really resents having to do that. It makes her feel very restricted. I usually write how I feel something should be written and conform to the instructor's demands only in the forms of technical merit, i.e., margins, font size, proper pagination if required, and spelling.

The irony here is the open admission by some writers such as Amber that they feel little or no ownership of their discourse, despite so much professional discussion among teachers of writing about helping students maintain that ownership. Discussions of teacher influence can lead to insights into what makes writing enjoyable. Bonnie records her path toward her own identity as a writer:

> Sara told me that when she writes a paper for a class, usually she writes what she thinks the teacher wants to hear. Only when she is writing a journal or other personal writings, does she enjoy writing and let it help her organize her thoughts to see her emotions more clearly. I can relate to her feelings because my writing style was that way for a long time. Only when I got to college (and began to take classes that made me really care about what I was writing), did I begin to integrate my personal and public writing identities. Writing became a better tool for me to express myself. I would write things I truly cared about and when I turned my paper in, I felt that I had really learned something.

Here Bonnie affirms what textbooks and teachers tell writers: that we can write to learn, to discover what we had not known before.

The student papers in this unit on individual writing processes tend to be so rich with insights that they can be the basis for continuing class discussion until the unit winds to a close. Then, as a way of summarizing, the focus for discussion can turn to what students have learned about writing and how they can use that knowledge to become better writers. Some discoveries recorded in the papers may need some further elaboration to help students think about all the issues involved in their discoveries. For example, in his paper Steve reached the following conclusion:

> I realized from this assignment that I need to develop a consistent writing routine that allows me to make mistakes and have time to find and correct them. And as far as my prose or essay writing habits, well, I just need to get them. I need to not just think up the first drafts, but also write outlines, or even write out first drafts days before the finals are due. Let me repeat that so my brain understands what I just wrote. I need to write first drafts before they are due. WOW! A revelation. An epiphany! Life really does work. Well, I still need to work on it, but at least I am aware of the problem. Thanks for this assignment.

Steve acknowledges in this paragraph that revision means giving himself more time and starting earlier. But there is also evidence here of another insight into writing: its heuristic power. It's an affirmation of the often-quoted comment attributed to Edward Albee, "Writing has got to be an act of discovery. . . . I write to find out what I am thinking about." Whether or not Steve actually came to that WOW! revelation at the moment of writing, it introduces for discussion the powerful claim for the generative force of writing to help us articulate ideas. For some writers, free-writing in some form can be a helpful tool they haven't made use of, and this can be introduced into the class talk to see if it helps some writers add a strategy to their composing processes. It's important to stress, however, that while free-writing assists some writers, it's not for everyone. For Matthew, it's a standard technique: "I just start typing and then try and move things around and shape them so that they more or less make sense. . . . I hardly ever sit down and think about what I am going to write before actually beginning to type. I just type away." By comparison, the person he interviewed "would come up with a nice, handwritten outline that she could follow while she wrote." Once writers see how they currently write and what other options exist, there can be further discussion about considering new options that might also help. Matthew may need to recognize that for some types of writing, outlining has advantages he can make use of. Similarly, those writers who tend to depend on outlines can become more aware of the usefulness of occasionally forgoing outlines, as Jennifer V. notes:

> Throughout the writing process, the student that I interviewed does not rely on organization to structure a paper. There is never a formal outline. This aspect of the assignment has helped me to understand that this type of writing gives writers the freedom to express both the emotional and creative aspects of their writing talents.

Other generative tools for writing will surface as well and can be examined for how members of the class might add them to their repertoires for writing. One such tool that students may (or may not) recognize is the power of talk. For Nate, talk is so necessary during his composing that he quit his job on the student newspaper because he "missed discussing writing with friends before putting it in its final form. There was no time for that on the newspaper." For students in the class who also recognize talk as integral to developing their ideas (usually those who scored highly as E's in the Myers-Briggs), it's time to suggest that they meet with tutors in the writing center for prewriting conversation or that they consider forming writing groups with similarly inclined classmates so that they can meet and talk. To extend the consideration of the usefulness of writing groups, the class discussion can move to another aspect of composing strategies in which groups can help. In the papers they've written, some students will have identified their preference for—or aversion to—feedback during the time that they're drafting papers. Jennifer B. welcomes other readers: "When I show my work to someone else, usually a paper I am working on, I will allow them to read it over my shoulder as I type. They can then interject with their comments as I write the paper." On the other hand, Trisha notes that "I do not like to show my work to my friends or classmates," while for Amy, the person Trisha interviewed, "writing is not as personal. She likes to show her work to her friends and expects honest, constructive criticism." For those in the class for whom feedback is useful (and not a painful, anxiety-laden experience as some will acknowledge), peer response groups can be formed for future writing.

Class discussions can also return to preferences introduced earlier with the Myers-Briggs typing, both to recognize strengths and to become aware of the need to attend to possible weaknesses. Intuitive types should think about recording more detail in their writing just as sensing types will want to consider whether their writing rises above the details they collect to larger generalizations. In terms of what counts for proof in their writing, judgers may be overlooking useful and appropriate appeals to emotion just as feeling types should also seek out facts and logic in their arguments. Students can also begin to recognize conditions that are more likely to lead to success—for example, that some of them will work better with structured, detailed assignments and that others will find easier entry into open-ended assignments that permit them to roam more freely. The literature on connections between Myers-Briggs preferences and composing is rich with such connections. For writers, the benefit derives both from acknowledging their preferences in terms of strengths and their recognition of the need to balance those preferences with more attention to what their writing and writing habits may lack. As a result of all this talk about writing and writing about writing, students will find that they have come to know more about themselves as well. Even for writers who profess little interest in writing, learning about oneself is always a useful—and interesting—outcome of a writing assignment.

Notes

1. Two sites on the World Wide Web that have short forms of the MBTI and that also score the test, with some explanation of the results, are the following: http://longwood.cs.ucf.edu/~porthous/mb_test.shtml and http://sunsite.unc.edu/jembin/mb.pl

Works Cited

Cramer, Sharon and Tom Reigstad. 1994. "Using Personality to Teach Writing." *Composition Chronicle* 7 (March): 4–7.

Jensen, George H., and John K. DiTiberio. 1984. "Personality and Individual Writing Processes." *College Composition and Communication* 35 (3): 285–300.

————. 1989. *Personality and the Teaching of Composition*. Norwood, NJ: Ablex.

Kiersey, D., and M. Bates. 1984. *Please Understand Me: Character & Temperament Types*. Del Mar, CA: Prometheus Nemesis.

Thompson, Thomas C., ed. 1996. *Most Excellent Differences: Essays on Using Type Theory in the Composition Classroom*. Gainesville, FL: Center for Applications of Psychological Type.

7

Self-Discovery to Self-Examination
Teaching the Personal Essay as Inquiry

Michael Steinberg
Michigan State University

Students are most likely to write—especially those students who are least likely to write—when they confront a personal problem that might be solved by writing. Writing must have a purpose for us to take it seriously, and the universal purpose that writing may serve is our fundamental need to understand the world.
—Donald Murray, *Expecting the Unexpected*

I

I teach personal essays in all my classes—graduate and undergraduate workshops, as well as in freshman composition. In the advanced sections, I'm free to present the personal essay as literary (or "creative") nonfiction. But in the freshman course, I always encounter resistance from colleagues. Even when I tell fellow comp teachers that there's value in teaching expressive writing, invariably someone will say that "My students love that 'touchie-feelie' stuff, but when I ask them to write a critical essay, they can't organize or focus their ideas, or come up with a clear thesis statement."

A personal essayist myself, I'm convinced this form is as intellectually challenging as any other academic or literary genre. And as a teaching writer, I believe that my colleagues' prescriptions—like the standard inductive or deductive argument, the literary/critical essay, and the compare-and-contrast theme—encourage only linear and logical thinking and discourage all but the most cursory thought and reflection.

I'm sure we've all read our share of student essays that begin, "In this fast paced, rapidly expanding and complex, technological society. . . ." Or "Huck Finn is a diverse and difficult novel that raises many social and political issues that still apply to our contemporary multicultural society. . . ." This kind of writing—what Ken Macrorie decades ago called "Engfish" (1970)—is typical of the kinds of academic prescriptions I mentioned.

Still, this doesn't help solve the problem that most freshman composition teachers face: that is, how can we get our students to write more thoughtful and reflective essays—personal and otherwise? Gordon Harvey (1994), a staunch advocate for the personal essay, explains this dilemma when he tells us that only in rare instances do his students' personal essays progress from "experience to idea." Harvey adds that "if a piece of autobiographical writing is an essay, it has already moved beyond private confession or memoir to some shareable idea for which the personal experience works as evidence" (648).

If Harvey is right, and I think he is, then those of us who teach personal essays could benefit from learning more about the kinds of strategies that are currently being used in creative writing workshops. I say this because I've found that associative and expressive approaches often help to nudge my students toward understanding what Harvey calls "shareable ideas."

2

I think this is at least a three-step process. First, students need to discover a personal problem or question that demands more exploration. Next, they have to find ways to shape their inquiries into focused narratives. Once students progress this far, then I think we can begin to show them how to connect their personal experience to more complex human issues.

With this goal in mind, I start the semester by asking students to write a series of exercises that will in five weeks' time lead us to a reflective personal essay. We begin with three icebreakers: in the first one, "Meet My Partner," students form pairs, write some "safe" disclosures, and then use these to introduce each other to the rest of the class. Next, they do a "Personal Writing History," which they share first in small groups and then with the whole class. And last, they fill out a "Student Information Sheet," which asks them to discuss their goals, intentions, and backgrounds.

The point of these exercises is to build community in the class, as well as to bank some trust for future writing critiques. But I also want students to know that their own experience, thoughts, relationships, and so on are important and legitimate subjects for writing. I've found that unless we encourage young writers to reflect on the significance of their own experience, it is practically impossible for them to discover meaning outside themselves.

To this end, I've developed a sequence of exercises and readings that in four to five weeks' time will prepare students to (hopefully) write more authentic and reflective personal essays. In order to expand my students' tool kit beyond the strictly linear and logical prescriptions they've learned in school, I assign a series of associative and reflective exercises. The four exercises that seem to to work best are "The Introductory Portfolio," "Only Connect," "Guided Writing," and a "Personal Inventory"—all of which I've borrowed from practicing fiction writers, poets, and essayists. These four in particular seem to lead some of my students toward the experience that many writers describe as discovering "what we didn't know we knew."

For "The Introductory Portfolio," students choose one significant object or item from each of four categories: family, friendships, school, and extra-curricular activities. The objects can be things that students have positive or negative responses to. First, students will write a short paragraph about each chosen object, and then they'll explain in a line or two *why* they've chosen these particular mementos, *why* they are important, and what *connections and relationships* these objects suggest. Next, they pick one object from the four and I ask them to describe a single memory. And finally, I tell them to write a short paragraph in which they reflect in some detail about *why* that memory is so important to them.

The main benefit of this exercise is that students will begin to see how a significant object not only can become a "trigger" for a rich memory recollection, but also it can act as a catalyst for reflective thinking.

Here's a short example. Under "Family," Jason writes:

> This is the alarm clock that sits on my dresser up north at our cabin. I bought this alarm clock because it wakes my father and me up when we go fishing or hunting. [The clock reminds me] of the feeling of being on a dead calm lake and watching the sun burst out from behind a hill. There's no one else around, the ghostly cry of a common loon echoes off the trees and surrounds you. The half-submerged fowl swims towards its nest in perfect grace. God created moments like this for fathers and sons.

Jason's paragraph works on several levels. It's scenic, concrete, and has some vividly rendered sense details. But perhaps what's more important is that last epigrammatic line where he's beginning to reflect on the larger meaning of his experience.

The other three exercises work in a similar fashion. "Only Connect" (the phrase is borrowed from E. M. Forster) asks students to describe in concrete detail *three* recent experiences, encounters, problems, and/or situations that "stopped them in their tracks." Then they write a paragraph explaining what connects the three experiences to one another. Finally, I tell them to write a short reflection that examines how and why these three experiences are related.

Those students who discover connections between three seemingly unrelated incidents are usually the ones who come up with the most thoughtful reflections. For example, John wrote about an encounter with a squirrel he happened upon while he was walking on campus, a phone call he received from his mother informing him that his father has a non–life-threatening aneurysm, and his own struggle to find a third example to talk about. In his final paragraph of reflection John explains that watching the squirrel skittishly dart away from the crush of bike riders and students on Rollerblades caused him to reflect on the differences between a big, impersonal university like Michigan State and his small-town upbringing. The phone call from his mother made him feel as if the aneurysm in his father's leg were one more obstacle making life at school a little more difficult. And, finally, John's inability to focus on this assignment forced him to confront the vague sense of confusion and dislocation he'd been feeling since he arrived on campus a month ago.

Poet Syd Lea, the creator of the prompt, says that the exercise works best when it acts as a catalyst for the writer's current obsessions or preoccupations. And that's exactly what happened to John. All three situations helped him to understand and articulate "what he didn't know he knew"; in this case that he was having serious difficulties adjusting to a big university. While most of my students aren't as self-analytical as John is, many do experience a similar sense of dislocation when they first arrive at a large, corporate place such as Michigan State. It came as no surprise then, when I learned that John dropped out of school after his first semester.

The next exercise addresses most beginning writers' tendency to use generic description in place of more precise and singular details. We've all seen (and probably even written) lines like "The beauty of the majestic mountains is awesome." Well, it's one thing to tell students that authentic details and examples come from our singular experiences and/or imaginations, and that we perceive the world through our five senses. But it's quite another to get freshmen to write from their own felt sense impressions.

Apart from being sound pedagogical practice, writing from the five senses often leads students to previously unexplored memories. Therefore, I use the "Guided Writing" prompt as a catalyst for triggering those remembrances. I begin by handing out a guidelines sheet that limits them to ten minutes of free-writing for each segment of the five-part prompt. For part one, I ask them to imagine they're in a room that's familiar to them. Then I tell them to pan the room, and using only moment-to-moment sense details, describe what they see. Next, I tell them to imagine or recall a sound that has in the past provoked a strong reaction like fear or surprise. Then I ask them to try and connect that sound to what they're feeling. I then send them back to the room (imaginatively) to look at an object they hadn't noticed before and direct them to pick it up and respond in sense details only. "The object provokes a memory, a real memory that involves another person (or people) and that evokes some strong emotion or feeling," my directions read. After they've written about that memory and the emotion it provokes, I tell them to return to the object and respond to it once more, again using only sense details. And the last direction reads: "Because of the memory association, your perception of that object should now be different, altered. Reexperience the sensual characteristics of the object."

After they've done the first five parts, I have students write a reflective evaluation of their responses. I ask them to consider questions such as "What worked and why? What successes/ problems did you have in writing this? Were there any unexpected surprises or discoveries? If so, what do you think triggered these?" The last question is: "Did you learn anything about your-self that you didn't know you knew?" As you'd expect, the richest associa-tions and discoveries occur whenever the writer finds a catalyst that triggers a dramatic memory recollection.

Here's a good example. Sara begins by scanning her childhood bedroom. She describes her writing desk, the stiff-backed chair she sat in, and her bed— "lopsided and broken from way too many hours of jumping on it." The sound she recalls is from a hide-and-seek game she and her father used to play. "I quickly run to my closet and hide inside," she writes. "The door squeaks and bangs. I hope he didn't hear that. Then I hear the signal . . . 'Ready or not, here I come.' I hear his familiar footsteps. . . . Unmistakable, slow but steady with a loud creak toward the end. I try not to move, not to breathe, but my heartbeat seems loud enough to give me away . . ."

When Sara revisits (imaginatively) the room, she suddenly notices the carpet. She bends over to touch it. Describing its feel and smell reminds her of a moment when she'd spilled red nail polish on it. "I recall watching it spill to the floor," she writes. "It looked like blood on my off-white, grayish carpet." Then she describes being so fearful of her mother's reaction that she gets down on her hands and knees and works for an hour to get the red spot out. When she can't remove it, Sara takes a pair of shears and cuts the stain out.

Next, she describes a disturbing scene in which her mother berates her for ruining the carpet. Sara writes, "I hated her for saying those things to me. I hated the way she made me feel. I hated the tears that streamed down my face as her horrid voice came out of her mouth and attacked me. I felt like I was in a forest, surrounded by wild beasts, who were circling me and even-tually attacked me until they had torn me limb from limb. And there was nothing left. I hated myself more than I hated my mother."

Finally Sara says, "I touch the carpet once more, feeling the energy that comes from within. I feel the roughness, which maybe is a symbol of every-thing I have done to that carpet. The carpet has been with me through every-thing. When I was overjoyed, I would jump on it, when I was mad I would beat it, when I was sad I would cry on it, and when I ruined it, I cut it out. The carpet holds every secret, every memory I have ever had in my room. For that I am grateful."

Had Sara responded to only the first five questions, her piece would still be skillfully scenic, powerfully evocative, and full of vivid sense details. But in her reflective evaluation, she makes several unexpected discoveries, which in turn yield the following reflection:

> I never expected to get such strong feelings from writing this. The strong memories I had about my mother and the hurt I felt came out of nowhere. I never thought my carpet would have that much meaning to my life. I think scanning the room and seeing my carpet brought back the memory. . . . I can see that I felt like my mother valued the carpet more than she did her daughter. . . . I think I internalized most of this and began to feel awful about myself. . . . I thought when I began to do this exercise that there were really no objects that could evoke those feelings from me. Writing this allowed me to see that I was wrong. . . . I found my memories buried—in my carpet.

Once students are comfortable writing associatively, I assign the final exercise—a "Personal Inventory." I've designed this one to serve as a bridge or transition to the personal essay; I use it to show students that often their richest autobiographical writing comes from some combination of *self, family, place,* and *culture.*

First, I give them a handout sheet that includes five categories: Childhood/Self, Family, Place, Culture, and Universal. Under each I've listed specific guidelines. For example, under "Childhood/Self," I ask students to quickly recall in a line or two a variety of songs, smells, tastes, and so on associated with childhood memories. I also ask them to record their earliest yearnings, obsessions, and desires, as well as to list specific people who'd left a lasting impression. Finally I ask, "What did it take for you to be accepted? What rules and conditions were set by your parents, friends, teachers, and clergy?"

Under "Family," I tell students to write about their parents' expectations and to list specific agreements and/or disagreements. I also have them quickly record family rituals, myths, legends, stories, and props. For "Place" I list questions like "Where did you grow up? How connected/disconnected were you to that place? What memories and associations—sights, sounds, smells, tastes, textures—can you recall?"

For "Culture," I ask about the influence of nationality or ancestry. I also tell them to note the expectations that characterized their particular "Culture." I have them list specific props, myths, legends, stories, and foods, and I ask if they see themselves in agreement with or at odds with the larger culture they're living in now. And for the last category, "Universal," I list three questions: "What are your particular beliefs about the world you live in?" "Do you believe there's a particular way everyone should be living?" and "Why or why not?"

Once students complete these, I have them choose one item in each category to expand and develop in a paragraph or two. And finally I tell them once again to "reflect on why this is significant, and how it has affected you."

The goal of this last exercise is to get students to use their personal discoveries and associations as a way of examining broader issues of family, place, and identity. And by asking them to write and reflect on the larger issues of "Culture" and "Universal," hopefully I'm nudging them toward using their personal experience and opinions to serve as a way of making broader human connections.

Here's an example from a student who struggled with this exercise. In his early exercises, Jeff, a transfer student, had been hinting at some troubling conflicts within his family. In this prompt, though, Jeff uncovers a disturbing incident that becomes a stimulus for some revealing and unexpected introspection. Jeff writes that at an early age he'd witnessed his father stumble home late at night from the bar and then, in a drunken rage, strike his mother. After describing the incident, Jeff discovers that

> ... this was the moment when I decided that family would not play an important role in my life. Being by yourself, I believe you learn much more. You learn who you really can trust and who is really a good person. You learn that because you look at people more closely than others do. I also learned how to take care of myself at an earlier age than most. Once college came, I was ready—unlike many others. I do not wish my life on others, but I am going to make it one way or another.

It comes as no surprise then, that Jeff views himself as being at odds with "Culture," as well as finding himself confused about "Universals." In his final summary, Jeff discloses that he's fearful of the random violence he sees, and that he's both awed by the technology of today's world and apprehensive about his own future. He concludes:

> Now is not the time for me to answer what I think of the world. I have only been here twenty years and have only left the country a handful of times to go to Canada. For the majority of those twenty years, I was not much concerned about the world. I was more concerned about myself and who I was. That is not experiencing the world. As time passes, I will be much more prepared to answer for my views on the world.

Here, Jeff admits his self-absorption and lack of worldly experience. Yet at the same time he's struggling to acquire the knowledge and experience that will allow him to move beyond this self-conscious, confusing phase of life.

John, Sara, and Jeff's strong responses, and their subsequent attempts at self-examination, convince me that the prompts I've just described can lead students to unexpected and sometimes disturbing discoveries. As a result, when my students begin developing their first essays, they're now more eager to learn strategies that will shape those discoveries into reflective personal essays.

III

One of the problems all writers confront is figuring out what to write about. Inexperienced writers tend to write in broad generalities because they haven't yet learned how to delve more deeply into a subject or topic. Donald Murray continually counsels his students to limit their topics and then to explore the specifics. Natalie Goldberg's general advice is that "you stay with something because that's how you deepen your life; otherwise, you are always on the surface" (1991, 186). For our first essay I ask students to write a reflective piece that expresses how they overcame and/or adjusted to some particularly troublesome problem, obstacle, or predicament. To keep them focused on this one idea, I first ask them to write a few discovery drafts that describe the problem and the struggle. Once they accomplish this, I raise the stakes by telling them to examine the struggle and explain how it's helped them grow.

I begin by handing out a set of prompts that ask my students to consider topics such as first loves, first adventure, first day of school, first experience of death, and so on. I also point them toward subjects such as important landmarks, turning points, moments of insight or truth, crucial decisions, making right or wrong choices, meeting the right or wrong person, and so on.

Here are some representative prompts:

1. An incident when you felt failure, disappointment, or shame

2. An event or incident that caused great sadness, loss, or pain

3. Something/someone that caused you to feel angry, hostile, or alienated

4. Something you did that you were sorry for later

5. A positive or negative relationship with someone—another person your own age, a teacher, a coach, an important adult, a lover, a best friend, a family member

6. A relationship in which you felt hurt, betrayed, misled, or undermined

7. A time when you had to do something that went against your gain or ethics—that required you to do something you didn't want to do

8. An experience when you were the center of attention—the star, the hero, the winner

My hope is that in the brainstorming and early drafts students will write openly and freely, without censoring their ideas. Yet at the same time, I'm hoping that at some point in the process—and it's always different for each of us—each writer will discover a catalyst or trigger to unlock the kinds of vivid associations and memories that the previous exercises did. If/when this occurs, the writer can then start looking for a controlling idea or thematic center to the piece.

Let me illustrate by discussing two student essays, one that didn't succeed and one that did. Early last semester, Chris, a freshman, wrote a rough draft about the disappointment he'd suffered a few years ago when his high school girlfriend broke up with him. In the second paragraph Chris says: "My girlfriend's decision surprised me because it came without any previous warning signs." The rest of his draft is a chronological summary of their relationship and the break up.

One problem is that Chris hasn't begun to reflect on the reasons for the break up. He's still too caught up in narrating the details of the story. To nudge him toward asking more pressing and thoughtful questions, I suggested that in his next draft maybe he could speculate on some of the reasons *why* his girlfriend broke up with him. I asked him if he recalled any specific arguments, complaints, or disagreements that in retrospect may have been forewarnings.

The common problem teachers face is that, like Chris, many students never move beyond their preliminary thinking. As a result, their essays tend to be chronological narratives that don't *inquire* into a problem so much as they *describe* a troubling encounter, problem, or relationship. I think this occurs so often because the majority of freshmen have not learned how to establish a narrative "stance." By this I mean that they usually begin their personal essays in the past and continue to narrate the story from the point of view of the child/adolescent who is living through the experience. That's exactly what Chris was doing. When we met in conference, I told him that his narrative needed to be told from the point of view of Chris the adult, as he is looking back and trying to understand the break up. If he could establish this stance, I told him, then perhaps he'd be able to discover how the break up has helped him to learn something about himself.

Though he tried to take my advice, Chris's subsequent drafts never went much deeper into the issue. Like other inexperienced writers, Chris was simply unable to discover the central problem or issue within his narrative. As Peter Elbow (1995) says, "Unless there is a felt question—a tension, a palpable itch. . . . or a sense of a felt problem, nothing holds the reader's experience together—however well the text might summarize the parts" (296). This explains, in part, why some students have difficulties revising their pieces.

The next example, however, is from a student writer who did discover "a felt problem." And as Elbow suggests, this early discovery made all the difference to the piece's subsequent success.

I began to get a hint of what Jason's essay would be about when in an earlier exercise he wrote about an incident in which he was driving to work

and accidentally killed an old man on a bicycle. At the end of a free association, Jason wrote, "Old man, I hate you because you made me kill you . . .
I hate you man. Man mankind, I hate you. You won't help, my friends won't
help. I hate you all . . . Jason, you were going so fast, I hate you. And look
what you did to my beautiful green car."

In his initial brainstorming, this event was a kind of subtext running
beneath the surface of the narrative. Toward the end, Jason discloses that "I
have to still keep dancing around that subject that I know is coming up. I've
written about that incident before. I thought I got over that. I guess not.
Wow, is that a discovery." Then he proceeds to dance away again. Like
many essayists, he circles his subject; in this case, he's all the while eliminating generic things such as friendships, family, school, and so on. Finally,
Jason concludes his brainstorming by writing, "The music has stopped and
it's staring me right in the face. I never was a good dancer."

In his rough draft, Jason narrates the story of the accident. In the free
association he'd only hinted at what had happened, but now he recreates the
entire scenario—from the time he gets up in the morning to mow the lawn to
the aftermath of the accident. As Jason is driving to work, he sees the sign
for a local movie theater and begins to think about getting his friends
together that night for a movie. Out of the corner of his eye, he spots an old
man on a green bicycle. The man has just crossed over one lane of traffic,
and Jason sees that he is not going to stop. Then, he describes the moment-
to-moment sensory details of the accident:

> What the hell does he think he's doing? Then he looked across his right
> shoulder and his light blue eyes looked into mine and said, 'Hi, how you
> doing? I'm going to screw up your life today.' The rear tire of his bike
> crumpled as it struck the right side of my front bumper. I knew what was
> happening. My stomach felt like it would burst open, and my mouth went
> dry. I wanted to puke. I wanted to pass out and wretch all over myself.
> Then I wouldn't have had to see my wiper laboriously removing the blood
> and brain particles spilled on my windshield from the old man's head hit-
> ting the front right roof support . . . I'm sitting in my running car noticing
> that there are no cars between me and the road. I thought about running, not
> caring what it took to get away. I turned the car off and tossed the keys out
> of the window. I knew if I thought about it too long, I would run. I gath-
> ered every bit of life force . . . so I could walk into the clinic and call my
> parents.

The remainder of the draft quickly summarizes the aftermath, and in the
last segment Jason briefly mentions his shock and disappointment when he
watches a friend drive past the accident without stopping to help. He also
hints—almost in passing—about the recurring nightmares he's having, and
he briefly mentions "disturbing scenes" with his parents. Finally, in a short
phrase, he alludes to the threatening phone calls he received from the old

man's young granddaughter. "To this moment," he reveals, "I can't remember a night that went by that I didn't wake up choking back my tears." In the draft's concluding paragraph, Jason writes,

> Through all this I survived. I went through more pain than most adults have felt in their entire lives and I survived. I'm a better person for it as well. I can honestly say I care next to nothing for myself when other people need me. I don't know how that change happened but it did. When my friends need me I'm there, probably because one saw me after the accident and didn't stop to help me. Because of this accident I can overcome any pain. It all pales in comparison to the pain I will feel for the rest of my life. I can do anything because I'm not afraid to try anymore. Life is too short and too precious. Especially the life of a friend or of a family member. That little granddaughter taught me that.

Jason has done what most young writers do in a rough draft; he recreates the story and at the end he summarizes, and perhaps unconsciously formulates where he needs to go in his next draft. The missing part, of course, is the struggle he went through to get to the point where he was able to say, "Because of the accident, I can overcome any pain."

One of the most difficult things to learn—even for experienced writers—is how to read our drafts so that we can locate what Donald Murray calls "the informing line." This is similar to what Elbow calls "a felt question" or "palpable itch." Like many students, Chris was not able to discover this. That's why he couldn't take his thinking any further. Jason, however, senses that he's writing about an urgent issue. He also knows that in order for him to understand what he learned, he needs to delve deeper into the accident and its consequences.

In his revision plan, Jason notes that his draft is "linear and safe." He says he needs "to trim some of the details preceding the accident and get to that scene sooner." He also writes that "I'm just rambling along not saying much. No one needs to know about that old lady in front of me. Who cares what the drive looks like. That has nothing to do with what I'm trying to say. . . . I know what I want to say. . . . about the effects of the accident . . . but I'm drowning myself out in detail."

Knowing that he needs to make more connections between the accident and its impact on him, in his next draft Jason drops the linear story and starts writing associatively. In his opening paragraph, Jason establishes his stance as that of the young adult looking back on this incident. He writes,

> It's amazing how killing someone can change a person. On the morning of . . . I woke up an average seventeen year-old. I was selfish, immature, and cared nothing about what happened outside my little atmosphere. Yeah, I had friends and a family and yes I did love them. I only loved them

because I needed them. How does someone change? Close your eyes, give
me your hand and I will show you.

   That first line is a self-evident comment, but it helps him to pose the
important issue of change and struggle. By establishing this point of view,
Jason is allowing himself to think more reflectively. By the second page of
the draft, he has already described the accident. By the end of the draft, Jason
says a bit more about the nightmares and he discusses the disturbing calls
from the young granddaughter. Finally, in his concluding paragraph, he hits
on an important disclosure—one that was notably missing from the rough
draft.
   "Through it all I survived," he writes. "My mom and dad left for work
in the morning and my boss gave me an extra week off. In retrospect, he
almost killed me. I would sit home clutching a loaded .357 Magnum. Wondering if I deserved to live I looked down the barrel."
   Next, Jason wrestles with thoughts of suicide. "If I killed myself," he
speculates, "I would not only have killed the old man and myself but also my
parents and probably one of my friends. Imagine a selfish child like myself
doing something for someone else." And in the last two sentences Jason
concludes that as a result of the accident and its aftermath, "I try to do as little damage to the world as possible." In hopes of making up for the life he
has taken, he writes that he's decided "to become a veterinarian."
   Quite often, I've found that inexperienced writers only begin to discover
their real subjects toward the close of their early drafts. In Jason's case, he
was now ready to explore the aftermath of the accident more fully. Consequently, I could begin to suggest specific strategies for limiting and shaping
his next draft.
   In our one-to-one conference, I asked Jason if he'd be willing to examine in more depth and detail the thoughts and emotions that transpired *after*
the accident. Could he take a look at who he is now as a result of having
survived this trauma? In other words, how did this experience change him
and what did he learn from it? My final suggestion was to urge Jason to
focus more on the struggle—specifically on *how* he was able to make it
through this trying experience.
   In his final draft, Jason made three critical changes. First, he begins the
essay with a dramatic flashback. It's a vivid and unequivocal scene in which
he describes himself sitting at a table, looking down the barrel of the gun.
Then he cuts right to the accident and quickly moves to the aftermath.
Finally, in his ending Jason examines *why* he decides not to commit suicide,
and he also discusses his decision to become a veterinarian. In this new draft,
then, Jason is starting to write about how he came to terms with the effects
this experience has had on him. As a result, his piece has evolved into an
honest self-interrogation that in the end extends to a larger issue.

Having changed the title from the generic "Surviving" to the more descriptive "Change of Venue," Jason writes in his new introduction,

> I sit in my room, alone in my house clutching a loaded .357 Magnum. I am wondering if I deserve to live. I look into the barrel. It's the darkest place I've ever seen. Darker than any place on earth, darker than any hell. I'm not the same as I was a week earlier. I've gone through some horrible metamorphosis and come out of it a diseased creature. Let me show you how this happened.

This is a vivid and powerful moment, and it sets the stage for all that follows. Jason quickly moves from his rejection of suicide to the accident itself. By the halfway point in the essay, he's already discussing the aftermath: that is, his struggle to survive and understand this catastrophe. Using the accident as a catalyst for reflection and self-disclosure, Jason writes more openly about the nightmares, the threatening phone calls from the man's family, and the accusatory calls from the granddaughter. That's when he begins to entertain thoughts of suicide. Here he continues to interrogate himself; he reveals his fears that the man's family will come and kill him, he ruminates about the relief his own death would bring him, and he discloses guilty thoughts like "I don't deserve the relief death would bring."

But the essay's turning point comes when after a month spent "wallowing in my own misery," Jason decides to do what he calls "some digging." And he comes up with some startling information. He discovers that the old man had a fatal disease, he was going blind, and he'd just had his driver's license revoked. Surmising now that the man had nothing to live for, Jason concludes that this was a planned suicide and that he, Jason, just happened to be the random agent of the man's death.

Beginning his final summation, Jason makes another important discovery. "I started thinking," he writes, "what kind of society could turn out an individual who cared nothing about how his suicide could effect his family, friends, and the person who was forced into killing him?" Next, he reflects on why he has decided to become a veterinarian. "I'll gladly save the life of an animal," Jason says "because no animal will ever scar me so badly as humanity has and will. Maybe by saving the lives of animals, I can make up for the life, parts of me still believe, I took."

Finally, in his last paragraph, Jason realizes that he was right not to take his own life, that he does appreciate the value of life in a way that he didn't before, and that he will do all he can for his loved ones because "life is too short." But at the same time he reveals that he is still bitterly disillusioned with society and with humanity. He now believes that "one person cannot make a difference" and that "society will inevitably destroy itself." Jason concludes the essay by saying, "I still dream horrible dreams, I still hurt, and I still survive."

IV

I know that most students are not as confrontational and self-reflective as Jason is. Nor do they have such violent and traumatic experiences to write about. In fact, one of the dangers in asking inexperienced writers to write reflective essays is that the assignment might shut them down. Some do not wish to examine their lives, probe their darker side, interrogate their insecurities, or disclose their deepest demons and obsessions.

In defense of my methods, I can only say that I do not ask students to reveal these more painful disclosures simply for the sake of confession or therapy. I ask them to reflect because I know that only by confronting our truest selves—the selves that struggle to make sense of the world—can we understand our shared humanity. And we can't connect with others' struggles until we come to terms with the thoughts, beliefs, and shaping experiences that have helped form our identity and values.

Jason's piece is an example of what's *possible* for young writers when they learn how to reflect and make associations with larger human issues. But whether the majority of students succeed or not, I'm convinced that those who make an honest effort to deal with this kind of essay will come away with a deeper appreciation of what it means to write reflectively, not to mention what it means to be human. And at the very least, they will have learned some strategies for shaping future writings. That's why I agree with Gordon Harvey when he writes that

> This move from experience to idea, and then, through painful revision, from a dull idea and simple, narrative structure to an interesting idea and structure, bringing general insights out in the particulars and erasing narcissism, is precisely the great challenge and the great value of the personal essay as a Freshman writing assignment—this, and the broadened sense it gives us of what can count as evidence for ideas. The fact that students won't likely be asked anywhere else in college to put their personal experience through this process is all the more reason to assign a personal essay in Freshman Writing. (648–649)

It's hard to think of much better reasons for asking our students to write reflective personal essays.

Works Cited

Elbow, Peter. 1985. "The Shifting Relationships Between Speech and Writing," *College Composition and Communication* 35 (3): 283–303.

Goldberg, Natalie. 1991. Interview. In *Coming into Fullness: On Women Turning Forty,* ed. Catherine Roundtree, 186–95. Freedom, CA: The Crossing Press.

Harvey, Gordon. 1994. "Presence in the Essay." *College English* 56 (6): 642–54.

Lea, Sydney. 1992. "Only Connect." In *The Practice of Poetry,* eds. Robin Behn and Chase Twichell, 17–19. New York: HarperCollins.

Murray, Donald. 1989. *Expecting the Unexpected: Teaching Myself—and Others—to Read and Write*. Portsmouth, NH: Boynton/Cook.

8

The Degrees of the Lie

John Boe
University of California-Davis

Can you nominate in order now the degrees of the lie?
Shakespeare, *As You Like It*

When I am commenting on student papers, I sometimes fantasize about the rubber stamps I would like to use in place of laborious handwritten comments. My favorite imaginary stamp says "LIE" on it. To date I have no such stamp and instead resort to polite circumlocutions, such as the following comment I recently wrote about the last paragraph of a student's "personal statement": "I find it hard to believe this, hard to believe that you believe it." (The last sentence of her paragraph was something like "I see my ongoing path as a Human Development major possibly leading me into a career as a teacher, an opportunity which will no doubt offer me all I desire."[1] This was no doubt an easy lie for me to spot because my own thirty-year career as a teacher hasn't yet quite brought me all I desire. So I had to suggest that perhaps she didn't (or shouldn't) really believe what she was saying. In a less polite but more efficient world, I could have just used my "LIE" stamp.

In their papers, college students often seem not to know when they are lying. So the teacher has to tell them. Sometimes this process involves convincing them that they are lying. Learning to notice when you are lying (to others and to yourself) is an important part of education. The goal is not to avoid lying—for various reasons, including the ambiguity of the truth, this is impossible—but to be aware when you are lying. Writing teachers are well situated to help students learn to know when they are telling the truth (their truths, even their culture's truths) and when they are lying.

Students lie in many different ways, so I offer here a provisionary catalogue of the lies most frequently found in the writing classroom: the lies of

86

voice, style, false knowledge, epiphany, sucking up, argumentation, inattention—and, finally, the lies of the teacher.

1. The Voice Lie

There's a moment in William Coles's classic "novelization" of a writing course, *The Plural I*, where Coles tries "to render the feel of a certain way of beginning a writing course with a very particular group of students" (74). Coles reads a student's paper out loud to the class and then asks what sort of voice speaks in this particular paper. The class responds with the predictable, "I think he proves his point pretty well," and Coles agrees, "No question. It's well organized. Clear, logical, coherent, well organized. It's neat." But Coles insists they abandon such shopworn English paper clichés, and he asks the class again, "Would you mind taking up the question of who's talking in the paper?" Coles then has someone read aloud a couple of sentences from the paper. Then follows this dialogue, beginning with Coles's question:

> "Look, how old do you think the writer of those two sentences is pretending to be?"
> "How old?"
> "Well how big then? Do you think he's really the size of the Jolly Green Giant?"
> [The student] looked at [Cole] with a puzzled, queer half-smile.
> "What would you say to Jim here, if he slid up to you in the snack bar and said: 'You know, Sam, the question of the amateur's place in a society of professionals is one that has greatly been changed by the scientific and cultural revolutions of the nineteenth and twentieth centuries'?"
> They looked at each other and snickered. (21)

In my own classes, I've often borrowed Coles's rhetorical trick, asking a student, for example, how he would feel if his friend came up to him in the snack bar and said, "Implicit in this experience was the realization that maturation was occurring" (or some such sentence taken from the paper under discussion). We don't write exactly as we talk, but when the distance between the written voice and the spoken becomes a gulf, it signifies the voice lie.

Of course we try on voices (like clothes), but (again like clothes) some voices do make us look foolish. (Probably we should try neither to dress nor to talk like a fifty-year-old when we are eighteen, and vice versa.) Many students believe they are supposed to write in some correct academic voice: wordy, not first person, abstract, without story, anonymous, impersonal, and above all—boring. Sometimes the students are correct in this belief—they might in some course be rewarded with a good grade for writing like the world's most boring sociologist.

There is a pedagogical purpose for trying on voices that are not like your own (for example, learning the traditional voice choices for certain professional disciplines). But it is nice to have one place in the university (the writing class) where students can experiment with finding more authentic voices. The easiest way to demonstrate the student use of fake voices is through listening to sentences together. Thus Coles has a student read a certain sentence out loud and then he repeats this sentence and points out the lie of the voice: How old do you think the writer of these words is? Likewise, I will sometimes read some particularly pompous passage out loud in a cinematic "voice-over" voice or in an "advertisement" voice, in some kind of recognizable variant of one of society's many "fake" voices we all know so well. My student listeners instantaneously recognize how such a lying voice fits the voice in the student essay. My students are neither made uncomfortable nor "shamed" by this occasional, brief, and spontaneous practice. They know it is not their voice that is being parodied but rather a fake voice they have unconsciously adopted. I think they are grateful to have their easily corrected lie pointed out with light-hearted humor.

Writers of course can have different voices, and no doubt "voice" is in some sense constructed, but for many of us the supposedly romantic idea of being able to "find your voice" makes intuitive sense, helps us to write how we want to write. Many students feel they've been discouraged from writing in their own voice in their previous academic experience and so respond happily to the idea of using a more authentic voice; they express surprise and delight in being allowed and even encouraged to write in their own voices.

It's easy to get students to try to use their own voices. You need only make them perform (or tell) the rough drafts of their papers. I almost always do this with at least the first paper in a class, so that by the second or third class meeting, each student will have stood up in front of the class and told (without notes) a version of their would-be first paper. Students find it easy to BS when they are writing; after all, they have been trained to do so by years of schooling. But when they have to talk their rough drafts out loud in front of their peers, they inevitably start sounding like themselves. And with my encouragement to try to keep the same quality of voice in their writing, they subsequently end up writing in voices recognizably their own.

Having students tell rather than write their first drafts also avoids what I like to call "the lie of the audience." Many of my colleagues, of course, see this device as a successful fiction, and I believe their claims of success in assigning papers that ask the student to see as the audience for their paper some fictive group: an architectural consulting firm, a judge, an editor. When I have tried designating a fictive audience, I have often been troubled and not received papers I wanted to read. I myself find the task of writing to some imaginary audience very difficult (which may be why I often can't make a success out of this kind of assignment). But when students perform their rough drafts, their audience is made real, does not have to be imagined.

Talking to a group, you can easily know when your audience is bored or befuddled, entranced or amused. Even with assignments that ultimately demand that students write for a specialized audience, it is useful to start off by speaking to actual human beings.

I am part of the audience for the students' oral presentations (and will be the total audience for their final written presentations), so I always offer my responses. (That they don't have to write a rough draft for me to read and that I don't have to read it is a labor-saving side benefit.) I ask the student questions, give my suggestions, solicit additional comments from the class. In such class sessions where students tell drafts, we are not bored, for it is fun to have everyone in the class stand up and talk. It gives us a chance to get to know each other, to look at and listen to each other.

But if you get students to write in their own voices, as Peter Elbow admitted in an interview, you may at first be disappointed:

> The writing I see from my freshmen sometimes seems too naive. I compare student papers with my colleagues and with the graduate students I teach with; I look at some of their students' papers, and I say, "My freshmen aren't writing such wonderful papers." I'm not sure what to do about that. I'm getting them to be themselves on paper—and when they are themselves, guess what? They are naive. . . . I hope I'm not wrong about all this, but I just feel so strongly—I yearn so strongly—that it's *got* to be possible to be yourself and sound like yourself and *still* be smart and sophisticated. But I certainly haven't learned how to make it happen in 14 weeks in a required freshman writing course. (Boe and Schroeder 1992, 22–23)

But when I get them to use their own naive voices, I get papers I like better; I get less boring, if less "intellectual" papers. And one of my major goals as a writing teacher is to get my students to write papers I can read with pleasure.

It is a matter of my pedagogical integrity to believe in the possibility of self-knowledge (which necessitates the perhaps old-fashioned belief in the existence of a self). If the students use their own voices, then when they write and see what they have written, when they speak and hear what they have spoken, they begin to know who they are. And as time and education goes on, they discover how complex they are.

2. The Style Lie

The style lie is a sentence-level version of the voice lie, exemplified in the lies of the big word, the big sentence, and the big paragraph. I once heard a history professor convincingly claim that what made for a college-level "A" paper was "the big paragraph": the fully developed and supported paragraph. The goal is to talk like a grown-up, to be big. So students often prefer the

Latinate to the Anglo-Saxon, the thesaurus to their own vocabulary, the long sentence to the short sentence, and the long paragraph to the small paragraph.

Students know that simple sentences and paragraphs tend to suggest simple thoughts ("See Dick and Jane"). But they often don't know how to organize big paragraphs, and they often don't know how to write complex sentences. So the big paragraph is long rather than developed, and the long sentence is made by connecting short sentences with coordinating conjunctions. Students will thus write compound sentence after compound sentence. They write the compound sentence (a+b) because it is easier to write than the complex sentence, in which the main point comes in the independent clause and modifications of this main clause are subordinated into one or more dependent clauses (a is a function of b).

The word *complex* comes from the past participle of the Latin verb *complecti* and can mean "entwined," "braided," "plaited," "woven," or even "embraced" (literally *complecti* means "folded with"). The crucial fact is that "complex" implies at least two elements brought together, synthesized into one. The elements are not combined just by adding one to the other, but are combined in a complicated way, as in knitting or weaving. While students quickly get the fact that they need to combine more than one element in order to make a long sentence, they don't as quickly master the intricacies of weaving complex sentences, of building long sentences without the crutch of "and," of using parallel structure, of employing sophisticated modification, of synthesizing numerous elements (words and phrases) into a single sentence. So they overuse compound sentences, and with this style lie attempt a content lie: pretending to analyze a relationship in order to see how the elements are woven together, but really only using "and" to separate items into a sequence.

The frequency of the common splice is part of this same stylistic impersonation, for the comma splice sentence is just a compounding of sentences without using the "and," an attempt to say to the teacher, "Look, I can write the long sentences you want if I am allowed to join short sentences together with commas." I do try to show my students how to write various kinds of long sentences, but I first tell them just to write the simple sentences they are able to write. While the resulting style may not be the intellectual style of the imaginary college "A" paper, it is, by virtue of being manageable, a better starting place. Why not start with grammatically correct simple sentences (and simple thoughts) and then try to build them into more complex sentences and thoughts?

Occasionally a facile student will have perfected the long sentence (can write complex sentences, can use parallel structure) but still hasn't discovered complex thinking, the way to real content. These are the most infuriating papers, full of gray flannel sentences with no content, no self, no voice: Eddie Haskell trying to bullshit his way to a "B."

My colleague Eric Schroeder uses such a paper to train TA's. This paper, "The Wonderful Word Processor," is 1500 words of mechanically clean, competently written sentences, which say over and over, in a multitude of graceful ways, that the word processor is wonderful. For example:

> As any writer knows, one of the most agonizing things about revising a report is having to type the whole thing over again, even though there might only be a couple of minor changes. The word processor eliminates this problem. Through the use of the computer, all reports or papers may be saved in computer memory, most likely in the form of a floppy disk.

New TA's usually want to give this paper at least a "B" (after all, it sounds like college-level writing, is more sophisticated than much college writing). They are fooled by the lie of style. "The Wonderful Word Processor" deserves no more than a "D," because content is the heart of writing. (But since it is easier to teach students to polish their style than it is to teach them how to find interesting content, writing teachers spend more time teaching style.)

The authors of papers like "The Wonderful Word Processor" are often shocked to be caught in their lie; some of their previous teachers and TA's have given such elegant crap a "B" or even better. But the writing teacher's job is to be like the child hero in "The Emperor's New Clothes," to say to the student, "Hey, underneath this style you're naked: there's no content here."

It's not only students who try to hide the simplicity of their ideas behind the complexity of their style; professors do it all the time. But shouldn't we all be more honest and admit how simple our ideas and thoughts are, how rare and new a complex idea is? Such an approach is antithetical to much academic writing, which is based upon dressing up simple thoughts so they seem to be profundities worthy of merit increases. The idea here is a familiar one. Richard Lanham has, for example, demonstrated in his book and video *Revising Prose* the prevalence of "the official style." This wordy, passive, euphemistic, nominalized, "pretentious guff" does indeed seem to be the official style; that is, it is the most popular lie of style. But none of us, teachers or students, should use a writing style to hide our lack of ideas.

3. The False Knowledge Lie

Socrates's best trick was proving himself wise by admitting to be a fool. But since students are engaged in something important called "education," they feel they are supposed to demonstrate their learning. They don't want to appear foolish, so, reasonably enough, they lie. Certain writing tasks (like the "personal statement" or "statement of purpose") can seem to *require* these lies: students mistakenly think they are supposed to disguise their unworthy real selves behind some more respectable and pompous pose. More than once I have read in students' personal statements sentences that begin "My philosophy of life is . . ." and wondered how some twenty-year-old kid expected me to believe he had developed a philosophy of life when I am not sure that

Wittgenstein had a philosophy of life at age twenty and am pretty sure that
I don't have one at my present age.

But certain academic assignments can almost demand such lies, for
example a question like, "What is the meaning of *King Lear*?" Who could
claim to know what *King Lear* means (not to mention how and if it means)?
To such a presumptuous, stupid question, I would want to say "Nothing"—
just as Cordelia in responding to her father's stupid question says, "Nothing."
Sometimes students will lie even when given a better question in their
assignment (one that guides them into talking about what they think and feel
about *King Lear*) because they don't know what they think and feel. Or perhaps they thought and felt nothing when reading the play. So, out of reasonable self-interest they therefore lie rather than give Cordelia's answer. This
is the lie in the place of silence. Foolish honesty earned Cordelia banishment
and would earn a student an "F."

I love much reader-response criticism, especially how it privileges honest
responses, but when writing about writing ("literature") students often use "the
reader" as an excuse to lie, a way to avoid talking about their own thoughts
and feelings (which they fear may be inadequate). So my students will write
about what "the reader" feels at a certain point, and I will point out that I as
a reader honestly didn't feel the same thing. I will suggest that maybe if they
talked about what they felt at this moment, I couldn't accuse them of lying
about what "the reader" feels, but could perhaps instead engage them in an
interesting dialogue about why we responded in different ways.

We can encourage more honesty than we do, can encourage students to
articulate their confusions, to admit that *King Lear* (not to mention the
world) doesn't make perfect sense. Let's start by admitting we are fools.
Once you admit to yourself and to others that you are confused, maybe you
can become conscious of what is confusing you, maybe you can get in touch
with your own genuine responses, maybe you can discover some real feelings and thoughts about *King Lear* or about life.

4. The Epiphany Lie

This is the lie of false knowledge fictionally located in a discrete moment. I
once asked some students to write about a learning experience and received
mostly epiphany lies. The most memorable was an essay about the childhood
experience of being caught in a lie, which ended with the conclusion: "I
learned at this humiliating moment never to tell a lie." I thought this sentence
one of the more preposterous lies I had ever read and said so (politely). After
all, a claim always to tell the truth is an obvious and self-contradictory false-
hood. But I sympathized with the student's predicament: the assignment
asked him to write about learning, so he felt he had to locate clear learning
in some particular moment in his life; he felt he was supposed to write me
a parable, a fiction, a lie. So many student papers will routinely contain

claims about wonderful learning: "Now I almost always finish what I begin," "This experience of independence helped to show me what I want out of life and just how to get it," "It was not until I saw death that I first began to appreciate life," etc., etc., etc. Part of the students' problems may come from the assignment and insufficient guidance on the teacher's part; once "learning" is mentioned, students will often opt for the easiest solution—the epiphany lie.

Consider this claim, again from a student's statement of purpose for medical school: "Every day I walked out the door from my job as a volunteer at the hospital, I felt a little wiser, a little more human." What is the reader supposed to picture here? Are we supposed to believe that every day all summer in his five-day-a-week volunteer job, whenever he got off work he really said to himself, "Gee, I don't know, but somehow I feel a little wiser, a little more—I don't know—human"? I can easily believe his volunteer experience did make him wiser, even perhaps more human (whatever that's supposed to mean), but I have a hard enough time locating his transformation in any one moment in time (the epiphany), much less believing it happened over and over again at a precise time of day five afternoons a week over the course of an entire summer. Humans don't always have a clear location for where and when their learning occurred; more often we mythologically reconstruct the process after the fact because such a reconstruction makes for a nice dramatic moment in a narrative.

I often take my writing students to art exhibits on campus and have them write about the experience. I want them to say what they saw and how they responded to what they saw. But instead many of them can't help but write about what they have *learned* from this experience: They feel that they are supposed to pretend that this visit, often their first visit ever to an art exhibit, was a genuine epiphany. And so they tell palpable lies: "I learned to have a greater appreciation towards all artists for their unique styles of expression," or "I learned the depth and nobility of the artist's vision."

The narrator of Richard Ford's novel *The Sportswriter* (1995) accurately described the epiphany as a "minor but pernicious lie of literature," a lie

> that at times like these, after significant or disappointing divulgences, at arrivals or departures of obvious importance, when touchdowns are scored, knock-outs recorded, loved ones buried, orgasms notched, that at such times we are any of us altogether *in* an emotion, that we are within ourselves and not able to detect other emotions we might also be feeling, or be about to feel, or prefer to feel. If it's literature's job to tell the truth about these moments, it usually fails, in my opinion, and it's the writer's fault for falling into such conventions. (119)

One of the points of Ford's novel and of its Pulitzer Prize–winning sequel, *Independence Day,* is that psychological transformation (or learning) is real, but that rather than happening in the locatable moment of the epiphany, it is more realistically spread over a longer period of time—in Ford's novels, several days; in my experience, several years.

As you get older, it becomes clearer that learning is mysterious, and that what you think you have learned at one time, you find later on you haven't really learned (or have suddenly unlearned), and so you have to learn it again (and maybe again and again and for the rest of your life). Life isn't a Bible story, and the literary-psychological moment of transformation, the epiphany, is for the most part a fictional device, much like the fairy tale denouement, the story-resolving moment of magical transformation.

5. The Suck-Up Lie

Samuel Butler said that "Lying has a kind of respect and reverence with it. We pay a person the compliment of acknowledging his superiority whenever we lie to him" (159). Just as subservient employees lie to tyrannical bosses, students sometimes lie to their teachers, pretending to think whatever the professor thinks (and hoping to be rewarded with good grades). But the writing class is different and shouldn't encourage these sorts of academic lies, the everyday lies of respect and reverence.

This lie can also be called the "Give Him What He Wants Lie." What writing teacher hasn't been asked by a student, "What do you want?" The only good answer to this question is Roger Sale's: "I have no idea. I can't know what I want until I see something I like" (45).

The apprenticeship approach (education by imitating the master) is the model for much education, and it certainly works (though as Auden said about behaviorism, of course it works, but so does torture). In this model the professor professes, and the student takes notes, memorizes, and spouts back. The teacher is explicit about what is wanted and teaches the student what to say and do. This is the model for much education.

This approach is impossible in a class where the primary activity is writing rather than notetaking, studying notes, or reading a text. Every so often in a writing class, I see a student write down something I say, and I always want to peek because I can't imagine anything I have said that needed to be written down. James J. ("Jerry") Murphy, acclaimed teacher of rhetoric, would not *allow* his students to take any notes, would not allow them the comfortable pose of sitting there holding pens in their hands poised meaningfully over their notebooks—the point being that real learning needs to happen inside you and not in your notes. To students, learning can seem to exist only as externalized in notes. I've heard students blithely admit not to have understood or even paid attention to an entire lecture, but then claim they will figure the material out later when they read over their notes.

Giving teachers what they want is often effective (and part of the manners of education). Much of my own education has followed this pattern, so that I learned to try on ideas and voices (my teachers') as if they were suits of clothes. But I also learned that none of these suits were me. The problem with sucking up to the teacher is that if you do it assiduously enough it can become a mode of consciousness and not just a survival strategy. Education becomes brainwashing, and the students learn to like their torturers and to want to be *just* like them.

So the real danger of the "psych out the teacher" lie comes when accompanied by lack of consciousness, the lack of awareness that you are just trying out provisional hypotheses, adopting academic voices, or just sucking up. Especially in a writing class, the "Be Like Mike" teaching strategy is ineffective. My students aren't going to write like me, shouldn't attempt to write like me (in the way they might attempt to do chemistry like Professor Bunsen). In the writing class, they need to develop their own process, voice, style. Their writing is best when it best represents themselves, not when it imitates me.

6. The Argumentative Lie

This lie appears most obviously in the sophomoric debater or the shyster lawyer who glibly uses the misleading statistic, the straw horse, the assumption of what is to be proved. These are the lies of someone who wants to win an argument rather than discover the truth. Students resort to these lies when, under the burden of an assignment, they leap at the writing structure of the arguable proposition (any arguable proposition) with some evidence "to back it up." Often students have been taught to structure their papers with an "argumentative edge," but too often they haven't been taught to argue in the service of the truth, of what they really believe to be the truth. The soul-destroying habit of arguing what you don't believe is, unfortunately, a currency of our educational system. So, because students often don't care about what they are arguing, they often write competent, logical, and lifeless essays. They pretend to care in order to complete the assignment.

As Roger Sale explains,

> [T]he fallacy here lies in the assumption that when we speak or write all we need is an arguable proposition. In fact, of course, anything is arguable, and most broad assertions are demonstrable as well. Thus it is not a sign of liberality or broad-mindedness when a teacher lets a student say anything he likes as long as he backs it up; it is only a sign of weariness. . . . The fallacy, then, is that a proposition, simply because it is arguable, is therefore worth arguing. (49)

Sure, students should learn how to write an argument (or an argumentative essay); sure, they should have some command of logic and the use of evidence. Constructing an argument is a legitimate skill. But writing teachers are not primarily training debaters or lawyers, so they shouldn't be encouraging students to argue what they don't believe; teachers should be encouraging students to argue what the students believe to be the truth. And in writing such arguments, of course, students begin to figure out just what it is they do believe. Such writing as discovery is a different, more interesting, and more difficult task than formulating still one more tiresome but defensible "thesis statement."

As Sale points out, "Teachers aren't, or shouldn't be, in the business of being persuaded or dissuaded, and so they should turn the question around and ask, 'Does that seem to you true to your experience? Is that all that is true? Have you said best what you really think is the case? Is that what you *want* to say?'" (51).

7. The Lie of Inattention

If I can't tell students what it is I want, I can tell them what I don't want, which is to be bored by their papers. I often quote to my students something I heard Roger Sale say at a symposium on composition at UC Berkeley. Sale was talking about boring student papers, and he said he tells his students that if he sat next to them on a long bus ride, he is sure they would have an interesting conversation, so why do they insist on writing boring papers?

Writing becomes boring when the writer is bored, writing still another "paper" somewhere between their twelfth and sixteenth consecutive year of schools, years filled with endless boredom and boring papers and boring reading. Students often are bored and write on automatic pilot, forgetting on page two what they said on page one. On one page, "I have always wanted to be a teacher," on the next page, "I'm not sure about a career in teaching"; on one page, "My father is a great man," on the next page, "I hate my father"; on one page, "W.W.II was primarily caused by Hitler's aggression," on the next page, "W.W.II was primarily caused by economic forces."

We could, alternatively, attribute student boredom to mental laziness, an unwillingness to suffer the pain of hard thought. But I prefer to attribute the lie of inattention to "diminished consciousness." After all, thinking is hard. When you do hard mental work, it is difficult to keep paying attention; you tend to become bored. Such is my experience when I try to read higher mathematics. (Someone who can more easily do this kind of mental work could call me mentally lazy.) Students often can't pay attention to what they write and think because paying such attention is difficult.

Paying attention to a complex piece of writing means paying attention to contradictions. The pedagogical goal is not eliminating or ignoring the contradictions (this is the path of simple thinking), but rather becoming conscious of the contradictions (the path of complex thinking): thus, the writer acknowledges "I'm ambivalent about being a teacher"; "Although my father is a great man, I hate him"; "W.W.II was caused by Hitler's aggression, economic forces, and a lot more."

Writing teachers regularly get writing that avoids complexity, writing that comes across as naive, such as a student's claim that "The experience of giving birth is the best moment in any woman's life." Obviously the author of this sentence hadn't known any women who had had horrible experiences during childbirth (my mother herself didn't speak fondly of the experience, which she endured five times). If such a student is made to focus on what she has actually said and is told of experiences that contradict her statement, then she will admit she was lying (and that she doesn't know enough to make a claim about what women feel during childbirth). She might then write a more suggestive truth: "I think the experience of giving birth should be the best moment of any woman's life." Such naive lies abound on student papers, for example, "Life is always easy for a child: to make friends, laugh happily, and believe in fairy tales and the magic of its parents." Pointing out such lies to students forces them to pay closer attention to their actual writing and to the complex world they live in, where life is not always easy, even for children. Stylistically, complex thinking can be reflected in complicated sentences, sentences that subordinate and entwine, sentences that acknowledge contradictions and move toward reconciling them. Thus complex thinking can be metaphored grammatically by "complex" sentences. But complex thinking can also be metaphored psychologically as consciousness of your own complexity, consciousness of your "complexes."

Carl Jung coined the psychological term "complex," a term that is clearly a metaphor. Jung conducted a series of "Association Experiments" in order to prove Freud's hypothesis of the unconscious. He read lists of words to various subjects who were to respond with the first word they thought of. By timing the interval between the initial word and the response, Jung showed that the subjects were unconsciously influenced by certain words (words that created an emotional response), and thus the subjects were slowed down in their responses. Groups of words that caused these delayed responses were often linked to a theme; Jung called these linked collections of associations "complexes."

According to Jung, everyone has complexes, a range of inner voices, "unconscious personalities." Human beings are psychologically complex because they have complexes (or, as Jung sometimes suggested, complexes have them). Again, to be complex means to be a combination of more than one, to be entwined or woven. (On an emotional level, as Richard Ford pointed out, this complexity involves awareness that we are never altogether in a *single* emotion.) Complex thinking is analogous to the psychological understanding that your psyche is not just the ego complex, but is made up of a number of complexes, woven together in an intricate fashion.

To notice and even embrace contradictions is a first step in complex thinking. When you are bored by a writing task or by your life, you may not even notice the tension between "My father is a great man" and "I hate my father." The integration of this tension could make for a successful essay (not to mention a successful psychoanalysis). When you are conscious of your complexes, you are conscious of your complexity (I love my father and I hate my father, perhaps because I and/or my father have more than one "I"). Psychological complexity brings ambivalence and ambiguity.

So a complex piece of writing may say opposite things, but it is aware of the contradictions; it highlights the contradictions and searches, perhaps, for a resolution. Shakespeare and his dramatic characters are the paradigm for such complex thinking. Edgar in *King Lear*, for example, shows the complexity of his experience of the truth by making contradictory but equally accurate philosophical exclamations: "World, world. Oh world! / But that thy strange mutations make us hate thee / Life would not yield to age" (IV.i.10–12) and "O, our lives' sweetness! / That we the pain of death would hourly die / Rather than die at once!"(V.iii.185–7). Yes, life is painful and we welcome death; yes, life is sweet and we want to live.

8. Teachers' Lies

If teachers should point out their students' lies, they should also acknowledge (and confront) their own lies.

The easiest writing teacher lie is to claim to know how to teach writing. Some of the most successful writing classes I have ever taught have been those where I least knew what I was doing (teaching scientific writing, for example, or writing in the life sciences), when I was forced there to be honest about my expertise. It's best to be a little unsure in the writing classroom, where you rarely have lecture material to fall back on but instead must try to pull rabbits out of a hat, making up the course as you go along (depending on what and how this unique group of students writes). The truth is I don't really know how to teach writing even if most of the time in my classes students' writing improves (or so I and the students tend to think). What Aquinas said about teaching is especially true about teaching writing: Teachers don't teach, learners learn. As the teacher, I contribute to such learning by putting students in situations where, somehow, they improve their writing.

Teachers need to acknowledge the mystery of writing, which is a creative act. While it may be useful to provide process models, to break down every step in the writing process into charts and lists (as many textbooks do), it is also useful to acknowledge that sometimes you need inspiration, the breeze of an idea blowing in through an open window. Writing is in part a teachable craft, but there is also mystery, randomness, the muse. When most of us begin writing something, even if we are experienced writers, we can't be sure how it is going to turn out. It's also easy to fall victim to the self-aggrandizing lie that stresses the importance of writing, of college education, of what we few, we happy few, we band of teachers do. "Let me tell you how important writing is going to be for your career," we often say, as if we have an idea in hell as to what the student's career might be, or even if the student will have a career as opposed to a job. Why make explicit claims that what we do is so important? Why not just do it and let the students finally decide just how important it is or was? While I am serious about teaching, and I am confident that as a teacher I have done more good than harm, successful pedagogy does not demand extravagant PR.

The most obvious honesty for a writing teacher to embrace is to give honest responses to student writing. This ability demands what Peter Elbow describes as paying attention to "the movies in your mind." You let the writer know in marginal comments what you were thinking and feeling at various points in the essay. Thus readers of student writing need to develop the good reader's ability to pay close attention to the piece of writing while at the same time paying close attention to their own responses. You let the student know when you were honestly pleased, confused, bored, intrigued, skeptical.

Commenting on scientific or technical writing epitomizes for me the honesty involved in this process, for I am often forced to say I am confused, that I don't really understand, when I can't be sure how much of the problem is the fault of the writer's bad writing and how much is the fault of my scientific ignorance. I love the vulnerability of such a response, the explicit acknowledgment that perhaps I am being dumb.

The great paper-commenting moment of truth is the writing of the final comment, the final comment that sums up your thoughts and feelings about the whole paper in a hundred or so words. Here "telling the truth" is an act of creation, a transformation of your moment-to-moment reading responses into a final comment that, to borrow a metaphor I once heard Roger Sale use, "cuts to the heart of the paper." And if I can't always find my intuitive way to the heart of the paper, at least I can always say what I liked and what I didn't like in the paper and try to explain why.

My favorite writing classroom activity, which I learned from my experience as a student in English 1-2 at Amherst College, is to talk about actual student writing as a class. I'll photocopy some student papers or parts of papers and then discuss them with the class (writers' names removed). I'm amazed time and again that not all writing teachers do this. As the teacher I usually talk the most, trying to teach the students about writing from my responses to their actual writing. This demands a spontaneous kind of honesty, a willingness to give your immediate responses (trusting that "first thought is best thought," as some Tibetan Buddhists say). I know that I demonstrate in such classes my honest and passionate desire not to be bored, my pleasure in talking about writing (which is usually more fun and always easier than actually writing). I've been bored in classrooms far too often in my life as a student (who hasn't?), so I need to enjoy the classes I teach—which means being spontaneous and honest in giving my responses and evaluations of student sentences, paragraphs, papers.

I make lying and telling the truth explicit criteria in my classes. Like Diogenes (but less cynically), I search for the honest student. To start with, I offer my students the practical rule most of us liars try to adhere to: try to tell the truth if there is any good chance of your being caught lying. (How you define "good chance" determines your integrity.)

Most of the time, I try not to lie to my students, but I sometimes do, especially in my final paper comments. I'll sometimes find myself writing, as the beginning of an end comment to a good paper, "I really enjoyed reading this," when in fact I've already read twenty-five papers that day and might not genuinely enjoy one more student paper even if it were written by the undergraduate Marcel Proust. But I know I won't be caught in this lie, and it expresses a certain truth (for it is a paper I did sort of enjoy, a paper I think I would really enjoy if I had read it earlier in the day). This venal lie is less a sin than telling a friend I like her new haircut when I really don't.

I do acknowledge to my students and to myself that just by using language we are often lying (that, for example, language does not directly translate our feelings and sensations). So the complex truth is that while I advocate trying to tell the truth, I acknowledge the impossibility of doing so. All memory, all writing is unreliable. Pam Houston said it well in a recent interview (Goggins 1997):

> A lot of teachers talk about the difference between a reliable narrator and an unreliable narrator. *All* narrators are unreliable. Every time any of us tells a story, we're unreliable. To think that we're not, to think that we can tell the truth, that we know how it really happened—is ridiculous. Everybody tells everything through their own personal window and a whole set of agendas. Which is what makes us interesting, which is what makes a story interesting.

As wise people know they are a fools, honest people know they are liars.

Your individual lies become, over time, your personal myth (your life stories), and they are embodied in your style, voice, personality, and complex life. (And of course there are also cultural lies—what cultures assume to be true—and even species lies, for example our "natural" belief that objects *have* color.)

If you study writing, you study lying, and you realize that truth is complicated. Mark Twain pointed out a frequent mistake: "The man who can't tell a lie thinks he is the best judge of one." On the contrary, the best judges of lies are those of us who have not only frequently told lies (in our teaching and writing), but have also had formal postgraduate training in the telling of lies (studying writing and literature). Plato had it right about poets, he just didn't go far enough: all writers are liars.

Note

1. The student examples of such lies are all based on reality but are composites, generalized out of specific examples found in the writing of many students. In other words, the student lies in this essay are made up.

Works Cited

Boe, J., and E. Schroeder. 1992. "An Interview with Peter Elbow: 'Going Two Directions at Once.'" *Writing on the Edge* 4 (1): 9–30.

Butler, Samuel. 1957. In Flesch, 159.

Coles, William. 1988. *The Plural I—And After*. Portsmouth, NH: Boynton/Cook.

———. 1995/96. "Response to 'The Shaming Game': Composition Pedagogy and Emotion." *Writing on the Edge* 7 (1): 73–78.

Flesch, Rudolph, ed. 1957. *The Book of Unusual Quotations*. New York: Harper and Brothers.

Ford, Richard. 1995. *The Sportswriter*. New York: Vintage.

———. 1996. *Independence Day*. New York: Knopf.

Goggins, Jan. 1997. "'All Narrators Are Unreliable': An Interview with Pam Houston." *Writing on the Edge* 8 (1): 83–96.

Lanham, Richard. 1992. *Revising Prose*. 3rd ed. New York: Macmillan.

Sale, R. 1970. *On Writing*. New York: Random House.

Twain, Mark. 1957. In Flesch, 159.

9

Writing Snapshots

Toby Fulwiler

The University of Vermont

Grammar A. In a small book called *An Alternate Style,* which is now out of print, Winston Weathers describes conventional English grammar as having "the characteristics of continuity, order, reasonable progression, and sequence, consistency, unity, etc. . . . promoted in nearly every English textbook and taught by nearly every English teacher" (6). He calls this conventional grammar, Grammar A.

Grammar B. Coexisting with Grammar A, Weathers suggests, is "an alternate grammar, Grammar B, with characteristics of variegation, synchronicity, discontinuity, ambiguity" (7) that challenges readers by deliberately defying expectations of continuity, order, and so on. In fact, readers of twentieth-century literature expect the fiction of Toni Morrison, the poetry of Adrianne Rich, the drama of Tom Stoppard, and the essays of Margaret Atwood to be some version of Grammar B—alternate styles, many would argue, that convey the ironies and complexities of twentieth-century life more successfully than the more conventional Grammar A.

New Journalism. But Weathers's real focus is nonfiction, so that he talks about the long tradition of literary figures who, in their nonfiction, wrote in Grammar B: from William Blake and Walt Whitman to D. H. Lawrence, Marianne Moore, and John Dos Passos—a grammar better suited to conveying multifaceted and multidimensional ideas in multifaceted and multidimensional

I would like to thank members of my writing group for thoughtful help in revising this piece: Glenda Bissex, Mary-Jane Dickerson, Laura Fulwiler, Corrine Glesne, Michael Strauss, and Jill and Rob Tarule.

prose. He specifically credits Tom Wolfe's *The Kandy-Colored Tangerine-Flake Streamline Baby* (1964) as the catalyst that sparked the subjective and experimental revolution in reporting called New Journalism. From the mid-1960s on, alternate-style essays appeared with regularity in the pages of *The New Yorker, Esquire, Rolling Stone,* and *Vanity Fair*—major publications that introduced Grammar B into mainstream American culture.

Mixed Media. The interest in and acceptance of alternative grammars to express unconventional ideas accelerates swiftly in the 1990s with the proliferation of alternate modes of electronic expression that differ radically from linear, sequential, verbal language. Contemporary audiences grow up experiencing and understanding television "texts"—especially commercial advertisements—that convey fast, impressionistic, simultaneous, and often contradictory information. Not to mention computer graphics, the Internet, and the World Wide Web.

Options. Among the stylistic devices that characterize Grammar B:

Lists—long sequences of details, facts, objects that add immediate depth and specificity to verbal description

Fragment sentences—short pieces of sentences (subjects or verbs alone) that render quick impressions for either speed or emphasis

Labyrinthine sentences—long, complex, seemingly endless sentences full of appositives, parentheses, convolutions, and digressions

Double voices—the conveying of simultaneous and often contradictory attitudes toward a subject, often suggested through the use of parentheses or italics

and Crots—

Crots. *1. crot: bit or fragment; independent unit of thought [archaic].* According to Tom Wolfe (1973): "As each crot breaks off it tends to make one's mind search for some point that must have just been made. . . . In the hands of a writer who really understands the device, it will have you making crazy leaps of logic, leaps you never dreamed of before" (19).

Prose stanzas. Think of crots as independent prose stanzas on a related subject (like this), one connected to the other by white space and leaps of reader logic and faith. A self-explanatory structure. Or as the most complete and independent of paragraphs, each a whole thought, without obvious connections to the paragraph before or after. (Like this.)

Tiny chapters. Think of crots as tiny chapters, perhaps numbered, titled—certainly autonomous—the many parts of which make up the whole book on a single topic. Instead of a whole book, a whole essay. (Like this.)

Miniature stories. Single crots satisfy weary, impatient, or media-trained readers by telling small stories within larger stories—each, at the same time, advancing a plot, developing a character, complicating a theme.

Tiny scenes. According to Theodore Rees Cheney, author of *Writing Creative Nonfiction* (1991): "A creative nonfiction writer will typically conceive of his or her story as a series of scenes connected by a series of summaries—drama connected by narrative. He or she will plan an article or book around a series of scenes, selecting those events that seem to have the greatest dramatic potential, and then organizing them in what seems the best sequence (not always chronological)" (9).

Verbal snapshots. Think of crots as snapshots in words, a photo album, scrapbook, slide show, pictures in an exhibition—each the work of the same maker, each a different view, each by some logic connected. When writing snapshots, you write short prose stanzas—typically fifty to one hundred words each—each telling its own small story or showing its own particular scene, each separated from the others by white space, numbers, asterisks, or dots, sometimes numbered, sometimes not.

For example. Margaret Atwood (1994) wrote snapshots to emphasize the dangers of men's bodies in the following passage from "Alien Territory" in *Good Bones and Simple Murders*:

> The history of war is a history of killed bodies. That's what war is: bodies killing other bodies, bodies being killed.
>
> Some of the killed bodies are those of women and children, as a side effect you might say. Fallout, shrapnel, napalm, rape and skewering, anti-personnel devices. But most of the killed bodies are men. So are most of those doing the killing. Why do men want to kill the bodies of other men? Women don't want to kill the bodies of other women. By and large. As far as we know.
>
> Here are some traditional reasons: Loot. Territory. Lust for power. Hormones. Adrenaline high. Rage. God. Flag. Honor. Righteous anger. Revenge. Oppression. Slavery. Starvation. Defense of one's life. Love; or, a desire to protect the men and women. From what? From the bodies of other men.
>
> What men are most afraid of is not lions, not snakes, not the dark, not women. What men are most afraid of is the body of another man.
>
> Men's bodies are the most dangerous things on earth. (99–100)

Gaps. The white space between snapshots—numbered, titled, dotted, or not—puts readers to work. What just happened? Where is this going? What's next? What's the connection? What's the meaning? Working readers read harder, remember more, don't give up.

For more examples: Aldo Leopold wrote snapshots in *Sand County Almanac* (1949), using the almanac form for essay purposes. Joan Didion wrote snapshots to portray a lost Haight Ashbury hippie community in her essay "Slouching Towards Bethlehem" (1968). John McPhee wrote snapshots in alternating views of Atlantic City with Monopoly game squares in "The Search for Marvin Gardens" (1975). Norman Mailer wrote snapshots in *The Executioner's Song* (1979), each reflecting a passage or impression from interview transcripts with convicted killer Gary Gilmore. Annie Dillard wrote titled snapshots detailing the follies of polar explorers in "An Expedition to the Pole" (1982). Gloria Steinem wrote snapshots to portray Marilyn Monroe as more person than sex goddess in *Marilyn: Norma Jean* (1986).

Composing piecemeal. Snapshots allow busy writers to compose in chunks, in five- and ten-minute blocks between appointments, schedules, classes, or coffee breaks. And five or ten or twenty chunks—reconsidered, rearranged, revised—can tell whole stories.

Composing nonetheless. While it's fun to write crots fast, random, and loose, putting them together in the right order—some right order—some order—is demanding, essential, and easier on note cards than computer. Assemble and arrange as you would pictures in a photo album, playfully and seriously: Begin at the beginning; alternate themes; begin *in medias res*; alternate time; begin with flashbacks; alternate voices; consider frames; alternate fonts; reinforce rhythms; experiment with openings and closings, type, and titles.

Thin. Snapshots, like lists, fragments, clichés, and blue jeans, worn too often or too long, wear thin.

Revision. In all my college writing classes, first-year through graduate, I assign snapshots as one of several revision moves in second or third drafts of both personal and research writing, often showing samples from my own published writing (1988); and I often ask students to start writing snapshots for the last fifteen minutes in a class as a start on their next draft, me wanting them to share samples, get the hang of it before striking out on their own.

Assignment, First-Year Composition: Explore and explain your intended college major or the career you hope to enter after graduating from college. Write draft 1 in whatever form or style suits you. Write draft 2 by interviewing professors and seniors in your potential major. Write draft 3 as snapshots, interweaving dreams and goals with interviews and research. (Write draft 4 any way you please.) Here are four snapshots from sophomore Sonya's eight-snapshot final essay:

1. What I care about is the environment, and what I want to do is teach younger children to care about it too. That's what brings me to college, and to this English class, writing about what I want to be when I grow up.

2. My first teaching was this past summer on the Caribbean Island of South Caicos. In the classroom one morning, I tried to teach local teenagers about the fragility of their island environment, but they did not seem to hear me or attend to my lesson, and I left class very frustrated. Later on, we went to the beach, and they taught me back my morning lessons, and I felt so much better. I thought then I wanted to be a teacher.

4. The School of Education scares me. A lady named Roberta and professor named Merton gave me a list of classes I would need in order to major in education. "Environmental education is not a real field, yet," the professor said. I realized it would take four years and many courses and still I wouldn't be studying the environment or be sure that I would ever teach about it in public schools.

5. The School of Natural Resources excites me. Professor Erickson is my advisor, and in one afternoon, she helped me plan a major in "Terrestrial Ecology." I now know, for the first time, exactly what I'm doing in college. I need to study natural resources first, later on decide whether I want to teach, work in the field or what.

Comment. Sonya liked her snapshot version best and stuck with that on her final draft. These excerpts show us telling scenes from her first-semester search for a major, revealing her basis for choosing one major over another without editorializing. By showing us snapshots of the highlights, and skipping most of the complaining that characterized earlier drafts, we experience more directly her reasons for majoring in natural resources rather than education.

Assignment, Senior English Seminar: Write a profile of yourself, as you see yourself today and as you would like to present yourself to others. Draft 1 is wide open. Draft 2 is based on memory and artifacts. Draft 3 is snapshots. (Draft 4 is up to you.) Following are seven of twenty-five snapshots from Becky's personal profile:

My mother grew up in Darien, Connecticut, a Presbyterian. When she was little, she gave the Children's Sermon at her church. My father grew up in Cleveland, Ohio, a Jew. When I went away to college, he gave me the Hebrew Bible he received at his Bar Mitzvah.

The only similarity between my parents' families is freckles. They both have them, which means I get a double dose. Lucky me. My mother once told me that freckles are "angels kisses." Lucky me.

I am a Protestant. I have attended First Presbyterian Church of Boulder, Colorado, for most of my life. When I was baptized, Reverend Allen said:

"Becky is being baptized here today, brought by their believing mother and their unbelieving—but supportive—father."

When I was little, I was terrified of the darkness. Sometimes, I would wake up in the night and scream. It was my mother who came in to comfort me, smoothing my hair, telling me to think of butterflies and angels.

When I am in Vermont, I attend North Avenue Alliance Church. I chose it because it is big, like my church at home. The last two Sundays I have sung solos. The first time, I sang "Amazing Grace." The second time, I sang "El Shaddai," which is partly in Hebrew.

I have always said my prayers before going to bed. Lying silently in the dark, talking to God. Like the disciples in the Garden of Gethsemane, I have been known to fall asleep while praying. Now I pray on my knees, it is harder to doze off that way.

I wear a cross around my neck. It is nothing spectacular to look at, but I love it because I bought it at the Vatican. Even though I am not a Catholic, I am glad I bought it at the Pope's home town. Sometimes, when I sit in Hebrew class, I wonder if people wonder, "What religion is she, anyway?"

Comment. These snapshots portray Becky's mixed religious heritage, strong commitment to Protestantism, and current participation in Christian rituals. Each focuses on a single small event—a cross necklace, prayer, a church, etc. Each actually tells a small story, complete with beginning, middle, and punch line. At the same time, the cumulative effect of these seven snapshots reveals Becky's broad tolerance, education, and interest in a spirituality that goes well beyond separate religious creeds. This theme emerges as one experience is juxtaposed against another, past tense against present tense, without editorializing, allowing readers to supply the connective tissue by filling in the white spaces for themselves.

Assignment, Graduate English Seminar: Write an essay on place. Draft 1, visit a place in the local community and tell its story in whatever voice, style, or form you choose. Draft 2, find all new material and eliminate both first-person pronouns and value judgments—let the place speak for itself. Draft 3, write snapshots. (Draft 4, whatever.) Following are three of sixteen crots in Kerry's essay on a nature trail in Burlington:

I. Deep boot and paw prints are frozen into the mud. It is January 29th, and the temperature is 10 degrees. Standing on a rise, I see the broad face of Mount Mansfield some twenty miles to the east. Closer in, I see the brick buildings and no-longer smoking stacks of Winooski, a former mill town close by the banks of the Winooski River. The Central Vermont Railroad bridge is on my left, the curve of the river called Salmon Hole on my right. Today the Riverwalk looks frozen, glassy, and strangely still.

III. To get to Riverwalk from downtown Burlington, walk north on North Prospect Street until you come to Riverside Avenue. Cross Riverside and continue on Intervale Road to Charlebois Truck Parts. Across the street, you'll notice a wooden fence and sign: Riverwalk Nature Trail. Descend the stairs, cross the footbridge, and follow the trail east along the river, to Salmon Hole, just west of downtown Winooski.

V. This morning I am stopped in my tracks by the sight of a small dark animal bounding toward me, across the river ice. My camera hangs closed in a bag around my neck, my notebook, too, is closed, my pencil useless in my mouth. I stand dumb, dumbfounded, as the deep brown creature hops my way, stopping suddenly short, no more than three feet from my frozen boots. Though I've never seen one before, I know this is a mink. Twenty seconds, no more, and it is gone, darting back down the river bank, disappearing down the snow encrusted ice.

Comment. Kerry's snapshots resemble actual scenes from a photo album, with the viewer's eyes jumping easily from one photo to the other—some wide angle, some close-ups; some still life, some in motion. Each snapshot is first person, present tense, and highly descriptive, placing the reader riverside with the writer. Kerry's plain style, with simple language and more compound than complex sentences aptly suits her reverence-for-nature theme. Her final snapshot is reflective:

XVI. I have waited two months to articulate my thoughts on this place that has become my regular oasis from traffic and commotion. It is now late March and most of the ice is gone. Buds are appearing on the trees and the warm air carries the scent of the moist earth. As the sun warms my face and mud clings to my boots, I realize that Riverwalk touches me in many ways. At first, I wondered if I had a right to be here. Now, though still unsure, I'm comforted by what I've learned. I hope, like the lumber of the once-new stairs, I've become weathered and less intrusive through time.

Comment. Unlike most of Kerry's other snapshots, which stand by themselves, her final one only makes sense in the context of the others. It concludes her story as might the conclusion of a more conventional narrative.

Ownership. Students own snapshot writing quickly. They take it in, play with it, make it their own. They do this, I suspect, because it's not conventional, not Grammar A, not academic—it's OK to own it.

Snapshooting as a subversive activity. Revising from narrative/summary to scene/snapshots works differently for each writer, for each assignment, but neither writing ability nor grade level will tell you why. Snapshots are not suitable composing strategies for all papers; after all, a lab report fulfills reader expectations in one economical way as does a literature review or position paper in another. However, snapshots do loosen, in a healthy and reader-friendly way, many more ponderous academic forms by withholding the strangle hold of theses statements, step-by-step transitions, overly logical arguments, and the illusion of absolute truths. Even when a final draft needs to be carefully Grammar A, a version of Grammar B along the way may help discover other possibilities.

The advantage of snapshot essays? The snapshot form, when fresh and unexpected, surprises both writer and reader in powerful ways. It encourages writers to see subjects in manageable chunks, to compose in particular scenes, to use specific details, and to look for moments of both periodic and final closure. Snapshots allow the covering of large amounts of time in small amounts of space. They forgo wordy, rambling, generalized transitions— often painful both to write and read. And they demand high reader engagement, making readers forge their own transitions, make their own inferences, write their own conclusions.

The disadvantage of snapshot essays? In long essays, snapshots can become tedious both to write and read—unless crafted with exceptional skill. Snapshots sometimes encourage too-hasty and two-dimensional glimpses rather than in-depth investigations, allowing writers to forgo synthesis or resolution, hoping inference will do that for them. The ease with which snapshot essays can be composed is also the danger. In the hands of hasty or inexperienced writers, snapshots become the easy way out; in the hands of committed or experienced writers, they take more work than at first appears.

A last assignment: On the last day of a recent advanced writing class, I ask thirty-two juniors and seniors (yes, clearly too large for a writing class) to compose a class portrait in snapshots ("crots," they insist—they love the rough erotic potential of the word and always prefer it to "snapshot")—one anonymous crot apiece (which, times thirty-two makes a good semester summary), among which I find these:

> Crot, crot, crot. After 13 weeks of reading, writing, revising, and reading about reading, revising and writing, we summarize it all, a classful of crots composing a classful of crots.

> They're pretty simple to write. Soundbites written down. Voicebites. Snapshots of *ourselves by ourselves for ourselves.*

> My personal voice in a single crot? Why not? Get on with it. Get to the point. Skip the small stuff. Learn me by learning my words.

Draft on top of draft. Do we ever stop rewriting? No. Our class is one big rewrite—talking, exchanging, producing, revising. How do we learn to write? "Rewrite," his voice says again, "try crots."

Ambiguity. Frustration. Relief. A never-ending cycle. Draft after draft. Again and again and again. But when it works, it works, and you know it. Free at last! Free at last! By writing crots, we're free at last!

Works Cited

Atwood, Margaret. 1994. *Good Bones and Simple Murders.* New York: Doubleday.

Cheney, Theodore Rees. 1991. *Writing Creative Nonfiction.* Berkeley: Ten Speed Press.

Didion, Joan. 1968. *Slouching Towards Bethlehem.* New York: Farrar, Straus & Giroux.

Dillard, Annie. 1982. *Teaching a Stone to Talk.* New York: Harper & Row.

Leopold, Aldo. 1949. *A Sand County Almanac.* New York: Oxford University Press.

Mailer, Norman. 1979. *The Executioner's Song.* Boston: Little, Brown.

McPhee, John. 1975. *Pieces of the Frame.* New York: Farrar, Straus, & Giroux.

Waldrep, Tom, ed. 1988. *Writers on Writing II.* New York: Random House.

Weathers, Winston. 1980. *An Alternate Style: Options in Composition.* Rochelle Park: Hayden.

Wolfe, Tom. 1973. *The New Journalism.* New York: Harper & Row.

10

Transforming Connections and Building Bridges
Assigning, Reading, and Evaluating the Collage Essay

Sheryl I. Fontaine and Francie Quaas
California State University, Fullerton

Understanding the Nature of Organization

In creating writing assignments for college writing classes, teachers commonly search for ways to help their students improve the clarity of their writing and the explicitness with which they articulate their ideas and the connections among them. Whether teachers assign essays according to genres—autobiography, explanatory, argument—or according to strategies—narration, cause and effect, analysis—they most likely expect the essays' organization to make clear the relationships that students have discovered among their ideas and wish to convey to readers.

It seems self-evident to say that if teachers want students to write well-organized, clearly articulated essays, then writing assignments should require that students create logical organizational structures through the use of conventional rhetorical devices. In this manner, students demonstrate their understanding of how conventional organizational patterns such as cause and effect, induction, deduction, and chronology, and devices such as adverbial transitions can help the writer to arrange and present information effectively.

But what about that quality of organization that comes, not from the structures that writers put their ideas into, but, rather, from the relational power that is generated when particular ideas and concepts are placed side by side? Putting idea A after idea B, the writer necessarily creates a different connection for the reader than if this order had been reversed or if idea F had been placed in between. And though transitions like "As a consequence of B, A takes place" or "We come to understand B once we see the way it is distinguished from F" may explain such connections to the reader, the connections will only truly work for the reader, on another level, if they can be intuited without the use of the directional transitions.

To help students understand organization in terms of the structuring power of conventional patterns *and* the structuring power of conceptual relationships, we recommend that in addition to using writing assignments that focus on the demonstration or imitation of conventional organizational structures, teachers also create assignments that focus students' awareness on the relationships and connections that they create whenever they place ideas on the page. Another way, then, for students to come to understand connections in their writing is by creating texts in which connections are developed for the reader not through conventional rhetorical methods but through the structures that naturally emerge among adjacent ideas and concepts. One such text is the collage essay.

What Is a Collage?

Like the photographer who creates a collage from a collection of photos taken over a long period of time and in various settings, the writer uses a collection of texts that have been written over time and for various purposes to make the collage essay. Highlighting and selecting sections from these various texts, the writer then spreads them out, setting them up against one another, moving them around, looking for connections that were not, could not have been, there initially when the words were in their original context or if they had been placed differently. Unlike a conventional essay in which structure emerges for the writer, in part, from the use of focusing heuristics and, in part, from the rhetorical patterns and devices that are available, the collage essay obliges the writer to seek and identify connections—parallels, oppositions, distinctions—that emerge when segments of different texts are placed in the context of a newly emerging text, serving as catalysts to stimulate new meanings. In the end, a collage "consists not of a single perfectly connected train of explicit thinking or narrative but rather of fragments: arranged—how shall we say—poetically? intuitively? randomly? Without transitions or connections" (Elbow 1981, 148).

In making the collage, the writer's goal, then, is to identify, through the course of arranging and rearranging, reading and rereading the segments, an organic structure from which will emerge a conceptual melody, a strain of meaning, a center of gravity. The "interplay between the text fragments 'recreates' their meaning and transforms them into a new piece of writing that, while maintaining the voice of the original author(s), brings new light and meaning to the text through the 're-visioning' by the collage author" (Quaas 1996a, 2). In this way, a "collage is like an abstract portrait by Pablo Picasso or Georges Braques. Each individual fragment—body part, piece of newspaper, words from a book—at once becomes part of the newly constructed portrait and retains the shadow of its connection to its original whole. By rearranging expected fragments (ears, eyes, legs) and introducing unexpected ones (newsprint), the constructed portrait is not a representation but an abstraction, a re-creation, a re-visioning" (Fontaine 1995, 1).

What most characterizes the collage essay for the reader is, first, the physical appearance and cognitive/psychological effect of accumulated segments of text and, second, the absence of introductions, transition, identified chronologies, or causal connections. Ultimately, the juxtaposition among segments and the unexpected absences between them create responses and reactions in the reader that will give the whole collage a general effect or impression.

How to Make the Collage Assignment

Preparations for the collage assignment must begin long before the actual writing task is given to students. Because the text of the collage is created from selected segments of students' previous writings, the more writing students have available from which to make their selections, the richer the collage will be. This writing can be formal essays or informal exploratory writing, journal entries, reading responses—any kind of writing that the teacher would like to make available for students' collages. The more varied the kind of writing from which students can select, the more multidimensional the collage.

The first part of the assignment, once enough writing has been completed to offer students adequate selection, is to have students read through all of these texts, underlining or bracketing sections that grab their attention, perhaps because they are most unlike other sections, most clearly written, or most strongly voiced—at this point, the idea is merely to select without analysis.

Once this first-round selection is complete, it can be helpful for students to cut out those underlined or bracketed sections of text so that they can physically remove them from their original contexts and begin to create the new one. This new context is constructed as the student writer places the segments next to one another, looking for the relationships among the segments and the emergent strain of meaning from the whole. This is the point at which students experience the organic nature of text organization. By first reading and rereading the segments, searching to identify the center of gravity that unites the segments, students can then arrange the segments together like the pieces of a puzzle. With this puzzle, however, the pieces are not cut from a preidentified image; rather they will be put together to create an image that is yet to be discovered. The meaning or significance of any particular segment will be influenced by the segments that are placed next to or near it. And as the segments provide catalytic energy for one another, the writer will "organize" the collage and the reader's movement through the various pieces toward a final grasp of the whole.

Anticipating Reaction and Guiding Response

In making the collage assignment, it is helpful for the teacher to anticipate the reluctance of students who have devoted their academic lives to demonstrating their knowledge of conventional structural patterns and devices. What the collage essay assignment asks them to do is to forget momentarily all of those patterns and devices. It asks them to rely on the way pieces of text can create predictable responses from readers, responses that will move the reader through a text and toward an understanding of the writer's central idea. Teachers should be prepared to reassure students by providing demonstration collages on which students can rehearse the reading process and practice identifying the center of gravity (see Fairgrieve 1993, Fontaine and Hunter 1992, 19). Students might also use segments of a class collage, identifying together a central meaning that emerges (Quaas 1996a, 6). Having worked to develop the necessary critical response skills, students can then read one another's drafted collages and even approach their own with a more constructive eye.

Classroom peer response may be the most reliable form of feedback for students' drafted collages, next only to the teacher's own response. Because "the collage asks the reader to build the bridges or connections or threads" (Elbow 1992, 4), students must be encouraged to show writers how they experienced the collage as readers. Using Elbow's "movie of the reader's mind" (1973, 85), students describe and demonstrate how the text is "creating" structure for the reader. Indeed, it can be additionally helpful to have writers make their own "movies" of their own collages. This description can then be used as a way for writers to see their collages with some analytic distance and can also be used as a point of comparison and discussion with the reader's "movie."

Feedback from sources other than the student's teacher or classmates can be limited in its helpfulness—unless the tutors or friends who respond have created collages themselves. Otherwise, the student writer becomes the expert and must be willing and able to explain what a collage is and how it is expected to "work." If the student writer doesn't have this expert knowledge or is not convinced of the nature of the collage, tutor response can be startled, at its best (Quass 1996a, 1), and disastrous, at its worst, as tutors mislead writers, advising them to insert transitions, write introductions, or provide conclusions.

Problems of Evaluation

Ultimately, as with any writing assignment, students must hand in their collages for evaluation. And because this kind of writing is likely to be so different from other writing that has been evaluated for the course, it is important that instructors make their expectations and criteria clear. Peter Elbow argues that "when [a collage] works it is terrific. Indeed, there is often a deeper impact on readers because the collage invites them to create actively out of their own consciousness the vision which organizes those fragments—the sparks which cross those gaps. But when a collage doesn't work, it seems merely opaque or annoying—a lazy copout" (Elbow 1981, 148). While we may agree with Elbow's analysis about the identifiable impact of a successful collage, students may need (and deserve) more concrete evaluation criteria. We can think of several options available to the teacher who is at the point of evaluating students' collages. Surely other options exist.

1. Ask students to turn in their personal "movies" of themselves as readers of their own collages and a statement about the emergent meaning of the text. Use these as a comparison point once you have read the collage. Evaluate the success of the writer's intentions.

2. Read the collage holistically to determine whether a meaning does emerge. Evaluate how well the individual textual segments support this meaning or, conversely, to what extent they derail it.

3. Evaluate the collage in terms of the writer's willingness to set aside traditional conventions. Has the writer effectively relied on internal relationships rather than external rhetorical conventions to create this text?

In some writing programs, portfolio readers are also expected to evaluate students' writing. If this is the case, the readers must be given adequate information about the process, nature, and expectations of the assignment to make a reliable and valid evaluation of its success. The assigning teacher may want to distribute the original assignment to the other instructors along with a description of evaluation criteria and an explanation of how the collage fits into the goals of a college writing class. Needless to say, while they should be prepared for a variety of reactions to the collage, teachers also need to know that they have the support of the Writing Program Administrator when making the assignment and including it in the final portfolio.

A Demonstration Collage

In order to make the idea of the collage more concrete and to include in our chapter the perspective of students who have written collages, we have created one from the responses and reactions that students and tutors recorded after having written and read numerous collages themselves. This particular collage integrates many voices, sometimes in groups and sometimes alone, into a single chorus. As you read through the collage that follows, be aware of the way you are constructing a meaning from the segments and from their positions in relation to one another. At the end of the collage, we will provide our own sense of how it worked as a whole, something against which you can place your own reading experience.

Voices Searching for Meaning[1]

"I [don't] understand what [is] going on."

"Why is this written like this?"

"I thought it would be easy to do, but I was very fooled."

"I felt it was something different. I was looking forward to trying [the collage]."

"I thought it would be easy to write because you don't need to analyze or go into detail about a topic."

"It seems nice the way that everything ties in, but I'll bet it's not that easy to put things together when writing your own collage."

"When I first read a collage essay, I thought it was kind of weird."

"I thought, 'they really know what they're doing, and they have probably done it before.' I wonder if my collage essay will turn out as well as theirs."

******

"I am a little nervous about writing a collage because I think it's going to be complicated, and I am not used to this format."

"I am a little bit intimidated because I have never written a collage before."

"I feel happy about writing a collage essay because I have never written one before."

******

You have spent a great deal of time over the past six weeks of the semester reading and writing about how you currently use writing and about your writing process. You have read and responded to a number of selections from Natalie Goldberg's *Writing Down the Bones*. In addition, you have completed a number of prewriting activities, and you have read a number of essays, both professional and student authored, about writing. All of these activities have laid the ground work for this collage assignment.[2]

******

1. Unless otherwise noted, the segments of this collage are taken from completely anonymous student and tutor responses to questionnaires. Both groups knew that responses might be quoted in this essay. Those who did not want to be quoted did not fill out a questionnaire. A practical note: each collage will differ in its citation of sources. The essay that follows provides footnotes at the bottom of each page; the authors feel this is serviceable compromise between endnotes and no documentation at all.

2. Quaas, F. "The Collage Assignment," 1.

"Preparing for the collage essay takes months of planning."

"Everything you write in your journal and the freewriting you do in class will all help you."

"I learned that doing a lot of prewriting really helps you in your final draft."

"I would tell other collage writers that doing a lot of prewriting will help a great deal."

******

"My advice would be to be honest with your feelings and opinions when writing your journal. Don't write what you think the teacher wants to hear. This will only make it more difficult for you to decide what to do in your collage because the ideas won't be yours."

******

******

Over the weekend you began highlighting passages in the readings, as well as passages from your own reading responses and journals that you found interesting, provocative or amusing. These selections of text will help you begin to create entries for your collage. The entries may be organized in any fashion you like. The format should mirror the way this assignment sheet is set up. In other words, you will separate blocks of your text or that of another writer with "***" or "---" marks.[3]

******

"A collage essay is an essay in which you have blocks of writing that have the same topic. You create a collage essay by collecting blocks of writing from your journal. Then you group the blocks together by organizing them and eliminating blocks that don't have the same topic. You can also use quotes from the reading to illustrate your point."

******

"I don't like writing the collage essay. It is frustrating trying to get my ideas to fit together, and it's even more frustrating trying to figure out how to fit in stuff from other authors."

"I like writing the collage. It's just a little harder than I thought to organize and put ideas together."

******

"Don't think this essay is going to be easy. You need examples from the texts and from your own experiences as well as your own thoughts. You need to reread through your journals to get the right quotes to express your feelings on the topic."

******

3. Harnick-Shapiro, B. "Collage Assignment," 1.

"My greatest struggle was in organizing the essay. I had all these underlined passages, but I didn't know how to start making sense out of them."

"It's your [essay] and your voice. There are no clear-cut rules; it's a relationship with yourself. What is it you wanted to say?"[4]

******

"After you highlight passages from your journals, number them, and try to put them in some order. They might not make sense together the first time you try this. If that happens, keep on trying. Eventually you will find an order that does work and does say something."

******

"At first it looks easy, but you will be clueless as to what topic to choose in the beginning."

"Write as much as possible. Express all you know about writing. Do not worry about what you are going to write about. When the time comes, you will know the topic."

"It was interesting how prior phrases could fit together to form a new essay that sounds as if the phrases were meant to go with that topic."

"[Writing] is an act of intellect; it is thinking with language' it is a craft . . . I write to learn, to discover what I have to say that I did not know I had to say in ways I did not know it could be said."[5]

******

"I learned a way of writing differently. I learned that writing doesn't always have to be the same old boring thing to get a message across. I also re-learned things that I had already read about and forgotten."

******

"After writing this collage essay, I have learned that what you write in your journals is really important and what you say really counts. You should always try to write your ideas in some kind of sequence. This assignment has helped me understand the importance of organization and the idea that my thoughts need to go in some kind of logical sequence when I'm writing."

******

"You really have to put your effort into doing the essays and journals, especially the collage essay. It was a totally different kind of essay compared to the kind of essays that we have done in the past. When you first look at it, it might seem easy because all you have to do is pick out some statements you like from your journals, but remember that it is not enough. You have to be sure that all the statements you choose relate to your topic and to each other."

4. Goldberg, N. "Writing Down the Bones," 157.
5. Murray, D. "Write to Learn," vii.

******

Collage writing is like the collages you did in elementary school. You remember cutting out pictures from an assortment of magazines, then pasting all the pictures on to another piece of paper in some sort of pattern that was meaningful to you.[6]

******

"I can't decide what sentences I should put in the collage or where to put them. I have a hard time picking out my main point. In the first draft I have more than one main point, so I know that I have to narrow my focus down."

******

"When I first started working on the collage, I thought that all I had to do was read over my journals, pick out a few statements that I liked, then type them out. But when my peer reviews came, I realized that I was wrong. There was much more to it than that."

******

"Writing my own collage was different than I thought it would be after reading other student collages."
"I thought it would just be a couple of opinions put together. I didn't think that it all had to make sense together. I didn't realize that it was a real essay, but it is."
"Collage essays don't just come out, even though the student essays seemed like they just wrote it, like it was natural. I've learned that they take a lot of work and a lot of time."
"I thought that using quotes from other authors would be an easy thing to do, but it's not."

******

You will need to engage in a constructive thinking process as you examine the work of other writers in order to provide an analysis and interpretation of the texts you have selected and to integrate those texts into your own in a meaningful way. In order to produce a successful collage, you will be required to make clearly implied connections between the blocks of text selected for the collage. The blocks cannot be on the page helter skelter. They must have a theme or a current that dominates and provides focus for the collage. Thus you will need to have a clear understanding of the meaning of the texts selected from other works, as well as a clear understanding of how the block of text is being applied to your collage.[7]

******

"Once I started writing my own collage it seemed difficult because I wanted my ideas to be in order, not splattered everywhere."

6. Quaas, F. , "Discovering the Collage," 1.
7. Quaas, F. "Collage Assignment," 2.

"I found that collages are a good way to put a lot of ideas together to create one main idea."

"Collages are almost put together like a puzzle, and sometimes what is in one spot should be in another."

"I had trouble creating a smooth pattern. I had to make sure I wasn't repeating something I had said earlier. This essay was fun, but it was also frustrating."

"I struggled with everything. It seemed easy at first, but when I had to categorize things and put them into a certain order, it was difficult for me. I could not piece all the phrases together to make it sound complete."

"I learned that you really have to make your paper flow; one idea leads to the next."

"I learned, or tried to learn, to put phrases together as organized as possible."

"I spent a lot of time trying to get the blocks to flow together. I had to find phrases that would fit that particular topic and blend in with the next block of text."

"My biggest struggle on this essay was making it all fit together. Sometimes my blocks didn't fit together, but I wanted to use them anyway. This was difficult to overcome."

"Putting together the bits and pieces of quotes or sections of writing I chose was difficult. It was especially difficult to eliminate pieces that did not fit in or belong, especially if I really liked that fragment or piece."

******

"I like my collage essay. I feel like the essay is personal. It's not just a bunch of words."

******

"The collage essay was a first for me. It was something different and challenging. You choose thoughts that you have written before. You read all your journals and underline everything you think is important. Then you put everything you underlined into categories like "details" or "being specific." Then you pick a category and put the sentences in an order, changing and putting in thoughts to make your collage better. You need to take sentences out that don't fit and freewrite about your topic to get new ideas."

******

"The collage helps students with connections because leaving them out makes you more aware of them. Making a collage flow without some kind of implied connection is harder than making an essay flow. Students can often make the ideas in an essay seem to flow together, even though in reality the ideas presented have nothing to do with one another, and the quotes selected aren't connected with the main point the author is making."

******

"The biggest thing I learned was how to organize and structure my essay to make sense. I had to use a lot of brain power to make sure the sentences transitioned well into the others. That was hard work."

******

"I would tell collage writers to cut apart the rough draft into strips in order to arrange them. It helped me a lot. It was visual, and I was able to try out new ways of using the text."

******

"I believe the most difficulty I had in this essay was putting the blocks in order. If I had just listed all the quotes on paper it would have been hard to pick them out. So my advice is to write the quotes on flash cards. This makes them easier to move around. Also, instead of looking at 20 or 30 blocks of text, you can deal with four or five at a time. The less you have to deal with, the easier and faster you will be able to finish."

******

"When I was working on my collage, I asked a lot of different people to read what I had written to see if they could find my point."
"Having a friend read your collage is very helpful because sometimes you might think your ideas follow through nicely, but others may think differently."

******

Collages encourage "aesthetic reading." The gaps in the structure of the collage allow the reader to engage with the text in ways that are not possible with traditional essays and offer the opportunity to contemplate the meaning of the individual blocks of text as well as the meaning of the entire collage. Further, the gaps challenge our existing reading schemata and encourage us to modify our expectations while reading.[8]

******

In nonaesthetic reading, the reader's attention is focused primarily on what will remain as the residue after the reading—the information to be acquired, the logical solution to a problem, the actions to be carried out. In aesthetic reading, in contrast, the reader's primary concern is with what happens during the actual reading event. . . . In aesthetic reading, the reader's attention is centered directly on what he is living though during his relationship with that particular text.[9]

******

"My first exposure reading a collage was pleasant, but confusing. Collages sound good, but I didn't get the point. Later still, I was even more confused about responding effectively to collages in the Writing Center."

******

Readers who are simply looking for explicit answers in their reading will be disappointed by the collage. They will miss the point of the collage because

8. Quaas, F. "Discovering the Collage," 2.
9. Rosenblatt, L. *The Reader, the Text, and the Poem,* 25.

they have not made the thought contribution necessary to make the connections between the blocks of text and to understand the main point of the author. [10]

******

"In general I find collages irritating, not difficult, because they seem so fragmentary, incohesive."

"My first reaction was confusion. I wasn't sure how to look at organization or how the student was supposed to organize the collage."

******

The implicit principle of the essay is to lead the reader's mind from point to point, to create bridges. Here is an essential contrast with the collage—in which the essential principle is non-connection or brokenness. The collage asks the reader to build bridges or connections or threads. [Whereas] in the essay the speaker is always building these bridges or connections. [11]

******

"Some collages jump around too much and the blocks don't connect to one another. Others are too connected and read just like an essay because the student doesn't understand the assignment."

******

"My first exposure to collage essays came in the Writing Center. I had no clue how to respond to the tutee who was desperate for advice, so I had to ask for the assignment sheet and for his idea of what the collage was supposed to be or do. The student had no clue. I asked other tutors in the Writing Center; again, no clue. I reread the prompt and the student's draft of the collage, and talked to him about how he had selected the quotes versus original material and discussed whether or not there was supposed to be linear connections between the ideas. My instinct told me there was not, though as a whole the piece would be unified, but that taken individually or in juxtaposition with one another, the separate entries did not have to necessarily obviously relate. This would correspond with my idea of a collage in visual arts. The student responded with a blank stare, which did not help matters."

******

"I like the collage genre in that it presents little snapshots or vignettes of life, and the reader puts them all together. The collages have to have some connections between the snapshots, but I like the disconnectedness of it."

******

"The collage essay was odd; the writing seemed well thought out and cohesive, but the paper structure was odd. I felt that the paper flowed, but not

10. Quaas, F. "Discovering the Collage," 8.
11. Elbow, P., "The Collage," 4

as smoothly as it might have because the blocks weren't grouped together well."

******

"I think that the strength of this type of essay is in its ability to help the student develop good judgement in order to pick out a representative statement, then provide a response to follow the statement, and finally organize all the text together into an essay."

******

"The most difficult part of the collage essay was organizing my thoughts and ideas and then putting them in a logical order. The collage essay taught me how to organize my thoughts."

******

"I really didn't think that I could form an essay out of bits and pieces of other works."
"I feel like I've accomplished a very difficult task. At first my writing was totally out of control. I've made myself work very hard to get through that, and now I think I have a good result."

******

"I think the collage assignment helped me develop skills for my future writing assignments because it made me focus on one main point."
"It helped me stay focused on one thing without going to other topics."
"I think the collage can help me write better essays in the future because of the techniques I learned, especially backing up my own ideas with other people's quotes."
"I learned how to back myself up better and how to organize things in a better fashion."

******

A Reading of the Demonstration

Over the course of several semesters of collage assignments, Francie Quaas, while in the course of doing research for this and other essays about collage assignments, invited interested students in her classes and tutors in the Writing Center to write in response to various prompts, which included sample collages, questionnaires, requests to write letters to other students, open-ended requests for reaction and commentary. From all of this writing, Francie began her own process of creating a collage—highlighting, selecting, arranging, sorting, rearranging—until a shape emerged that carried the essence of collage making, reading, and responding.

As the two of us read this collage, it loosely represents the way students and tutors have experienced the collage assignment and have reacted as readers to this unfamiliar genre. Sometimes the chorus of voices is reduced to three or four individuals who briefly engage a perspective; other times, a single voice is heard; and in the background runs a current of outside voices from the assignment prompt and professional texts. While we trust that something very close to this interpretation of "Voices Searching for Meaning" will have emerged for you, we are also aware that each reader filters the collage through his or her own knowledge and experience, resulting in a seemingly endless number of twists on the initial interpretation. Once you become practiced with reading collages and more at ease with the gaps and lack of transitions, you also become attentive to the ways your own experiences and expectations create an interaction between your own reading of the collage and the current of meaning created by the collage writer.

Adapting the Collage

There is no single "right way" to do a collage; there is only a single sensibility of what one is and how it should be helping students to understand the nature of organization, how organization effectively constructs the movement and meaning of a text. The variations on the assignment are endless: include writing from formal essays only; include writing from exploratory writing only; include the writing of others, students or professionals; create collages in small groups (Elbow 1992, Donovan 1994); add other media to the collage such as photos or found objects; perform the collage in a uni- or multivocal reading.

However you adapt the collage to your class and your program, keep in mind that it is an assignment that allows you and your students to break the conventional rules of organization in order to understand how concepts and ideas interact to create structure and organization in a different way. The more playful and freewheeling you can be, within the expectations that you lay out for yourself and your students, the more likely it is that the collages your students create will provide them with experiences and knowledge about writing that, like meaning that emerges from the segments of a collage, wouldn't have occurred with quite the same intensity had the rules not been broken.

Works Cited

Donovan, E. 1994. "Furthering the Collaborative Collage." March 16 Presentation at Conference on College Composition and Communication. Nashville, TN.

Elbow, P. 1973. *Writing Without Teachers*. New York: Oxford University Press.

———. 1981. *Writing With Power*. New York: Oxford University Press.

———. 1992. "The Collage as a Mode of Collaborative Writing." March Presentation at Conference on College Composition and Communication. Cincinnati, OH.

Fairgrieve, J. 1993. "Seeking Aunt Beast: A Collage Essay." In *Writing Ourselves into the Story: Unheard Voices from Composition Studies*, eds. S. I. Fontaine and S. Hunter, 177–192. Carbondale, IL: Southern Illinois University Press.

Fontaine, S. I. 1995. "Guidelines for Creating the Collage Review." Unpublished document. California State University, Fullerton.

Fontaine, S. I. and S. Hunter. 1992. "Rendering the 'Text' of Composition." *Journal of Advanced Composition* 12 (2): 394–406.

Goldberg, N. 1986. *Writing Down the Bones*. Boston: Shambhala Press.

Harnick-Shapiro, B. 1995. "Collage Assignment." Unpublished document. California State University, Fullerton.

Murray, D. 1985. *A Writer Teaches Writing*. Boston: Houghton Mifflin Co.

———. 1996. *Write to Learn*. Forth Worth, TX: Harcourt Brace.

Quaas, F. 1995. "The Collage Assignment." Unpublished document. California State University, Fullerton.

———. 1996a. "De-mystifying the Collage: Exploring the Reactions of Students and Tutors to Collage Essays." Unpublished document. California State University, Fullerton.

———. 1996b. "Discovering the Collage." Unpublished document. California State University, Fullerton.

Rosenblatt, L. 1978. *The Reader, The Text, The Poem: The Transactional Theory of the Literary Work*. Carbondale, IL: Southern Illinois University Press.

11

"Habits of Opposite and Alcove"
Language Poetry in the Composition Class

David Starkey
North Central College

Words say, Misspell and Misspell your name
Words say, Leave this life
From the singer streams of color
but from you
a room within a smaller room
habits of opposite and alcove

—Michael Palmer,
"Baudelaire Series"

Gary: Although I admit their ability to write abstractly, it is for the very same reason that their writings fail.

Joan: This seems like just a bunch of images slapped onto a page with no coherence. . . . The author's responsibility to her audience is to leave the reader with some kind of point or message. I believe that is why this work is unsuccessful.

Clay: I was, like, Huh?

By the middle of every term, I'm ready to see a change in the style and outlook of my writing students. Typically, they have found an adequate voice to use in their papers. If my teaching has gone well, that voice retains some of the characteristics of their own personalities; if not, the voice is the bland pseudo-academic, or "acanemic" voice (as I call it), which they learned in high school.

I value writing that takes risks, that is willing to cross genres and experiment with new voices, new outlooks. Yet unless I jolt them with what seems to me the most high-voltage writing of our time—language poetry—my students are tenuous about their experiments. Because they gravitate toward the safety of the middle, their boldest writing comes when I push the boundaries as far out as possible. I've found that by exposing students to writing that they are likely never to have seen before—work that flouts conventions of grammar, syntax, and meaning—they are shocked into reexamining their own perspectives as writers.

In his "Lexicon Rhetoricae," Kenneth Burke states, *"Form* in literature is an arousing and fulfillment of desires. A work has form in so far as one part of it leads a reader to anticipate another part, to be gratified by the sequence" (124). If Burke is correct in assuming that one of our chief delights as readers comes from this gratification of expectations, then the work of writers like Michael Palmer can hardly be said to give any pleasure at all, for one of the central projects of language poetry is to arouse expectation, only to disappoint it.

Naturally, those of us who have spent our teaching careers trying to get our students to fulfill the expectations they raise in their papers—and penalizing them with poor grades when they don't—are likely to want to know *why* a writer would dedicate herself to derailing standard syntax and logic. Composition teachers struggle heroically to help their students make sense of things; yet occasionally both students and teachers become so obsessed with hammering square pegs into round holes that the inherent messiness of the world is forgotten.

Language poets, on the other hand, celebrate this messiness. They distrust Truth with a capital *T* and constantly look for ways to undermine what they see as our false sense of security that things are as they appear. Clark Coolidge (Hoover 1994), one of the most radical language poets, puts it succinctly:

> I have the sensation that the most honest man in the world is the artist when
> he is saying I don't know. At such moments he knows that, to the questions
> that truly interest him, only the *work* will give answers, which usually turn
> out further questions. (652)

Of course those familiar with expressivist composition theorists such as Peter Elbow and Donald Murray will recognize this sentiment. Invention and exploration, a willingness to accept uncertainty, a foregrounding of the writer's imagination, a focus on process rather than product: all are qualities shared by two very different types of thinkers, though one group has focused on strengthening the bond between writer and reader while the other has challenged it. If little has been made of this connection, it nevertheless seems an obvious one. As Lester Faigley (1992) remarks,

> In retrospect, the process movement was aligned with certain trends that have
> since been described as postmodern, especially in its conception of the text
> and the relationship between writers and readers. Process theory views the
> text as open-ended, as potentially always changeable instead of as a static
> object. Similarly, the widespread practices of peer review and multiple drafts
> have tended to make classroom readers active participants in the production
> of texts, reducing the distance between writers and readers. (225)

Faigley's *Fragments of Rationality: Postmodernity and the Subject of Composition* provides a useful context for relating language poetry to composition, but the writing theorists who have most successfully linked postmodern writing with college composition are Winston Weathers and Derek Owens. [Another important book, *Elements of Alternate Style*, edited by Wendy Bishop, had just appeared at the time this chapter was completed.] More than half of Weathers's 1980 volume, *An Alternate Style: Options for Composition,* is given over to examples of alternative styles, yet the ideas crowded into the first section have proved a fecund source for many writing teachers. Most important, Weathers advocates the use of what he calls "Grammar B": "an altogether different 'grammar' of style, an alternate grammar . . . with characteristics of variegation, synchronicity, discontinuity, ambiguity, and the like" (8). Although he nowhere mentions language poetry, among the models Weathers holds up for emulation are important language predecessors such as Laurence Sterne, Gertrude Stein, and John Cage.

Like Weathers, Derek Owens (1994) declares that he has no desire to impose alternative styles on his students: "If, after tasting an array of oppositional forms—those 'resisting' writings—they choose to remain with the conventional (as I have, on many occasions), fine. But at least the decision will be theirs, not mine" (17). Writing fourteen years after Weathers and covering some of the same ground, Owens turns to more contemporary models of alternative style, and he focuses on language poetry in his discussions of experimental discourse; the ideas of Bernstein (1986), Hejinian (1987), Silliman (1986), and others inform much of his thinking.

One of Owens's most forceful arguments for the relevance of language poetry to composition is that there are already so many analogs in daily life: "We're more used to nonlinear paths of reading than we might realize, as in our lives we are constantly reading texts, scribal or otherwise, in ways that disrupt their intended linear flow" (164). He points to the practice of channel surfing while watching television, the way we often skip from one section of the newspaper to another and read it as a "patchwork of texts," and the generally unsystematic nature of our ordinary thought processes. The raw material of language poetry is all around us: we simply need to open our eyes and ears to be aware of it.

Carly: I find that I am sympathetic to experimental writing because it
    does promote creativity and individual expression, but at the same

time it can cause laziness. Example: a student turns in a blank paper or with one word on it for an essay because that is how the student felt.

Debra: This writing is so unstructured, it would be difficult to grade. There would be no set standards.

Ken: Most papers are assigned to show a student's knowledge of a subject. The student could be an expert on the subject, but the prof would not get that idea if the student wrote this way for another class. Papers need to be made up of concrete facts, not individual ideas.

Serina: In my bio class, he's been telling us to write plainly, eliminate unnecessary words. What's the point of writing a paper to inform people when they can't understand a word of it? Say what you mean.

Before going any further, let me acknowledge the validity of these students' reservations and introduce a few of my own. Both Carly and Debra point to a conspicuous problem: the dilemma faced by any reader, but a writing teacher in particular, when responding to and evaluating work that so consciously flaunts conventional ways of making sense. For all its theoretical ingeniousness, there is a marked nose-thumbing quality to language poetry, a sense that, as D. H. Lawrence (1964) playfully remarked of revolution, "it would be fun to upset the apple-cart / And see which way the apples would go a-rolling" (517). Lee Bartlett (1986) rightly observes that the "impulse behind much of this material . . . is as much a reaction against a prevailing aesthetic, an attempt to provide a critique of the American 'workshop poem,' as anything else" (743). So, if a student claims that her work accomplishes its purpose—no matter how obscure and solipsistic that purpose might be— what right does an instructor promulgating the values of language poetry have to disparage that work? In fact, a writing course based entirely on the principles of language poetry—that is, one in which writer and reader remain profoundly skeptical of each other, in which meaning is erratic and provisional—would face a situation analogous to the fate of the radically expressivist class described by C. H. Knobloch (1988), in which "conceptual exaggeration . . . lead[s] to misguided classroom practice" and "students end up cynical about the manipulating liberalism of their teachers while teachers eventually blunt their energies struggling against institutional realities whose power they have not fully come to terms with" (133–34).

Carly's remark about the one-word essay alludes to Gertrude Stein's famous refusal to sit an examination for William James at Harvard because it was a lovely day and she didn't feel like writing. Although James awarded Stein's "performance" an "A," few composition teachers would probably agree with his assessment. I told my students the anecdote when we were discussing Stein's work, and immediately there was delight in the classroom. My overwhelmed and overworked first-year students naturally find appealing the notion that language poetry might be a shortcut around the toil that normally goes into writing a traditional academic essay.

Clearly, though, to equate creativity with lazy or haphazard thinking is counterproductive. Having taught language poetry to high school and college students of varying abilities, I must concede that not all students are ready to grapple with experimental writing. Despite its apparent linguistic anarchy, reading and writing language poetry requires a great deal of thought. For all their claims of egalitarianism, language poets like Ron Silliman are often as erudite and patronizing as the elitist "follower[s] of received European forms" they despise (xxi). I believe that training students who are not yet capable of writing a simple argumentative essay in the ways of fragmentation and idiosyncratic juxtaposition is simply wrongheaded.

Of course many theorists, including some of the contributors to this book, would disagree with my reservations; Derek Owens points out that "*no* composition course [provides the necessary tools to survive in academe], no matter how concentrated its focus, any more than the student who has sat through two semesters of Introductory Lit courses understands the depth and complexity embedded in the term 'literature'" (193). Yet one could reply that the student with two semesters of introductory literature who is dropped into a seminar on, say, *Finnegan's Wake* is better prepared than the student who has not taken any preliminary courses. Here Owens, who was teaching in the expository writing program at Harvard when his book was published, lets his enthusiasm carry him away. If students are largely unaware of the conventions they are violating, they obviously cannot appreciate the liberation that language poetry can provide. In any case, they are unlikely to have the skills to manipulate language with sufficient expertise to produce anything other than a muddle. Avant garde writing is, literally, "advanced" composition—writing that pushes beyond the current boundaries of what is acceptable—and the language poet as pedagogue becomes potentially detrimental when he or she forgets that fact.

In *An Alternate Style*, Winston Weathers admits that the writer of Grammar B "must be concerned not to bore her reader, and therefore she—far more than the writer in the traditional style—must be concerned with variation, variegation" (40). Yet, frankly, inventive linguistic variation and variegation are not always possible. Some writing *must* allow the possibility of boredom. Certainly there would be a great danger in teaching this as the *only* method of writing. Future lawyers, scientists, doctors, engineers, and business people need to talk and write clearly, with a minimum of ambiguity. As one of my cynical colleagues has observed, "If language poets were in charge of day-to-day communication, America would collapse."

Essays that argue long, difficult points may not always be fun to read; yet such essays are sometimes necessary. My student Ken is right: "Most papers are assigned to show a student's knowledge of a subject." For the avant garde writer, the startling ellipsis, the clever *non sequitur* are always legitimate options. She knows that her aesthetic enables her to avoid the logic of conventional academic discourse precisely because she believes that such logic is inadequate to her purposes. However, students who attempt to employ these same rhetorical devices in their political science or biology classes are likely to find their instructors remarkably unsympathetic.

> A white egg, and a colored pan and a cabbage showing settlement, a constant increase.
> A cold in a nose, a single cold nose makes an excuse. Two are more necessary.
> All the goods are stolen, all the blisters are in the cup.
> Cooking, cooking is the recognition between sudden and nearly sudden very little and all large holes.
>
> —Gertrude Stein, from "Milk"

> The lowly cabbage strives and the turnip in the garden yearns to be a person. You know, things like that. Systems betray, or are, as in a "made place," made betrayals. I was organized by addition and addiction. I found a penny in a calla lily.
>
> —Lyn Hejinian, from *My Life*

Because of my reservations, I have yet to base a course solely on language poetry, and I've never incorporated the work into "basic" writing classes. I have, however, found limited yet productive ways to introduce students to ideas that help them, as Owens puts it, to "locate habits of perception or pinpoint interests" they might never have considered.

One of the chief difficulties I encountered when I first began bringing language poetry into the composition classroom was that students became inordinately preoccupied with line breaks, occasionally to the exclusion of all other concerns. Even when I specifically and emphatically asked them to translate what they'd learned from language poetry into prose, they often ended up breaking their lines anyway, turning their work into something that *looked* like poetry. Since I'm more concerned with the disruptions of thought and syntax *within* sentences and paragraphs than typographical playfulness, I now only bring prose poems into the classroom. Fortunately, they aren't difficult to find; Ron Silliman, Susan Howe, Bernadette Mayer, Rae Armantrout, and Barrett Watten have all experimented extensively with the form. In a book like *O/two: An Anthology*, edited by Leslie Scalapino, perhaps half the work is in prose. Charles Bernstein voices the sentiments of many language poets when he says, "I've always preferred the term 'writer,' which is more neutral [than 'poet'], and which refers anyway to the medium, since there is some difficulty in separating out what the difference is between poetry and writing" (431).

I normally introduce language poetry in the middle of the term, after students have developed some confidence in their own work, and after I've had the opportunity to discuss a few of the methods of invention, drafting, and revision traditionally sanctioned in the process classroom. I also want to have carefully assessed my students' writing skills so that I can gauge how much or little emphasis to place on the avant garde. I begin by passing out several prose poems, which I tell students are essays written for Freshman English, and which my students must read, analyze, and grade. Because students are likely to have trouble articulating criteria without some guidance, I give them a series of questions to answer about the pieces. These questions, culled from grammar and style handbooks, focus on unity, supporting examples, point of view, diction, clarity, tone, and so forth, that is, the qualities by which most composition teachers judge most of the essays they grade. So that I don't influence their initial readings, I have students do this work at home, and I don't talk about language poetry beforehand. Whatever bewilderment the lack of a formal lecture may cause is more than compensated for by the freshness and candor of the students' interpretations.

I've used work by most of the poets discussed so far; however, because the poetry is so volatile, it's impossible to predict what will work well and what won't. Recently, I used Gertrude Stein's prose poem "Milk" (though Stein is not a language poet, per se, she is their most important precursor) and a chapter from Lyn Hejinian's "autobiography," *My Life*. In order to give some initial validation and context to Stein and Hejinian's complex writing, I indicated to students that the assignment that inspired Stein's "Milk" was to describe ideas and feelings that were evoked for her by a common household food—cereal, for example, or apples or milk. Hejinian's putative assignment was to choose one year from her life and to write a short autobiographical essay that explores that year (in fact, the chapter I chose, "When one travels, one might 'hit' a storm," *is* meant to evoke the author as an eighteen-year-old).

Michael: Her prose is firmly tied to the world—but it is a world constantly under construction, a world in which the equation of word and thing can no longer be taken for granted.

Cliff: I do know that it lacks clarity and unity, but does not sacrifice coherence. . . . "Milk" succeeds in making me want to read on through sheer mystery.

Bob: She's proving that she's seeing it by a continual athleticism, leaping free of the gravity of the familiar.

Gloria: Its tone is one of fond memories being recalled: imagine a "daydream" voice as the way she would read it aloud.

Jackson: I go from word to word, seeing the shapes of the printed words, hearing the sounds inwardly, noting rhymes, assonances, alliterations. Where an image is suggested, I see it inwardly.

Nina: Its strength is that it is abstract and leaves itself open to interpretation.

Robert: It's not "snapshorts" (moves; don't copy nature), and it's not "the pathetic fallacy" (though it includes much of the artist's process). And it ain't abstract.

Each of these quotations are responses to prose poems from Stein's *Tender Buttons*. However, the comments of Michael Davidson, Bob Perelman, Jackson Mac Low, and Robert Grenier appear in *The L=A=N=G=U=A=G=E Book* (Bruce and Bernstein 1984, 197, 199, 202, 205), while Cliff, Gloria, and Nina were students in my composition class. Aside from a more sophisticated critical terminology, the chief difference between the students and the language poets' responses seems to be that the students (not surprisingly, considering the prompts I provided them with) are trying to read Stein's work within the framework of the traditional college essay. The students privilege content—"what she's trying to say"—over form, while the language poets focus on the formal characteristics of the work.

I've found this difference in perspectives can be a good starting point for class discussion. Of course, the most common reaction to the readings is frustration and puzzlement. A typical student criticism is that the writers are "totally self-involved." For the most part, I agree with this particular censure, and that provides a productive leaping off point for another conversation about the responsibility of an author to her audience. Other negative remarks, such as "I had no idea what was going on" or "They don't stick to their point," can also generate valuable dialogue about effective organization, the power of a logical argument, the need for continuity, and effective transitions. I like to nudge my students even further: Why does logical writing appeal to us? What makes it "better"? Are we responding to some innate call for order and design, or have we merely been trained to value linear arguments above all others?

Yet I don't want to make language poetry primarily an example of what *not* to do. I point out that one of the things this sort of writing does is force the reader herself to become more involved; the writer takes only so much responsibility for making meaning. There is a political component to this as well, as George Hartley (1989) notes, "Language writing is often posed as an attempt to draw the reader into the production process by leaving the connections between various elements open, thus allowing the reader to produce the connections between those elements. In this way, presumably the reader recognizes his or her part in the social process of production" (xiii). Students tend to like the freedom language poetry gives to *writers,* but just having been in the position of a critical reader of the text, they are hesitant to take on similar responsibilities as *readers*. They are, however, quick to make observations similar to Owens's, that there are many experiences that can best be expressed by disjunctive writing. For instance, one student, very much in the middle of the process himself, commented that Hejinian had "nailed emerging adulthood."

Inevitably, after I have asked students to try writing some language poetry themselves, class discussion moves to address the question of how useful it is to write like a language poet outside of this particular section of first-year composition. As earlier comments will suggest, students are deeply skeptical. Though they can envision such work succeeding in a creative writing class, they find language poetry's day-to-day value as a form of discourse problematic at best. Students are more sympathetic, however, when I ask them to consider language poetry as a kind of directed freewriting or brainstorming—one that insists that the writer take her thought and language in unexpected directions. Language poets would be appalled by the suggestion that their work ought to be transformed into something more orthodox, but students themselves are comforted by the notion of language poetry as part of a larger process, as a prelude to something more finished. Viewed as an invention activity specifically designed to generate a profusion of ideas that might be developed into more conventional prose, writing language poetry suddenly becomes attractive, for it has the sort of practical applications my students always seek.

As the term progresses, I try to refer to the insights of language poets whenever they can help illuminate our conversations about the writing process. I also allow my students to rewrite all or part of one paper—usually their least successful—using what they believe they've learned from language poetry. Frequently, the most effective revisions juxtapose small sections rewritten as language-oriented prose poems with longer passages in conventional prose. This arrangement forces the writer, as well as the reader, to periodically view her subject from an entirely new angle. In any case, I want students to follow Bruce Andrews's injunction, "Don't narrate, think!" I want them, that is, to be intensely aware of writing differently, of not falling into familiar patterns of storytelling.

Though students find it much easier to translate their own writing from Grammar A to this particular version of Grammar B, rather than to generate all new material, the results are still mixed. As anyone who has ever attempted to write nonsense verse in the style of Lewis Carroll knows, it's much harder than it looks to cultivate "habits of opposite and alcove." Too often, students fall into predictable utterances and routine rhythms. They aren't totally reenvisioning their work. What results is rarely what I would call pure language poetry, but it can be productive nevertheless. Compare, for example, a passage from Angela's original essay, which analyzes a Nike ad in *Seventeen* magazine, with a revision modeled on Lyn Hejinian's *My Life*. Here's the original:

> What takes up the biggest part of the magazines, besides the mass of advertisements, are the beauty sections. These sections are the main tie between editorials and advertising. The majority of the advertisements are for makeup, skin products, and other personal care products. Most of the advertise-

ments are kept to one or two pages for each brand name, yet there are those that extend to three or four pages. *Seventeen* also caters to the nation's health and fitness craze with a section called bodyline. This makes it possible for Nike advertisements to fit in.

And the revision:

> Check your life; find flaws and reality. Play dress-up. Examples of garb. Walk the catwalk. Masquerade—hide your face so the world can never find you. Tips for daily masks, assisted by the feature paints. What are your feelings? Excited? Want to see more? Want to keep flipping? Powerful names get what they want. Power equals money. Or should it be Power takes money?

I wouldn't necessarily argue that the revision is "better" than the original. The earlier version uses specific examples and is easy to follow. Moreover, some essential information is obviously lost in translation; still, the attempt to write like a language poet has forced Angela to quicken the pace of her prose. The passive verbs in the original all but disappear in the revision. Hurried questions replace measured statements, giving the paragraph a fragmentary, mosaic quality. And the writer's direct address to the reader makes the reader engage more immediately with the text. Angela may not employ this strategy the next time she writes an essay, but, at least she possesses the option to do so.

> Heavy with soot, the rain drummed on the tin roof of the garage, eager to fall into language and be solved in the manner of mysteries.

—Rosemarie Waldrop,
from *Inserting the Mirror*

Whatever reservations composition teachers have about this unlikely discourse, they should not underestimate the importance of its potentially liberating effect on students. Teachers who came of age in the fifties and sixties may remember their own delight in discovering Beat poetry (which was once reviled as frenzied gibberish), the sense they had of renewed faith in the power of language to express ideas and feelings that had seemed unutterable. I believe that something of the same excitement awaits students who read, respond to, and write like language poets. Like physicists smashing atoms in a reactor, students can learn a great deal from banging words together until they explode.

Yet these explosions are rarely fatal. My own experience mirrors that of Winston Weathers: instructors need not fret that exercises in alternative style will discourage students from ever correctly using punctuation and grammar again. Indeed, after thinking and writing like language poets for a while, my

students embrace the opportunity to write "normally" again, having come to
appreciate the virtues of convention only after they have been forced temporarily to renounce it.

Works Cited

Andrews, Bruce and Charles Bernstein, eds. 1984. *The L=A=N=G=U=A=G=E
Book.* Carbondale, IL: Southern Illinois University Press.

Bartlett, Lee. 1986. "What is 'Language Poetry'?" *Critical Inquiry* 12 (4): 741–52.

Bernstein, Charles. 1986. "Characterization." In *Content's Dream: Essays
1975–1984*, 428–62. Los Angeles: Sun & Moon.

Bishop, Wendy. 1997. *Elements of Alternate Style: Essays on Writing and Revision.*
Portsmouth, NH: Boynton/Cook.

Burke, Kenneth. 1953. *Counter Statement.* Los Altos, CA: Hermes.

Coolidge, Clark. 1994. "Words." In *Hoover*, 649–52.

Faigley, Lester. 1992. *Fragments of Rationality: Postmodernity and the Subject of
Composition.* Pittsburgh: University of Pittsburgh Press.

Hartley, George. 1989. *Textual Politics and the Language Poets.* Bloomington, IN:
Indiana University Press.

Hejinian, Lyn. 1987. *My Life.* Los Angeles: Sun & Moon. Hoover, Paul, ed. 1994.
Postmodern American Poetry. New York: Norton.

Knoblauch, C. H. 1988. "Rhetorical Constructions: Dialogue and Commitment."
College English 50 (2): 125–40.

Lawrence, D. H. 1964. "A Sane Revolution." *The Complete Poems.* New York: Pen-
guin.

Owens, Derek. 1994. *Resisting Writings (and the Boundaries of Composition).* Dal-
las: Southern Methodist University Press.

Silliman, Ron. 1986. "Language, Realism, Poetry." In *In the American Tree*, ed. Ron
Silliman, xv–xxiii. Orono, ME: National Poetry Foundation.

Stein, Gertrude. 1946. *Tender Buttons.* In *Selected Writings*, 407–50. New York:
Vintage.

Waldrop, Rosemarie. 1994. "From *Inserting the Mirror.*" In *Hoover*, 314–17.

Weathers, Winston. 1980. *An Alternate Style: Options in Composition.* Rochelle Park,
NJ: Hayden.

12

Beginnings
Voice, Creativity, and the Critical Essay

Art Young
Clemson University

My Blake paper was one that I felt benefited significantly from not only seeing other people's writings but from a second draft. I have included Cari's paper "Let Them Eat Blake" in my portfolio because it is one that significantly influenced the rewrite of my critical essay. Reading hers gave me more insight into what exactly I needed to do with mine. My first draft was called "William Blake: The Conscious Poet." This is a perfect example of what happens when you don't know what you are really supposed to be doing. My second draft "All the Little Black Boys" more effectively accomplished what the critical paper was supposed to and it more concisely told what I wanted to tell. I realized also in doing these two drafts that if I get off to a bad or confusing start, the rest of the paper usually stinks.

May I too be protected from a bad or confusing start.

I am rereading Harilyn (Lyn) Friday's portfolio, some months after she turned it in, the course finished for her, the grade of "B" secured. The passage I begin with is from the reflective essay that serves as an "Introduction" to her semester's writing in my advanced composition course. This passage gives me pause, because Lyn admits to confusion in her first draft of a critical essay on William Blake and then to her accomplishment in the second (and final) draft. The change in her titles is dramatic and, as I realize when reading further, emblematic of her experience with this writing assignment. So what is going on here? How does one move from "William Blake: The Conscious Poet" to "All the Little Black Boys"?

I wish to thank my former students Harilyn Friday and Cari McCall for permission to quote from their writing. They were enrolled in my "English 312: Advanced Composition" at Clemson University, Spring 1996.

William Blake: The Conscious Poet

William Blake was born in 1757 in London England, the son of a hosier. He was largely self taught and as a child wanted to become a painter. At the age of 14 he was sent to be an engraving apprentice and after seven years, he studied at the Royal Academy. In 1784 Blake established a print shop that went under after a few years and for the rest of his life Blake worked as an engraver and illustrator. The collection of poetry that Blake wrote called Songs of Innocence was published around 1789. The poem that I will analyze, "The Little Black Boy," is a poem from that collection of poems.

"The Little Black Boy" is a poem that in my view can be interpreted in two different ways. My initial impression was that the poem was about race relations in Blake's time. Slavery was very prevalent in Blake's time and it's only right that he would be concerned about slavery because it was an injustice. . . .

So here is the beginning of Lyn's first academic essay in English 312. The entire piece is about seven hundred words long. She writes it after spending a class session reading five poems from Blake's *Songs of Innocence* and five from his *Songs of Experience*, writing a one-page free-write, and participating in class discussion.

Lyn also had heard my imploring spiel: write this essay, please, for an audience of your classmates (fellow students and teacher); take risks; be creative; inquiry is our goal; we seek to learn from the texts we read in order to learn more about Blake's poems, about ourselves, about each other, about our classroom community. Delivering my spiel is important, but I know the meaning will be in the doing.

And Lyn writes an essay familiar to me because many of her classmates write similar ones. Her first paragraph summarizes the Blake headnote that everyone in the class has previously read. We are told Blake was a conscious poet and that slavery was an injustice, and the paper goes on to deliver more such "insights." The audience she writes for is distant or "unknown," both to her and to me. Her voice is disjointed. Lyn is trying to sound academic and authoritative—as if she were a scholar who has read one or more biographies of Blake, has studied his poems extensively, and now has something important from her research to communicate to us. But this is not Lyn; she had never read William Blake until this past week. She isn't sure why she is writing or to whom. Lyn knows she is not an expert on Blake, but she feels compelled to construct a voice that speaks as if she is. Even if she is honestly concerned about race relations, Lyn writes what she thinks the teacher wants or at least will accept. What Ken Macrorie called "Engfish" (1970).

Furthermore, she apparently has written many essays like this one for teachers throughout her schooling; thus she knows the formula for writing an academic essay. For Lyn, this is how you write "when you don't know what you are really supposed to be doing." This is how you write when you don't know very much about the subject but have to pretend that you do. In order to write an essay of more interest to her classmates, Lyn needs to know more about Blake's poems, she needs more options for writing the critical essay, and she needs the confidence that she has something of importance to say to this particular audience. She needs to become personally involved in the task and then develop a voice that persuasively expresses that involvement. In a former pedagogical life, I would tell her some of this and maybe more, and then we would move on to the next assignment.

This time around, however, we are just beginning. In fact, I give Lyn very little response to her first draft. Rather, I construct a "creative" assignment sequence that I hope will address Lyn's and her classmates' problems in the context of a supportive "writer's workshop" environment. Now, as reflective practitioner, I return to the students' portfolios to learn about my teaching from them.

In class, we read aloud the essays in groups of four and provide copies of our essays to the other three members of our group; we select one in each group to read to the whole class; we talk further about the Blake poems—historical background, possible interpretations, and the form of the dramatic monologue. Lyn likes Cari McCall's essay and suggests that Cari read it to the class.

Let Them Eat Blake

"A robin redbreast in a cage
Puts all Heaven in a rage.
A dove-house fill'd with doves and pigeons
Shudders Hell thro' all its regions."

> Auguries of Innocence
> lines 5-8
> William Blake

Innocence and Experience: these two unlikely cousins share an ideal likeness in their origin, yet in human affairs, the segregation of these realities manifest themselves for the purpose of exploitation; all is masked with the hopeful illusions of innocence. . . . Conditional to this exploitation is obedience to God's authority and His representatives on earth—the church.

Blake was a visionary whose lyrical style often masked a fiery assault against church practices which perpetuated society's ills with the rationalization that all must perform their duties with obedient hearts if they wish to go to heaven. . . . In "A Little Boy Lost," an innocent child declares his love of all living things equally. . . .

Although Lyn is not explicit about how Cari's essay "significantly influenced the rewrite" of her critical essay, I can now make some conjectures, especially as I read through Lyn's writing in this sequence. Lyn may have noticed and been influenced by Cari's clever title, her beginning with an invocation, her knowledge of literature ("Auguries of Innocence" was not available in the handout I provided), the sureness of the author's voice, and the focus on the social and political critique exhibited in Blake's poems. She learns from Cari that although Blake's poems may seem childish and inno-cent, some of them mask "a fiery assault against church practices."

In a five-minute, end-of-class free-write that day, Lyn reflects:

> I have to admit that this whole unit on analysis of poems has been particu-larly painful for me. I have never been good at analyzing socially conscious poetry written in anything but contemporary times. The reason for that is because I usually don't have the slightest clue as to the state of the society or times that the author is referring to especially if I'm dealing with a for-eign writer. . . . Now because I understand them [Blake's poems], I don't dislike them as much.

Lyn is learning what Blake's poems are about from Cari and from class discussion but continues to feel alienated from the academic activities asso-ciated with writing about them.

The assignment for our next class is to write a poem in the style of Blake's *Songs of Innocence*: "Write in the voice of an innocent child who does not fully comprehend the hostile environment created by adults; write using strategies similar to Blake's—a contemporary context, monologue form, dramatic irony, etc. Be prepared to 'perform' a dramatic reading of your poem for the class." Thus, I give them this new formula to open up the possibilities and limitations for writers in formulas, conventions, and genres.

Yes, they are surprised that I ask them to write a poem. They did not sign up for a creative writing class. They protest that they are not "creative." Some confess they like to write poetry, but they don't like to read it aloud to others. Trust me, I say. We are going to enjoy each other's poems, not crit-icize them. Our poems may help us understand Blake better; our poems may expand our possibilities as writers.

I wanted to penetrate the barriers that existed between these writers and their voices, their purposes, their audiences. This desire led me to ask them to write creatively in the middle of an assignment sequence designed to help them write more effective critical essays. And I was curious as well. What would the poems look like? How would the students "relate" to them? As a reader, would I find pleasure in reading my twenty-four students' writing? Would I experience a wonder similar to the one I experience when I read *Songs of Innocence and Experience*? Would writing these Blake imitations have anything to do with writing critical essays about Blake? I was moti-vated, my students might say perversely motivated, to explore the counterin-tuitive: to learn about writing a critical essay by exploring what it is not; to visualize the critical essay by looking in another direction; to experience cross-genre writing as a strategy for generating new perspectives on Blake and on ourselves as writers and readers.

James Britton, Nancy Martin, and their colleagues (1975) speculate that there is something about writing in poetic form that enables us to express our values. When we write in the "spectator" role we free the imagination to reflect on experience and engage language in such a way that meaning is shaped and reshaped by an active but disinterested mind. This activity is fundamentally different from composing transactional writing, the purposeful writing we do to conduct the world's business in the vested "participant" role. And my students often attest to the "freedom" of writing poetically. "There are no right or wrong answers," they say. Or, "it was easy to write but it took a lot longer than I thought." Or "there is no right way to write a poem." Precisely. And yet, for whatever reasons, many of them continue to believe there is one "right" way to write a critical essay, and they plead with their teachers to reveal the one correct formula.

Here is Lyn's poem:

Dear Santa,

Toys are nice,
Clothes are good,
But what I really want
is to get out of the hood.

Momma—she gotta go to work all day,
So when I come home I usually go outside and play.

Momma she tells me not to be playin outside,
out there—there ain't really no good places to hide.

You know—in case somebody starts cappin',
She just worries too much—ain't nothin gonna happen.

At least not to me—see I got it covered,
I got me a gat from this dealer I know named Trevor.

I know I'm only 8 but around here you gotta be careful,
You never know when you gon' get caught in the
crossfire of some people. . . .
So Santa remember:
Toys are nice,
Clothes are good,
But what I really want
is to get out of this hood.

Love,
Samuel

I read Lyn's poem with pleasure and wonder. It is playful and childish and informed by adult terror. This poem, I speculate, allows Lyn to tell something of what she knows in a form she creates for this particular writing task. It enables her to explore the world of childhood innocence and the world of adult experience in the spectator role. Lyn is expressing herself and her values rather than trying to interpret for others what Blake expressed two centuries ago. By writing in a voice not nominally her own, she may be learning something about the possibilities of her own interior voices. If I am correct in assuming that she has invested herself in the writing of this poem in a way not evident in the first draft of her critical essay, then she is learning what Blake is doing as a writer, thinker, and social critic and what possibilities she might have available to her in the same regard.

Students and teacher read their poems aloud to classmates—some more dramatically than others. Lyn performs well—the vernacular—the tension between sympathy and outrage. She hears the sound of her voice fill the classroom's space. Many students read poems that demonstrate engagement and passion—the risky side of freedom and commitment—the stretching of the personal imagination and the writer's vulnerability beyond the comfort zone. Still other writers, some of whom undoubtedly blew off the assignment, listen, chat, laugh, ponder, and applaud. There seems to be a general easing of the anxiety of participating in a writer's workshop. As Lyn's confidence grows, her "pain" with this sequence of assignments appears to be decreasing. We are building our own context for reading and writing, our classroom community that both exists within larger academic structures and apart from them. I am the authoritative teacher who designs and limits my students' writing assignments and enforces deadlines, and I am the counter-intuitive teacher who promotes the freedom of spectator role-writing as a way of creating a meaningful context for reading and writing.

The assignment for our next class is to revise the critical essay on Blake's *Songs of Innocence and Experience*. I do not want my students to simply edit their drafts, tinker with surface features, and add a sentence or two in various places, because that is not the kind of revising these initial drafts need to become effective essays. Rather, I want them to "re-see" their writing task, their audience, and their voice. I hope Lyn, and many of her fellow writers, will discover the originality and validity of her own experiences and draw on them to make the literature she reads more meaningful. I also hope that her writing will be a more authentic rendering of her own perceptions that will further awaken the curiosity of her classmates.

Lyn begins again. Here is the opening to her second (and, in this case, final) draft of her essay on Blake.

All the Little Black Boys

"The Little Black Boy,"—everyday of my life I have seen little black boys in every aspect of those words. Literally and figuratively I have seen "black" boys. People that have been deprived of light—all types of light.

People that have been deprived of justice—all types of justice. People that long to be in a better place and a better time—yeah, I've seen "black" boys. They're everywhere.

I really don't know where those words came from. I sat down to start revising my critical paper and something of an extended poem came out. I think that is the most succinct way that I can relate my interpretation of William Blake's poem "The Little Black Boy." After reading it several times and thinking about it I have decided that this poem is just as relevant for the 1990's as it was for the 17 and 1800's. I also feel that in Blake's time the meaning that is applied is not so different than the meaning that could be derived now.

When reading the first stanza of the poem the line that struck me first was the one that says "And I am black but O! my soul is white." To me that particular line indicates the innocence of the speaker. . . . Many things taint the souls of men and part of the attractiveness and beauty of childhood is the innocence, purity of soul and inner peace that children have. In contrast to that inner peace, the next two lines talk about the outer conflict of skin color. "Black, as if bereav'd of light" [and] "White as an angel." What do the words black and white mean?. . .

Lyn's essay gives me a pleasure similar to when I read her poem "Dear Santa." Then on rereading, I notice several things. In using her beginning invocation, she is echoing a strategy she saw Cari use in her draft essay and one that Lyn herself used in her poem. She is now more confident about her knowledge of Blake and his times ("17 and 1800's") than she was in her free-write of a brief week ago. Not only does she know more about Blake and more about how to write about him to classmates, but her writing exhibits the desire to participate in this classroom conversation. Lyn has found a way into this reading/writing task, has, in some sense, made it her own. She mixes genres, personal and academic knowledge, her words with Blake's. My interest in reading this essay is in learning more about Lyn as much as it is in learning more about William Blake. Because of what Lyn brings to the reading of "The Little Black Boy," my world promises to be expanded and enriched. Such authentic conversation is the source of my reading pleasure.

Lyn's first two sentences after the "extended poem" provide contextual cues that involve her readers in their common experience of the classroom. "I really don't know where those words came from. I sat down to start revising my critical paper and something of an extended poem came out." The common experience of revising the critical paper, the common experience of writing a poem and talking about where poems come from, the common experience of mixing colloquial and academic language in classroom talk—here is a writer building a context to communicate with a real and "known" audience. As Lyn comes alive in her writing, she brings William Blake's poetry to life for her readers as well. Distant, scholarly readers, desiring primarily to find out more about Blake and not particularly wanting to know the current conditions of this writer's life or her personal opinions on race and injustice, would perhaps vilify these first two sentences. But she is not writing to them. She may never in her life write to them. Yet, Lyn's writing, today, may very well make a difference in the perceptions and understandings of her twenty-four readers, while her first draft—written to a distant, scholarly audience (but never to be read by them)—surely would not. From her classmates, she can receive immediate feedback; she can surprise them or piss them off; she can inspire them to reread Blake or to vow never to do so again. Through her experience with racism and her readers' common experience with Blake, she can change, perhaps, her readers' ways of being in the world.

I read the twenty-four essays quickly but attentively. During the next class period, I returned the essays, but not before I made overhead transparencies of the first pages of Lyn's and two other students' initial and final drafts. I put them on the overhead projector, and we read them aloud, a different student reading each succeeding paragraph. Then we voted on which version was the most effective and discussed why we voted as we had. Next, the writers talked about the changes they had made between the first and second drafts. The votes were 22–2, 23–1, and 24–0 in favor of the second drafts. Lyn was obviously pleased, and the collective feedback seemed genuinely beneficial not only to the three identified writers but to the others as well, some of whom had been content to tinker with rather than revise their less than interesting first drafts.

When the two students who preferred Lyn's "William Blake: The Conscious Poet" to "All the Little Black Boys" were asked why (they may have suspected the vote was a teacher's trick question), they volunteered, perhaps a little defensively, that they personally preferred "All the Little Black Boys"; however, they did not think it fulfilled the assignment that most teachers expected from a critical essay as well as "William Blake: The Conscious Poet" did. And, of course, they may be right. How students should approach each writing assignment depends on the context, and for school writing, that context is dominated by teacher expectations. My approach to "teaching writing creatively" is to make the shift from "pretend" writing to "real" writing. Pretend writing is when we say to students, either implicitly or explicitly: pretend you are an expert with years of research behind you; pretend you are writing to a distant and unknown audience; pretend these people really care about what you are saying; pretend you have thoroughly considered other points of view; pretend to be objective; pretend you are fascinated with William Blake; pretend to write a formal, scholarly essay (because, who knows, someday you might want or need to write a *real* one).

Now, I'm still learning what "real" writing is and how to create a classroom environment that values it, because I believe that is one way to "improve" student writing. The example of Lyn, though instructive I trust, is not applicable to all students—my assignment sequence did not work the same for everyone. I don't clearly understand whatever causes and effects are involved (was writing the poem a key "intervention"? was working in small groups? was requiring self-conscious free-writes on their writing processes? was grading a portfolio that included their own and classmates' writing? was requiring daily writing in a variety of genres?). I do believe Lyn, and most of her classmates, wrote much more effectively and insightfully at the end of my advanced composition course (the William Blake sequence took a little less than three weeks of the fifteen-week course) for *an audience of her classmates in a context constructed by our community*, albeit deeply influenced by my guidance and authority. I read my students' writing between every class session (well, almost every session), and I listened carefully to their conversation in and out of class. I am aware always that there is plenty of time in my courses to display and impart my professional knowledge. What I must be careful to do is make plenty of room for the knowledge of students like Lyn and then to construct a pedagogy that supports further learning, language development, rhetorical understanding, and multiple ways of communicating. While I don't always succeed as well as I would like in this endeavor, when I do, I experience the reciprocity involved in teaching while learning and unfeigned pleasure in reading my students' writing.

Taking my cue from Lyn, I too fear bad and confusing starts—in the courses I teach, in my own writing, in my students' writing. I work through beginnings of courses by listening as well as talking, learning as well as teaching, and questioning whether our classroom communication is growing more authentic and whether we are learning to take ourselves seriously as writers and our readers seriously as thinkers. I revisited a beginning when I read the writing of Lyn and her classmates after the first three weeks of the course, and I revisited that beginning again several months after the course had ended as I reviewed their portfolios and wrote this essay. In such revisitings my students continue to teach me long after their particular class has ended and my planning for other classes has begun.

Works Cited

Macrorie, Ken. 1970. *Telling Writing*. Rochelle Park, NJ: Hayden.

Britton, James, and Nancy Martin, eds. 1975. *The Development of Writing Abilities*. London: Macmillan.

13

One, Two, Three, Testing
Using Cassette Tapes to Encourage Dialogic Exchanges

Alys Culhane
Coastal Carolina University

A Dialogue with Max

It being the third day of class, I asked my twenty-five first-semester composition students if there were any more questions about the syllabus. I didn't
expect a response because I felt we'd covered all the bases. But then Max's
hand shot up. "I still don't understand why you want to respond on tape to
our papers. It seems like this is going to be a pain in the ass."

Several of Max's classmates giggled.

Max looked around nervously, then continued talking. "I mean, this has
got to be time-consuming for you. And it's a real hassle for us. We gotta buy
these tapes, unwrap them, put our names on the boxes, put our names on the
tapes, put the tapes in an envelope along with our paper, and then when we
get the tapes back, listen to them. Wouldn't it be easier if we did this in a
more conventional way?"

Seeing that Max and his classmates appeared dubious, I relied on personal experience to stress that yes, indeed, the use of tapes was worth all the
supposed time and trouble. I explained that I had been using this particular
method of feedback for more than ten years.[1] I had initially been attracted to
this form of response because it allowed me to elaborate more than did written responses. For example, I could incorporate passages from various
sources into my comments—including student work, my own work, and
published texts. And over the years, I had become increasingly more reliant
upon what I saw as a more expansive feedback space.

146

In response to Max's concerns about time, I noted that as with written comments, responding on tape took between fifteen and twenty minutes per paper. "And in that space of time I can give you about five times as much feedback," I paused. "Any more questions?"

The students looked at me expectantly. Seeing that I had their undivided attention, I continued by saying that during this particular semester, I planned to do a research paper on the subject of using taped responses, and that the title would be "One, Two, Three, Testing: Using Cassette Tapes to Promote Process-Based Pedagogical Practices." I said that our audience would be the readers of a disciplinary anthology called *Teaching Writing Creatively* and further explained that the essays in this text would support the idea that writing instruction is as creative an activity as writing. Narrowing my focus, I added that our findings would be of use to those readers who were looking for more diverse and innovative ways of responding to student work.

" 'Our' findings?" said Max.

"Yeah, 'our.' I'm going to incorporate your responses into my paper," I said. Feeling that I needed to offer a rationale for my actions, I said that I thought that involving students in this project was a good idea since this was a writing project with a purpose; they'd help me determine what I might tell others about this particular method of response.

"What are you wanting to tell others?" asked Adam.

"I'm thinking that the use of taped feedback complements some of my beliefs about writing as it relates to teaching, my main premise being that students become more adept writers when teachers model good writerly behavior. In order to do this, teachers have to make writing and writing-related concerns the focal point of the course."

In finding that these students, as well as those in my other three classes, were fairly receptive to my ideas about the use of tapes, I laid out my game plan. I told them that I would write a page-long journal entry at the end of each taping session. And I'd have them periodically write me letters in which they evaluated this particular method of feedback. "Any comments about this?" I asked.

"I'm still not convinced that this is such a good idea," said Max.

"Well, all I'm asking is that you keep an open mind about it," I replied.

Smooth Beginnings

During week three, I responded on tape to ninety-nine student journals.[2] I had planned it so that during the first five weeks of the semester students would do a series of invention exercises. My intent was to show that buried in what they believed to be gibberish, were interesting and usable paper topics.[3] This was a premise that they read about in Peter Elbow's *Writing Without Teachers*. I was most concerned, however, that the writers put what was to them an abstract theory to practice.

Things went well at first. In part, I think, this was because I repeatedly went over what I called "taped-response logistics." I also made it a point to let students know that I was excited about responding to their ideas. As I had hoped, they had plenty of them.

My method of response was straightforward. I quickly scanned their entries and drew stars next to those ideas that I wished to comment and elaborate upon. I then put their cassette tape in my recorder and made note of the time, date, and title of the work I was responding to. While responding, I kept in mind that my purpose was, as Robert Brooke (1991) suggests in *Writing and Sense of Self: Identity Negotiation in Writing Workshops*, to model writerly behavior. As writers do, I demonstrated to students how to give feedback to one another. And I occasionally reminded them that in a few week's time they'd be doing as I was doing; reading one another's journal entries and making note of possible writing topics.

In addition to citing workable ideas, I suggested reasons why they might pursue particular topics. For example, I suggested to Jennifer[4] that she write a paper in which she explored the pros and cons of holding a full-time job while going to school. I added that her classmates would be receptive to her ideas since most were holding down at least one part-time job. Reading Becky's entries, I was struck by the fact that she was opposed to the use of computers. "Our technology is going to be the death of us," she lamented. I said this was a good topic because it was one that was timely, especially for college students. In reading Heidi's journal I noticed that she had a wide range of possible paper topics, including the near abduction of herself and two neighborhood friends, her bouts with anorexia nervosa, and, her most recent horrific family vacation.

Max's journal entries centered around his current obsession with rats and ferrets. He noted that, at last count, he had fifty rats and seven ferrets. Intrigued by this unusual subject matter, I said I wanted to hear more. I read Marvin Bell's poem "Gemwood" to him, adding that Bell was using the death of a rat to talk about loss. I enclosed a copy of Bell's poem in Max's envelope, and encouraged him to come and talk further with me about his possible paper topic and the poem.

In rereading my own journal writes, my initial response to the use of tapes was, early in the semester, favorable. I wrote that it took me 30.5 hours to respond to 99 sets of journals. In talking with colleagues, we figured out that commenting by hand on the same number of journals would take about the same amount of time. As I also noted, the advantage of the taped-response method was that I could pack more feedback in to a shorter amount of time. Yes, the use of tapes was really time-consuming. But I felt as though it had been time well spent, since I could not have said all I said on paper. Hoorah for technology. Hoorah for Memorex.

My students' first responses to my use of tapes were insightful. They commended me for taking the time to respond in what they considered to be a more personal manner to their work. Also, a handful, including Jennifer,

Becky, and Heidi, said that they had been convinced by the tone of my voice that their ideas were worthy of further exploration. Said Becky, "It interests me that you noticed that I mentioned five times that I hate computers. Maybe I will pursue it." And Jennifer commented that she found the use of taped responses convenient since she was able to listen to my comments on her drive home. She also liked the use of tapes because the sound of my voice left her in no doubt as to how I felt about certain topics.

A handful of respondents had reservations about this method of evaluation. For example, Max was dubious. He remarked that my pauses made him feel as if I was having a hard time finding good things to talk about in his work. He also pointed out that my voice sounded "passionless" and that "I could show a little more enthusiasm for his work."

Reading over the ideas of these writers, I noticed that most focused on an aspect of response that was not a part of written commenting—voice. What these student writers appeared to be seeking was affirmation. In this way my verbal cues were adding an extra dimension to paper comments, a more traditional form of response. I was most pleased because this realization compensated for the fact that I didn't have the time to meet and talk with the one hundred or so writers who were enrolled in my three classes.

Reflecting Upon the Middle Portion of the Course

From weeks six to ten, my students did a series of drafts in which they elaborated upon ideas of their own choosing. Not surprisingly, the majority chose to work with topics that they had generated in their journals. All were required to come to class with a draft each week. I mainly responded on tape, and when students requested it, met informally with them in conference sessions. During week ten, I again asked students to write me a response in which they commented on the use of taped feedback.

On the positive side, Jennifer said that listening to the tapes made her feel as though she had more options (in terms of revision) than she originally thought. Heidi indicated that my use of explanations and examples was most helpful. And like Rebecca, others noted that after listening a few times to the tapes, that they felt like they knew me better.[5]

There were also negative comments. One student said that she'd rather receive a paper marked in red, so that she would better be able to see her "mistakes"; another claimed that she had to listen to her tape several times in order to fully grasp what I was saying, and yet another intimated that my "umms, and ahhs" were too distracting. Lastly, Max wrote about what he called "demoralizing feedback," saying, "I am finally convinced that this business of 'comments on tape' is a waste of time. After I listened to my tape I felt like there wasn't any hope for my paper. You sounded really mad at me. I didn't have these kinds of problems in high school. I really don't know how to use quotes right yet. But I'm willing to learn."

After reading my students' letters, I set aside a class period to talk about their concerns. I made note of their positive comments in order to affirm that their insights were (as I believed) accurate. Yes, I was trying to get students to see themselves as writers; yes, I was using examples to make my point; yes, I was talking not just as a writing teacher but also as a writer. At the same time, I also took into account their more negative suggestions. In response to those who felt as though they weren't getting enough grammatically related feedback, I explained that I was, in my comments, intentionally focusing on revisionary concerns since many students had ideas that I wanted to hear more about. As for difficulty in finding specific suggestions, I said that I would pause between comments so that those who needed to could write comments on their drafts. Since Max was the only one who really seemed to be discouraged, I scheduled a conference with him. I said that if I sounded mad, the reason might be because I was getting frustrated by the fact that on that particular evening I had to tell three of his classmates the same thing that I'd told him—that using research sources without citing sources was what we in the academic community call plagiarism. I added, "If the paper isn't written in your voice and you don't acknowledge your information sources either directly or indirectly, your credibility as a writer will be called into question."

"Well, I didn't know this," said Max.

I suggested to Max that he set his draft aside and write in his own voice about the subject of raising rats and ferrets. To further encourage this, I suggested that he elaborate on his ideas. "I don't think that I can do this if I don't have someone to explain things to," he said.

"Why not ask one of your group members? Why not Joe? He's read your drafts carefully and really likes what you're doing. Or you can talk into a tape recorder, and play back your comments."

"I'll ask Joe," said Max.

Sifting through my reams of mental data, I saw that the main reason why I was first attracted to this form of response still held true: it enabled me to make writing the subject of my ongoing discussions with students; in addition, my use of tapes was bringing my student's concerns about process pedagogy to the forefront of class discussion. Questions then, that my students were asking me to more explicitly consider were: How do I show that writing involves revision? How do I demonstrate that a "movie of the mind" response (to use Peter Elbow's phrase) is a valid form of feedback? And how do I illustrate that writing involves mediating between one's own ideas and the ideas of others, not copying them down verbatim?

Ironically enough, it was in making a justification for this method that I began to see that there was another equally important reason why I was using tapes: this particular form of response encourages dialectical conversations, or discussions (which in the best sense of the word involve a more egalitarian exchange of information). This was something that I had not considered until this particular semester.

The End of the Taped-Response Road

During weeks ten to fourteen the focus of the course was on copyediting, not revision. I told my students that I would give content-related feedback on tape; however, if they needed assistance with copyediting, I would comment directly on their drafts. Jennifer, Becky, Heidi, and Max were among those who asked for revisionary feedback. In regards to her paper on anorexia, I suggested to Heidi that she think more about how she was using examples to reinforce her argument. After reading Jennifer's paper on commuting, I suggested that she ask the housing office for more specifics as to the number of University of Wisconsin-Stevens Point students who commute to campus. Along the same lines, I encouraged Becky to ask the counseling office for information as to the number of students they annually talk to about drinking problems. And I talked with Max for twenty-five minutes about his poem on his mother's ambivalent feelings towards rats, suggesting that he try harder to put himself into her shoes.

On the last week of class, I asked students to write me a final assessment as to the use of tapes, adding, "Let's give the use of taped evaluations a grade."

Jennifer, Heidi, Becky, and Max's comments were similar to those of most of their classmates. Heidi and Becky said that when listening to my feedback they often wished that they might be able to immediately respond to what I was saying. Heidi recommended that I have students put responses on the reverse side of the tapes. Heidi's final grade suggestion was a "B"; Becky's was a "B+". Jennifer also suggested that I put written comments on the papers. Her final grade suggestion for taped evaluation was a "C+". Max conceded that listening to the tapes was useful, but suggested that I schedule more one-on-one conferences. He gave the idea of taped responses a "B-".

During the last class of the semester, I provided my students with an overview of my research paper findings. I said that their concerns about taped responses were legitimate. I added that I was also pleased to see that they appeared to me to be interested in ironing out the bugs of the taped response system. I noted that what struck me as most interesting was the fact that my class was student-centered in that we were engaging in a real dialogic exchange. What I said I was hearing was that "you believe that taped responses alone are not enough; they need to be used with other forms of feedback. This includes one-on-one and informal conferences, and written responses."

In an attempt to stress the fact that my students had helped me to shape my ideas, I added that I had changed the title of my paper. Previously, I reminded them, it had been "One, Two, Three, Testing: Using Cassette Tapes to Promote Process-Based Pedagogical Practices."

"And what is it now?" asked Max.

"One, Two, Three Testing: Using Cassette Tapes to Encourage Dialogic Exchanges." I concluded by saying that I would again use tapes. This was because I still believed that my use of tapes complemented my more process-based pedagogical practices. For one thing, I was able to talk at length about content-based concerns. For another, my use of tapes better enabled me to use oral response as a vehicle for talking about how to respond to workshop drafts. I also discussed how the use of one's voice is related to the voices of others. I added that, in part because of their feedback, I had decided that I would use them with other forms of response. For example, I would continue to conference because this seemed to me an ideal method of interaction. I was quick to add that time-wise, I thought that tapes were the second-best option. As always, Max had the final word. "So what grade are you going to give taped responses?" he asked.

"I'll give it a "B". It works well, but there's room for improvement."

"Cool," he said.

Notes

1. I have also used the taped-response method in creative writing and literature classes. I used a composition class as my model here because this was what I was teaching at the time I was doing this particular research project.

2. Journals have always been an integral part of my teaching pedagogy. To this end, I, like Toby Fulwiler (1987) and Ken Autrey (1991), have stressed the fact that journals can be used to generate ideas. In an attempt to honor this premise, I have my students keep their entries in binders and turn in those entries that they most feel like sharing.

3. As I had done in teaching Introduction to Creative Writing, I decided to let the students in my freshman composition courses write in the genres of their choice and dictate their own writing schedules. This was an attempt to further blur the distinctions between the two types of writing courses, as I'd learned there was much to be gained by reading and writing poetry, fiction, and nonfiction.

4. In this chapter I primarily focus on the work of four individuals: Jennifer, Becky, Heidi and Max. This is because in looking over my notes, I saw that their comments were most representative of my students as a whole.

5. In speaking on tape, I often give students a brief description of the setting I am in. I also give them some clues as to my mood, since I think this better puts my comments into context. For example, a statement like "I am tired" might help a listener to better understand why a given response is unusually short, or why I have missed what they see as being a central concern. I've also come to believe that sounds alert them to the fact that it is a real person who is responding to their ideas. To this end, background noises have included, at times, barking dogs, a maintenance man commenting on the sorry state of my garbage disposal, and a buzzing smoke alarm.

Works Cited

Autrey, Ken. 1991. "Toward a Rhetoric of Journal Writing." *Rhetoric Review* 10: 4–90.

Bell, Marvin. 1987. *New and Selected Poems*. New York: Atheneum.

Brooke, Robert. 1991. *Writing and Sense of Self: Identity Negotiation in Writing Workshops*. Urbana, IL. NCTE.

Culhane, Alys. 1997. "13 Ways of Looking at an Egg: An Exercise in Generation and Revision." In *Elements of Alternate Style: Essays in Writing and Revision*, ed. Wendy Bishop. Portsmouth, NH: Boynton/Cook.

————. "Envisioning Revision." 1994. *The Wisconsin English Journal* 36 (3):12–14.

————. "An Essaying We Will Go." 1995. *The Wisconsin English Journal* 37 (2): 21–23.

Elbow, Peter. 1973. *Writing Without Teachers*. New York: Oxford University Press.

Fulwiler, Toby. 1987. *The Journal Book*. Portsmouth, NH: Boynton/Cook.

Murray, Donald. 1989. *Expecting the Unexpected*. Portsmouth, NH: Boynton/Cook.

14

Reading as a Writer, or What Happens When the Lights Go On
A Triadic Approach to Understanding the Development of Literary Values in Students

Patrick Bizzaro
East Carolina University

The course in question is an upper-level literature course for creative writing majors, the goal of which is simple enough, according to the syllabus: "To examine a selection of literary magazines with the intention of determining editorial preferences." But then things get a bit tricky: "Students will be required to match their stories, poems, or pieces of creative nonfiction to a magazine and then submit a piece of writing to that magazine for possible publication." And then things get slightly perplexing, working counter to the lore of teaching creative writing: "Students will also be asked to examine why they matched those particular works to that magazine. To do so, students will write a short narrative focusing on the development of literary values that are reflected both in their writings and in the journals to which they have submitted their works."

I would like to extend my appreciation to the following students who participated in this project and whose writing is presented, with their permission, in this chapter: Anthony Atkins, Ron Cherubini Jr., David Cloughley, Corey Daniels, David Dilts, Jennifer Martin, Carole Mehle, and Vickie Morgan.

Like Bizarro (not Bizzaro!) of *Superman* Comic Books, who confusedly reverses commonly known facts and beliefs, I have always tended to work, if not in reverse, at least backwards. While many writing teachers work from theory to practice, I have often worked from practice to theory. In this particular instance—and against the advice of many of my poet and novelist friends—I am continuing an effort I began nearly ten years ago in preparation for writing *Responding to Student Poems* (1993) by asking young poets and fiction writers in my classes to reflect upon what they do when they read and write.

To compositionists, this activity must seem a natural consequence of the effort they make in teaching students how to write. But to creative writers, such reflection seems counterintuitive for, as many would insist, there are some things writers should not know much about, and one of those things is how they write. As Randall Jarrell is reported to have remarked, a poem is one way of forgetting how you wrote it. Ron, a student in my class, articulates this view with particular clarity, reinforcing the context of the assignment I asked him to complete while at the same time repeating the lore that has been passed on to him by some of his other teachers: "Finding out how to turn on the light in the dark room that houses my literary values is a joyous discovery. However, the mystery that went along with stumbling around in the dark room that houses my values has me wondering if I am somehow less creative now or . . . just in control now of how I channel my creativity."

I gave the above assignment to Ron and his classmates without really knowing the theoretical principles the assignment drew upon. It seemed to me a task worthy of my students' best efforts. And I knew they wouldn't mind doing it, since students long to see their work in print and even the simple, if often tiring, task of submitting works to a magazine is exhilarating for most. What I later discovered, however, and hope to detail here, is that by asking students to determine as best as they could the literary values of those who edited the journals we studied, students would inevitably reflect upon and confront their own literary tastes, employing what Ann Berthoff (1996) has called "triadicity."

Triadicity in the Course in Creative Writing

Though triadicity is a concept Berthoff has worked at defining on several occasions, her recent article in *College English* is to my way of thinking her most successful articulation, a statement so compelling I have been drawn to it from my perspectives both as creative writer and teacher of young writers. My central concern as writer and teacher is that somehow the writing we do, whether we publish it or not, leads us to certain otherwise-missed opportunities to make observations about our place among others in the world. As a result, I feel obligated to improve whenever possible my methods for understanding the forces at play when I make decisions concerning what I value in a literary text, by published writers as well as by my students.

In "Problem-Dissolving by Triadic Means," Berthoff defines a triadic semiotic by contrasting it with a dyadic semiotic. According to Berthoff, a dyadic semiotic is "a view of the meaning relationship as two-valued"—that is, the poem, story, or essay, on the one hand, and what it means, on the other—and, as a result, a view that overlooks interpretation, treating it as simply "appended as a psychological factor" (9). Berthoff writes:

> The gap which opens up between those two terms—the signifier and the signified—cannot be defined in the light of a dyadic semiotic as other than an abyss. (Deconstructionists and the Posties throw different kinds of trash into that abyss, but the gap remains.) In a triadic semiotic, the meaning relationship is conceived as having three terms: the symbol (or *representamen*, as C. S. Peirce called it), its referent (or object), and the *interpretant*, Peirce's term for the idea which mediates the representation and what it represents. Triadicity sees the distinction between the sign and what it signifies not as a gaping abyss but as a relationship mediated by interpretation, which is thus the logical condition of any and all signification. (9)

The triad, then, is composed not just of the text and what it means, but also of the student's understanding of his or her means of making meaning from the text: "Triadicity recognizes that meanings are our means of making meaning" (9–10). From this perspective, then, the assignment I gave encourages students to see that the magazine they prefer and select as a match to their own writing is selected because the two sets of works are mediated by interpretation; between the student and the student's understanding of what something means lies the student's means of illuminating meaning, and Peirce calls that means of illumination the *interpretant*.

Inevitably, then, by requiring my students to perform two related tasks, I assured myself that a third task would be completed as well. By asking them to read literary journals to determine editorial preference and then to read their own work to determine if the editor's preferences would work to favor their literary productions, I invited students, albeit by chance, into the shadowy hallway that joins these two rooms, one of the editor's preferences and the other of the students' literary values as reflected in their writings. And the assignment produced narratives in which students reflect upon the development of their literary values in such a way that they would better understand why their writings are better suited to some magazines than to others.

As I have argued elsewhere, this reflection empowers writers by enabling them to understand that a foundation, in fact, exists for what they believe to be true about themselves as writers as well as a basis for retaining authority over their text.[1] I go farther perhaps than Berthoff and Peirce safely (and, perhaps, wisely) go by suggesting here that students will not happily entertain authoritative commentary by others until this space between the sign and the signified, the space Berthoff and Peirce describe not as an abyss but as a mediating idea or an understanding of how understanding has taken place, has been accommodated. So, from my perspective on learning, while teaching that aims at authoritative or appropriative responses to student writing may temporarily result in writing more to the tastes of the teacher, no permanent changes will take place in the writer.

My position is much the same as Berthoff's, however. Using I. A. Richards's term, "gangster theories," which treat discourse as binary code, Berthoff puts this view in more general terms, though terms that show our agreement nonetheless. She writes:

> Gangster theories make teaching impossible by undercutting attempts to keep the making of meaning central; they sabotage our efforts to make literature accessible and to encourage our students to see their writing as a means of discovering and representing the meanings which their interpretations create. Gangster theories foster killer dichotomies such as *fact/ opinion*, which as a binary opposition suggests that facts are self-evident and in no need of formulation and that opinion is merely subjective and therefore antithetical to fact. Gangster theories make it impossible to appreciate the dialectic of meaning and knowing, of representation and interpretation, and, indeed, of self and society. (10)

Gangster theories, thus, place limits on what a teacher can expect to accomplish in the classroom.

If these limitations are acknowledged by the teacher, the writing teacher enters an interesting predicament, a condition marked by ineffectiveness. As one graduate student told me last term upon completion of her thesis, a collection of short stories: "Of course I'll make the changes my teachers require me to make. Everyone knows you can always put it back the way you had it once you go home." For literature teachers, however, the context itself defines the problem. Every good student knows to give back to the teacher during test situations exactly that interpretation the teacher has given the class. In the instance of the literature teacher, less clearly perhaps than in the instance of the writing teacher, permanent change in the students' readings of a given text will not occur: as the cliché goes, if we've told our students the poem's meaning a thousand times and they still don't get it right on a test or in an essay, then who's the slow learner? As most teachers know, students will not understand literature that does not connect, in some way, with the students' prior experiences.

The assignment I gave my young writers, then, reflects an effort to get students past their loyalty to the teacher as authority for their understanding. In fact, this assignment is one that asks students to get the *how* out of the *what*—that is, they are asked to determine on the basis of what they value (simply put, what they enjoyed reading during the course) how they came to value it. In this way, I believe lights will go on for students who might otherwise leave the class in the same darkness they carried with them when they entered.

What Happens When Lights Go On

The exploration I report on here began as a journal assignment. Mixed in with a typical night's reflection in writing on matters such as "What kinds of poems (or stories) does this editor prefer?" and "Which is the strongest (or weakest) poem (or story) in the magazine and why?" was the assignment that students write a short note card on their histories as readers of poetry, fiction, and creative nonfiction. As often happens, one assignment gave rise to another, as the note card on their histories as readers gave rise to a revision of that card, focusing on the development of literary values, all in preparation for the final and much-feared reflective essay on why students matched their poems, stories, and essays to certain specific magazines.

In a class discussion of the above three assignments, it became clear to all of us (the class as well as the teacher) that a metaphor that quite naturally arises from reflections done in their note cards might allow us to examine if not more clearly at least more ingeniously the implications of the way students came to value certain aspects of the literature read for the course. As a result, we decided to explore and play with the metaphor of light. From our particular vantage point, when the switch is flipped, the light that enables an individual to see a room more clearly is an indicator not only of what is in the room, but of how an individual comes to see and know it—that is, from where in the room the individual observes what can be seen. This illumination, as we found out in our class discussions, does not happen in the same way for every person. Rather, in the same way that lights might come in differently by the use of different switches, my students' understandings of how they understand come to them in different ways.

We decided on the basis of those first note cards that, for some students, literary values seem to evolve over a period of time. We called this the *rheostat effect,* where as the switch is twisted counterclockwise illumination moves from low intensity to high. For others, preconceived values suddenly were changed, and students came to see things with new and different skills. This we called the *light-sensor effect,* in which the light switch is sensitive and responds to the movement in front of it. For some, and this happened during the course itself, certain literary preferences revealed themselves to the students. The awareness this kind of light made possible is what we described as the *clapper effect,* modeled after the television commercial that shows elderly people clapping their hands as they enter a room, turning on the light they know is there. And, as our discussion continued and our understanding of the implications of our metaphor deepened, we realized that there were all kinds of lights we might have chosen that describe the experiences writers have when they read since the light metaphor, like the interpretant, must hold the possibility for all kinds of illuminations; in fact, some experiences reported by students in that first notecard claimed to incorporate *all* of the kinds of lights we could think of. We decided to call the experience that incorporates all of the others the *spectrum effect*, since some individuals came to their understandings in a variety of ways.

Let's begin this discussion, then, by more fully exploring the occasion for each of the light metaphors and what my students found out about themselves as a result of trying to understand their means of understanding. I found that I was interested not only in what happens to and in my students when the light goes on, but also in how it goes on for different students.

Carole does an excellent job of explaining the rheostat effect. In explaining how that effect occurred, Carole added another layer to our understanding of the rheostat as a way of achieving understanding, that her use of the metaphor is an effort to suggest that certain of her literary values surfaced—that is, rose to consciousness. In Carole's instance, many of these values were previously unstated or unexplored. Carole writes:

> As these values of mine returned to the light of my conscious consideration, they were deepened and broadened; they evolved as I became better aware of how to consider my audience, the tone, the style, thus I feel the rheostat effect . . . I reacclimated myself with considerations that became latent, blew the proverbial dust off them and learned to see these [values] again. Not only did my consciousness return as I revised, it became present as I drafted. I became a better writer by allowing myself to consider elements I had forgotten were part of the writing process.

Reflection on what she values enabled Carole to remember what she values most about her experience as writer and reader and, as a result, go back to her writing with renewed enthusiasm and conviction. As she says, "The creativity returned to my writing."

The predicament of the creative writing student (and, perhaps, the literature student) is expressed quite well by Vickie in a statement that demonstrates her experience of the light-sensor effect. Vickie carried into the class a notion of what a poem is (and, therefore, what is *not* poetic) that reflects, perhaps, the literary values stressed by one or more of her previous teachers. Certainly, finding among poems published in the literary magazines subjects banned from her other poetry writing workshops enabled Vickie to determine for herself that, in fact, those subjects are worthy of her exploration. Vickie writes:

> Poetry that I was not interested in previously was presented in a whole new manner. . . . Reading and enjoying such a variety of work makes me want to try writing something humorous, witty and entertaining to the reader. In

the past, I have just avoided writing about certain topics that came to mind that were not traditional and concrete. Somehow I believe that writing students get the impression that the best publishable work is proper, well-versed and conservative. Anyway, I know that I was given that feeling because most of my classmates in college tried to write in that style or the works read aloud in class were similar to that.

Here Vickie describes her realization that, if treated with sufficient skill, "poems filled with personal relationships, current social issues, etc. can have deeper meaning or simply give the reader something to consider, and can also be a joy to read." This runs counter to advice offered by many writing teachers to not write what one of my colleagues terms "expressionist" poems about personal and "local" matters, as though there is no precedent for doing so and as if poems that do exactly that will never appear in print in journals we encourage our students to read and publish in.

What's more, Vickie's experience nicely demonstrates the distinction I want to make between a dyadic semiotic, in which the authoritarian teacher ignores entirely the *interpretant* by enforcing a narrow perspective on subject matter appropriate to poetry, and the triadic, which by providing students with a forum to better understand their methods of understanding likewise enables students to make breakthroughs of the kind Vickie has made. The dyadic allows students to successfully traverse the room of their understanding by taking a guiding hand; the triadic enables students to see for themselves how they got to the other side of the room.

The clapper effect, as treated by David, seems to draw upon literary values and tastes developed in the student by early experiences as a reader. Perhaps, as in David's case, these tastes are a product of listening intently to works read to the student by his or her parents when the student was a child. David writes:

> I believe in some cases these values have been a part of my make-up all along and it took a certain reading or passage to bring them to the surface. An example may be while reading, "a light goes on," and I say to myself, "Wow! I never thought about that or this subject in the way the author is presenting it."

For David, then, reading literature seems to have the effect we assume it can have for all of our students, the effect not only of giving pleasure but of educating as well—the kind of reading most people think of when we say students need to learn to read as writers. David writes, "I may not have agreed with a particular passage as soon as I read it, but upon rereading or thinking about it the next day I may find myself agreeing with what the author was trying to do with the character or development of the scene."

The majority of students in the class view their experience as resulting from the spectrum effect, where two or more of the above insights have occurred to them. For these students, as one wrote in her paper, "not only have [their] literary values revealed themselves, they have changed and evolved." Or, as Corey notes,

> The purpose in much of this course has been to find and explore the literary biases interwoven into each of the little magazines that are in question for publication. But to do this, the first and foremost thing that is necessary is to find out and interpret our own literary understandings as a reader and a writer. Being involved in the process of critical thinking towards these very different magazines has caused us . . . to become aware of our own literary values and understandings.

In this particular vein, no single literary critical theory influences the way the student has read a literary text, no "trash" has pushed them to view what they have read in a particular way. Still some students, like Tony, have to wrestle with the terms of their college educations. Tony writes:

> The literary values I brought with me . . . were strung loosely together because of my inability to accommodate any one subject position. Without being identified as an expressivist, Marxist, feminist, or some other aspect that labels me, it was difficult to evaluate other's writing, including poetry or short stories.

Still, in the process of writing this assignment, the majority of the students have seen the development of their values in more personal terms, understanding that the point of what they have read is not to reach some predetermined interpretation but, rather, to understand their means of understanding. Carole writes, "While being able to consider what I like and why, what I am and am not, may not be necessary for other classes, it has helped greatly in this one as we evaluated texts."

Even Tony, who seems quite involved in adopting as a method of analysis what Berthoff terms "trash," comes to see the assignment in terms of some other, highly personal, set of circumstances. Tony, who teaches tennis to support himself while at school, continues:

> This experience (of having the light turn on) was much like one I had on the tennis court. At 9:30 on a Tuesday night I was teaching a lesson with a thirteen year old. He had been playing rather well, but in order for him to generate more power he had to be instructed to step toward the ball with his left foot and to follow through by dragging his right foot around finishing completely open. He seemed to have trouble with this. I wasn't sure what to do next. I told him to close his eyes just before he hit the ball and concentrate on what he was supposed to do rather than on where the ball would end up. At the same time the "timer" on the lights surrounding the courts ran out. Once I turned the timer back he seemed to do everything right. He stepped to the ball, he finished high with an open stance, and

indeed, seemed to have more pace on the ball. It wasn't necessarily that the light came on for him, rather it was that the light went off.

Tony concludes quite interestingly, traveling perhaps down a longer hallway than anyone else in class from one room to the next, that "the literary values I have acquired because of the class have come to be brighter because of the darkness I was once in."

Some Conclusions

This chapter is an effort to connect practice with theory. By requiring my students to do an assignment that ends in reflection, I believe I have encouraged them to employ a triadic semiotic of the sort Berthoff believes not only to have certain benefits for students but to be necessary if teaching is to take place at all. To reinforce Berthoff's point, I describe in some detail one assignment with three parts, only the third of which is uncommon in creative writing classes. I believe many creative writing teachers ask students to submit their work to one magazine or another. Probably fewer require students to read honest-to-God literary magazines as texts for a writing course. And as near as I can tell, fewer still require students to reflect upon the development of their literary values, and those teachers do so only after deciding that the pedagogical lore of creative writing instruction is received, not required, and therefore not immune to scrutiny, unpopular as such scrutiny might be.

More than in composition courses, creative writing courses are, by design, dyadic. One characteristic of a triadic semiotic is that students would be encouraged to reflect upon their literary values. But is such reflection useful? Not for every student. Some students have become so accustomed to being told how to read and write, and even what steps to take in generating a poem, story, or essay that reflection might do more harm than good. The problem, in my estimation, is that teachers are more interested in making certain their students produce poems, stories, and essays that satisfy the teacher's expectations than in enabling students to improve as writers in some lasting way, even at the expense of having students write works the teacher might deem ineffective. As I have argued throughout this chapter, if the *interpretant,* the idea that mediates the text and the reader's interpretation of the text, is ignored, little learning will take place.

Still, the best conclusions about the usefulness not just of the assignment I describe here, but also of introducing students to their means of making meanings come from my students. Carole, who better than any of the others articulated the coming to light as a growing awareness or consciousness of her values, reaches yet one more important and substantial insight that the triadic approach to my course made possible: the distinction between "testimony" and "anti-testimony." For Carole, "testimony . . . is seeing others employ things within their writing you use in your writing. . . . As I read the fiction and poetry in *Quarterly West*, I felt that reinforcement; this was the first journal we read to which I felt connected." By contrast, "anti-testimony is contradiction" where "works seemed to go against my style. . . . These were things I read because I had to, not because I wanted to on my own." Carole concludes, "As I search for my place in the writing world, it helps to know things that have been happening to me are supposed to happen, that I am not alone."

Jennifer notes that by doing this assignment, "some literary values which weren't apparent to me at first were revealed to me. . . . I knew that I liked a certain style, such as the Southern-literature style, yet I never knew why." She goes on to write that "Things which were hidden to me were suddenly revealed and as a result the reasons as to why I liked that style were revealed to me."

Perhaps the best insights, though, were Vickie's, who understood that teachers working dyadically limited for her an acceptable range of subjects worthy of exploration in her poems. Though she might have reached the conclusions she reaches in her paper through some other medium, it can be argued that she could only reach those conclusions, nonetheless, by means of reflecting on her literary values in light of the works read for the course. I think Vickie would agree that by conducting such an examination, insights about the self are inevitable.

Vickie is not alone in that view, however. Clearly there are those among us, Berthoff included, who believe that by abandoning examination of this third place—that is, by teaching from a dyadic semiotic—we make teaching impossible.

Note

1. In *Responding to Student Poems*, I argue from the perspective that new models of response to student writing, based on tenets of poststructural theory, permit students to retain authority over their writing. Fashioning my study after Bizarro Superman, however, I worked from practice and now, years later, I see the theoretical bases for that study in triadic semiotics.

Works Cited

Berthoff, Ann E. 1996. "Problem-Dissolving by Triadic Means." *College English* 58 (1): 9–21.

Bizzaro, Patrick. 1993. *Responding to Student Poems: Applications of Critical Theory*. Urbana, IL: NCTE.

15

"Carom Shots"
Reconceptualizing Imitation and Its Uses in Creative Writing Courses

Hans Ostrom
University of Puget Sound

I

Imitation, as a technique for teaching creative writing, has about it the air of the old-fashioned. And why not? After all, as a formal concept of writing instruction, it dates back at least to Aristotle and his elaborators, Cicero and Quintillian. (James Murphy's relatively new edition of Quintillian's works is especially useful at showing the extent to which Quintillian thought carefully about the subject.) Less historically, more intuitively, we English-professor types are likely, when we think of imitation, to conjure up images of John Milton or Samuel Johnson imitating Latin poets in their composition books, thereby acquiring the gravitas of their later works. How very Miltonesque, how very Johnsonian and quaint is imitation, we may be inclined to think.

Across the English-studies curricula these days, imitation is a concept without a home, or at least it has struck me as such. In journals, at conferences, in the hallways, a person just doesn't hear creative writing teachers discussing its use much at all. Nor does one hear literature teachers talking about—for instance—having students come to know Shakespearian sonnets "from the inside," as well as from standard interpretation, by writing a sonnet, imitating His Willness, arm wrestling with iambs, rhymes, and quatrains, monkeying around with that courtly irony and wordplay.

And you don't hear composition teachers kicking around the idea of imitation, either. One might speculate that the creative writing and composition types see themselves as so intent on getting students to write "originally" or to "find their voice(s)" that imitation of models would seem heretical. To be fair, we must acknowledge that compositionists have fought so long, so hard, to define students' writing as the subject of a composition course that to reactivate imitation as a pedagogical tool might seem like the betrayal of a cause. No doubt issues of empowerment, canon formation, "gate-keeping," figurative colonialist teaching strategies, and so forth, contribute to the wariness toward imitation. And for literature teachers, questions of canon formation probably cut the other way; for instance, isn't there something indecent (a literature teacher may believe) about students imitating Shakespeare? Doesn't it sully the museum that is a literature course? And who would want to read such drivel?!

Therefore, while a variety of animosities, suspicions, and disagreements exist among the camps of English studies, imitation-the-venerable-but-not-venerated seems to be one concept that the camps, by default, can agree to ignore. It is true that John Gardner (1981), in *The Art of Fiction,* a book based on many years of teaching, cheerfully advocates the use of imitation and presents imitative exercises. But Gardner himself, like imitation, fell betwixt and between the camps of English studies because he was an odd amalgam of medievalist, novelist, conservative (*On Moral Fiction*), and rebel (the biker pose). Anomalous Gardner championed old-fashioned imitation; no net gain for the status of imitation resulted.

One conclusion to draw from the apparent plight of imitation, especially if you're a contrarian, is that a concept so grossly out of fashion must have a lot going for it. Indeed, I'd like to spend the rest of this chapter reconceptualizing imitation and explaining how it can be used in creative writing classes—even by teachers who have ideological and pedagogical reservations about it—perhaps, indeed, especially by such teachers.

II

Firstly and briefly, let me do a little foregrounding; it concerns what I came to regard as the need for "a safe place" in creative writing classes—especially fiction courses; it also concerns one tactic for advancing the "safe-place" strategy, something called a "microstory."

One aspect of undergraduate fiction writing courses that troubled me was how monumental each story became for the students. In my classes, they usually finish three or four stories during a fourteen-week semester, and while I used such compositionist tactics as peer review of drafts, precise workgroup protocols, and portfolio evaluation, it still was the case that a malaise hit the classes when stories were due to be presented to workgroups; a sense of anticlimax blossomed; and, psychically if not practically, there seemed to be too much riding on each story: A student would toil on a story for about a month, present it to her workgroup, have it evaluated by me, and no matter how good the response to the story was, the student might feel let down. And if the story fared poorly with the group or with me, the student quite rightly might feel as if she had nothing to show for a month's work. Even apart from the issues of malaise, anticlimax, and disappointment, I felt that—independent of stories and drafts of stories—more writing should happen more constantly in the courses. (I felt less strongly about this in poetry classes, where texts, by comparison, seemed to proliferate like rabbits.)

Consequently, I started introducing many opportunities for students to write more often, more experimentally, and with less of a "do-or-die" atmosphere surrounding their performance. The illustrative example I'll describe in a moment is "the microstory," sometimes known as a "slice," but first I should probably anticipate at least one objection to there even being a problem that the microstory or related tactics might solve. The objection is this: What's wrong with the sense that a lot is riding on a story (a devil's advocate might ask)? Why should we try to protect students from disappointment, when authors in "the real world" are disappointed all the time?

To which one might respond as follows:

1. We're there to teach, not to replicate the cut throat world of publishing; moreover, the "it will toughen them up" rationale can be used to justify all sorts of bad teaching: "So what if my lectures are boring? Corporate life is boring, too, so the students are learning how to cope with boredom." (I've even heard the "it will toughen them up" argument used to advocate a laissez-faire attitude toward sexual harassment, but that's another story.)

2. As Richard Hugo (1978) wrote in *The Triggering Town,* colleges and universities are as "real" as other environments and institutions.

3. We tend to construct a false economy of scarcity in writing classes, the implicit message being, "You'll all complete three stories; if you're lucky, one might turn out to be very good; and if you're really lucky, you might be one of the (at most) two students who become class stars." It is just as easy, more productive, and less pretentious to create an economy of abundance, in which every student is an explorer of language, literature, memory, the social construction of literary standards, authorship, memory, meaning, and so forth; an economy in which students' texts are less commodities that need to be "priced," as it were, and more of a means of discovery. Wendy Bishop fleshes out this viewpoint throughout her book, *Released Into Language,* and Pierre Bourdieu studies "the economy of taste" (also an economy of false scarcity) in his book, *Distinction* (1984).

4. The notion that most students are egomaniacs who think they can do no creative wrong and who need to be taught a cruel-world lesson or two is false. One of those urban folktales. Most of the students I've taught over the last fifteen years are hard on themselves; they doubt their abilities; they're frustrated by their imperfections; and even when they're defensive, it's usually out of insecurity or self-consciousness, not delusions of genius. Even if I were predisposed to rough up students in a Paper-Chase way (I am not), why would I bother to do so when they tend already to rough themselves up?

By "safe place," then, I do not mean a classroom that puts students' egos in a box of cotton, but I do mean a figurative place where this notion of exploration is explicitly more urgent than the notion of performance, or the notion that, in fourteen weeks, we should all of us be able to produce well-wrought urns of one sort or another.

Some years ago I started having students write impromptu pieces in class and, during intervals between the "major" stories, I had them write short-short fictions—one or two pages, three at most, with just a couple of days to work on them. I called these pieces "microstories" or "slices."

Often—and here's the rub—I'd combine imitation with micronarration. So, for example, after we'd read Italo Calvino's *Invisible Cities,* (1974) students would write a microstory evoking an invisible something, anything: college, planet, government, sport, car dealership. . . . Or, after we'd read some Gertrude Stein, students wrote microstories that, whatever else they did, needed to jazz around with language in some way, not necessarily Stein's way. Richard Brautigan's work opened the door to some micro-micro-fiction: pieces that toyed with the combination of whimsy and French surrealism found in Brautigan's work, often only a paragraph long. Sometimes I wouldn't have a specific imitation in mind, so the students and I would invent some options in class.

Obviously, this is a different sort of imitation from an "apprentice's" modeling of a "master's" work. Instead, it's more of a carom shot, one text playing off another; indeed, I came to appreciate how text-centered these microstory assignments were (the playing was the thing)—in contrast to the full-blown stories, in which the process seems inevitably so author-centered. The students, for their part, generally liked this sort of work—because it was short (students are pragmatists), because they'd get feedback from me rapidly, because the stakes were lower, and because (conversely, perhaps ironically) the room to grow seemed abundant. Microstories inspire a certain fearlessness.

Some interesting by-products emerged. Sometimes microstories would become the basis for one of the students' longer stories—a situation roughly comparable to that of the Roethke exercise described in Hugo's *Triggering Town*: so consumed are students, suggests Hugo, with the details of Roethke's tortuous, arbitrary poem blueprint that the subconscious mind takes over, students forget about "communication," and surprisingly, rare poems sprout like cacti in the desert. Concentrating furiously on the short, demanding form of the microstory, students sometimes unearthed equally surprising material appropriate for longer fiction.

In addition, because the microstories are indeed micro, students tend, on their own initiative, to be more precise with grammar, style, and usage. They polish without being nagged. Too, the microstories become not just a means of discovery but a manageable end in themselves. Usually, students may select three to five (revised) microstories from the eight or nine we write and include them in their portfolios. This shows that excellent fiction need not be long fiction; it gives students a broader range of material to "show" in their portfolio; and it allows them to see themselves as more versatile writers—and we all know how, oddly enough, young writers seem determined to define themselves so quickly and so narrowly.

As I mentioned, the imitative microstories arose in response to issues that manifested themselves chiefly in fiction classes, but I've used similar techniques in poetry classes, having students play carom shots off particular poets, poems, styles, forms, and so forth. Microstories constitute only one representative example, then, of a general approach to using imitation.

III

Now I want to turn to some broader conceptual issues concerning this general approach to using imitation. These are, I believe, issues to consider whether one finds my particular uses of imitation appropriate or not.

"Positionality"

The carom-shot approach to imitation I've illustrated here alters the position of students toward the texts imitated—alters it from an apprentice/master or a novitiate/sacred text model to one of inviter/invitee. That is, students are invited by a particular text to manipulate language in a similar way. The instructor is a go-between, shaping and delivering the invitation to imitate. The altered position gives students more author-ity, I would argue—more freedom, but also more responsibility.

"Complication of Reading"

Too often in creative-writing courses, interpretation is—at least implicitly—presented as "the business of critics," whereas the business of writers is implicitly merely "to write," as if in a vacuum. And even if students are encouraged to take themselves seriously as interpreters, too often the process gets stuck at the like/dislike stage—an up or down vote on Hemingway, or whomever. Or, when student work is "gone over" in the workshop, interpretation can shrink to two words—*work* and *flow,* as in, "This story really works for me," or "For me, the story didn't flow." Obviously, there are a variety of ways in which creative writing teachers can cultivate subtler interpretation. Carom-shot imitation can help the effort, however. For it is really engaged, complicated interpretation in its own right. One need not like what one is imitating, but one must know it, must begin to decode its linguistic and literary DNA.

For instance, many students react negatively to some of Richard Brautigan's writing, partly because of its unreconstructed sexism, partly because his persona of Beat-hippie-surrealist-dropout can seem one-dimensional, occasionally mannered. Nonetheless, I've had students who are cool to Brautigan write imitations that capture satisfying qualities of his writing. Moreover, they sometimes have embedded in their imitations crafty critiques of what they've found wanting. For example, one student wrote a microstory from (the recurring Brautigan character) Marcia's point of view, ending up with a Brautiganesque narrative spoken by a "someone" whose views of men, women, and hipsterdom differed sharply from Brautigan's. In some ways, the story became a miniature study in Bakhtinian mulivocality, if you will. At any rate, such a reading of Brautigan is necessarily complicated, layered, agile.

"Theory"

Because carom-shot imitation constitutes interpretation as well as text production, it also can crystallize questions of theory. Mimesis, multivocality, social construction of texts and of literary "standards," definitions of narrative, deconstruction, the politics of canon formation: these and other topics can emerge from imitations, because by crafting an imitation, students have adopted, however briefly, a certain stance toward literature, language, and writing different from their own but not wholly divorced from their own. Potentially, the students are at once invested in and distanced from the microstory (for example), and this complicated stance invites theorizing, but also anchors it to a specific moment, text, and discursive move. Put another way, imitation makes theory palatable for creative-writing students, who have been known to become sullen in the company of theory. And imitation of the sort discussed here is, after all, an explicit, concrete enactment of intertextuality, itself a concept of literary theory. And finally . . .

"Liberatory Teaching" (Paolo Freire's Term)

As enlightened and as composition-influenced as a creative writing course may be, the teacher will still likely emerge as a gatekeeper, as manager of quality control, so to speak. Maybe this isn't all bad. Even if it's good, however, it doesn't preclude the need to search for teaching modes that are more liberatory, wherein students are given more authority. From this perspective, I've come to appreciate how carom-shot imitation authorizes students, in ways already mentioned, but also because it's an area in which students can invent, can determine, what we (the class) do. When they define the options for carom shots, or when they revise ideas I put forward (as they often do), they're composing a curriculum. Imitation—an idea that, at first or second glance, would seem the opposite of liberatory—gives to or leaves with students considerable, appropriate power. (I did say that a contrarian would like imitation's possibilities.)

A microstory is something a teacher can write, too; few things can do more to make for a gatekeeper who's suddenly gateless than having The Boss complete an assignment, too. By contrast, if we bring in one of our finished longer stories, we're not really working alongside students. We look like ringers. We will seem self-serving. Or we may reify our position of power. Writing a short, experimental piece precisely when the students do is a different matter entirely, though. It demystifies the teacher, keeps her/him honest, and validates the purposes of imitation.

IV

Conceptually, then, imitation as I've begun to define it in this chapter becomes a multipurpose tactic for those teachers who continue to interrogate, rearrange, and even dismantle the old "creative writing workshop." It repositions students in relation to published texts and well-known authors, and it complicates students' reading practices. By fusing interpretation with text production, imitation also opens up theoretical issues but also grounds them in a specific practice. For reasons I've stated, imitation is potentially a liberatory teaching practice, and—in a more mundane, pragmatic vein—it can also serve as an effective invention site for whatever other texts students produce in class.

Although it dates back to the early days of rhetoric, imitation need be neither quaint copy book exercises nor weak stabs at parody. More broadly conceived, it is essentially a particular kind of engagement-with-the-text, one that creates a "safe place," one that depressurizes the workshop environment, one that's almost endlessly adaptable and variable.

Works Cited

Bakhtin, Mikhail. 1986. *Speech Genres and Other Late Essays.* Trans. Vern W. McGee. Austin: University of Texas Press.

Bishop, Wendy. 1991. *Released Into Language.* Urbana, IL: NCTE.

Bourdieu, Pierre. 1984. *Distinction: A Social Critique of the Judgement of Taste.* Trans. Richard Nice. Cambridge: Harvard University Press.

Brautigan, Richard. 1994. *Trout Fishing in America, Revenge of the Lawn, In Watermelon Sugar.* One volume. New York: Houghton Mifflin.

Calvino, Italo. 1974. *Invisible Cities.* New York: Vintage.

Gardner, John. 1978. *On Moral Fiction.* New York: Basic Books.

————. 1981. *The Art of Fiction.* New York: Vintage.

Hugo, Richard. 1978. *The Triggering Town.* New York: W. W. Norton.

Murphy, James J., ed. 1987. *Quintillian on the Teaching of Speaking and Writing.* Davis, CA: Hermagoras Press.

Shor, Ira, and Paulo Freire. 1987. *A Pedagogy for Liberation: Dialogues on Transforming Education.* South Hadley, MA: Bergin & Garvey.

16

My Other, My Self
Participants and Spectators in Introductory Fiction Writing Workshops

Lee Martin
University of North Texas

A few years ago, I started thinking about how my introductory fiction writing workshops might best serve the folks enrolled in them. I had tired of seeing too many good students work diligently at their writing only to receive mediocre grades simply because they lacked the talent they needed to write sophisticated fiction. I began to wonder whether there might be some other way to teach the course that might give my students another way to succeed. In the process, I gave some serious thought to the learning I wanted them to experience.

I generally encounter two types of students in these beginning courses: those who are genuinely interested in practicing the craft, and those—usually a larger population—who are there to fulfill English requirements. This last bunch is comprised, for the most part, of nonreaders and nonwriters. The course appeals to these students in ways literature courses don't ("too much reading"), and it seems preferable to composition courses ("too much writing"). Like Goldilocks choosing porridges or beds, these students imagine fiction writing will be "just right."

The realization that turns them into grumpy old bears is that writing literary fiction requires a good deal of study, practice, and skill. Perhaps, even more important, students start to see that they need a certain aptitude for the art in order to be successful. The truth that starts to sink in is that not everyone can write good literary fiction, no matter how dedicated to that purpose or how excellent their instruction. So often, in these introductory workshops, we are teaching fiction writing to students who will never write another story after the course has ended. All of them, however, will become thinking citizens of the world. That fact alone has caused me to reassess how I expect my fiction workshops to fit into my students' overall educations.

I've begun to see that the distinctions we commonly try to make between fiction and nonfiction dissolve when we look at both as forms in which writers think with language. For a while now, I've been convinced that my fiction workshops can teach the aesthetics of the craft while also asking students to demonstrate their learning by how well they can use fiction to think analytically about themselves and the worlds they occupy. This isn't to say I've lost interest in teaching students to become better writers and readers of literary fiction. In fact, because I now know that even if students fail as fiction writers, they will still take something useful from the course, my expectations for their stories are even higher than in past workshops. My resolve to consider students themselves to be equally important texts in my workshops has allowed the naturally talented writers to emerge and prosper while the less-skilled writers have become more likely to use fiction writing to help them build critical thinking skills.

I tell my students that somewhere in the stories we write, no matter how removed from our actual experiences, we meet some emblem of ourselves. A short story, then, presents an "other" in which we can find some aspect of the "self." James Britton's (1970) distinction between the roles of "participant" and "spectator" in communication acts offers us a theory by which we can better understand the learning that may take place when students write fiction and then reflect on that writing. If we consider the characters we create to be replicas of some part or parts of ourselves, we see the possibilities for learning that fiction writing presents. Indeed, Britton's idea that when we fuse the experiences of others with our own, we ourselves become more knowledgeable (116) helps me think about the way my students make meaning when they examine autobiographical sources by writing *about* the stories they have produced.

Central to my application of Britton to my students' learning is an understanding of his use of the terms *participant* and *spectator*. A participant, according to Britton, is someone enmeshed in experiences as they occur (104). When I was lost once as a child, for example, and I went to the first place I recognized—a dime store—I was acting in the role of a participant. It is a role that requires decision and action. A spectator, on the other hand, suffers no such demands. A spectator is "on holiday from the world's affairs, someone contemplating experiences *in which he is not taking part*" (Britton 104). Thus, when I relate my experience of being lost and entering the dime store, I no longer have to decide and act; I am free to tell my story and to watch it unfold from the vantage point of a spectator. We can say, then, that fiction writers are "spectators" of their characters, who are "participants" in the worlds of their stories—worlds that present situations containing their own demands for decision and action. If we imbue our fiction with aspects of ourselves—if we are ultimately both spectator and participant—it stands to reason that the key to learning something of ourselves and our worlds from the fiction we write lies in a successful merger of the two roles. This is what I hope happens when I ask my students to explore the sources of their stories.

Eve Shelnutt, in her essay, "Transforming Experience into Fiction: An Alternative to the Workshop" (1989), explains a teaching method she first used in the Honors College at the University of Pittsburgh. She asked her students to begin the semester by performing a series of memory exercises meant to put them in touch with personal experiences that would become the material of their stories. Later, after her students had written their first stories, she asked them to write an essay in which they examined the sources of their material and the processes by which they turned the actual moments of their lives into fiction. Her purpose, as she explains it, was to help students achieve "a perspective of distance" from autobiographical material so as to have "emotional control" over that material when they eventually transformed it into fiction (156). Although Shelnutt expands the focus of the workshop to consider not only the stories produced but also the means by which those stories come to be, her emphasis, as I understand it, is still on helping students become more sophisticated fiction writers.

My interest in Shelnutt's method lies more in how we can use it to create sophisticated critical thinkers. Students in my composition courses often use fiction to explore personal issues too sensitive to face in autobiography. These students feel safer writing stories because they can conceal themselves behind created characters and plots. I notice that often, after students have written short stories, they recognize themselves in their characters. I recall one student in particular who wrote a story about a recalcitrant girl who constantly rebelled against her mother. In this student's end-of-the-semester evaluation of her work, she wrote about how she had used that story to shape material she couldn't articulate in autobiography: "I wrote a short story because it was hard for me to admit that Amanda was really me as a child." Writing fiction, then, provides a protective shield of sorts that eventually dissolves for the writer: "Writing this story has given me a way to escape from the real world," my student noted, "yet the world I have escaped to was my own." In my introductory fiction writing workshops, I now invite students to experience similar moments of recognition by engaging in an analytical dialogue with their own stories.

Theorists have long underscored the crucial role dialogue plays in the learning process. Hans-Georg Gadamer suggests a connection between the understanding of a text and the understanding of oneself, emphasizing the dialectic exchange between text and reader: "One must take up into [himself] what is told to him in such a fashion that it speaks and finds an answer in the words of his own language" (from his *Philosophical Hermeneutics* quoted in

McNeil 1989, 87). My assumption in teaching fiction writing is that this same principle operates between text and writer. More recently, Ann Berthoff (1981) has championed the role of dialogic action in the making of meaning, claiming the importance of questioning to discovery and, consequently, to learning. "Language is an exchange," she proposes, "we know what we've said and what can be understood from it when we get a response" (72). Writing, argues Berthoff, should be a recursive activity. Students learn by returning to their texts, by questioning them from another angle. This mode of inquiry, this *dialogue* between writer and text, provides a valuable method for those of us who teach fiction writing to students who are not exceptionally talented, especially if we are looking for alternative ways to measure these students' success in our courses.

Fiction writers, no matter their talents, must first examine the significant moments of their own lives before they can begin to engage themselves with the crucial moments of their characters' lives. To help my students through this process, I ask them to begin the class by joining me in a number of journal writing activities in which we become observers of our own past experiences. The first class meeting begins with an activity I have borrowed from Shelnutt. My students and I list pairs of shoes we remember wearing in childhood, and then we write about single episodes that happened to us when we were wearing specific pairs of shoes. Other memory-recall activities, performed during the first few weeks of the class, center on significant places, scents we remember from childhood, gifts we received, people who left an impression on us. I reinforce these activities with readings of stories meant to highlight various elements of literary fiction. We look at how other writers have used setting and details, made point-of-view choices, created plots that have come naturally from characters' histories and present needs, and moved their plots to crucial moments in which characters' masks drop away—and we see something about the inner lives they ordinarily keep hidden. My purpose here is twofold: to get my students thinking about what literary fiction does and to steep them in the vital moments of their pasts so they will build up emotional reservoirs for them to tap during the writing of their own fiction.

After my students have recalled notable moments from their lives, complete with the often conflicting and ambiguous emotions associated with these events, I ask them to look away from themselves to created characters and plots. I tell them to write a name at the top of a page—any name—and to answer some questions about that person: "What's something this person has hidden in a drawer?" "What's hanging in this person's closet that they never wear, but can't bring themselves to get rid of?" "When's the last time this person cried?" "What does this person want to tell someone, but can't?" I read these questions aloud and invite my students to fill in the blanks. I progress at a steady rate, so they don't have too much time to ponder their responses. During one class period, students create three characters complete with histories, fears, desires. The triangles that begin to take shape suggest plots. I ask my students to write the opening of their stories by putting one of their characters in a specific place and having him or her engage in a specific action. By the end of the class, students should have a curiosity about their characters and what will happen to them in the course of their stories.

Naturally, this is trickery on my part. I'm convinced that it's impossible for us to write about a character without writing about ourselves. The illusion, of course, is that those people on the page aren't us, and in the early stages of the creative process, it's an illusion I'm willing to permit. We all know too well the protest of student writers: "But this really happened." Usually, when beginning writers are trying to faithfully render actual episodes, they are, of course, too close to the material to see it clearly. It becomes important, then, to let those experiential episodes recede into the background so the emotions connected to them can emerge with more clarity and complexity in the characters these writers imagine they are conjuring up from thin air.

I eventually expose my chicanery when I ask students to write essays that examine the sources of their stories. During an in-class writing assignment, I invite students to locate themselves in their fiction. "When you think of your story," I say to them, "what specific moments do you recall from your own lives?" I suggest that a story probably draws on several moments from our pasts, and I emphasize the importance of seeing how many of those moments we can connect with the emotions at work in our fiction. I give them an example by using one of my own stories in which an elderly couple in London become separated when the wife gets on a subway train and the husband doesn't. The relief and fear the nagged-to-exhaustion husband feels at that moment reflects my own feelings of abandonment when I was lost as a child, as well as the concern I have felt many times in my life when I have waited for loved ones to return from journeys. In thinking about my story, I could keep pulling out memory after memory from those I have stored; each one would somehow deepen my empathy for my characters and their dilemmas. In another round of journal entries, I ask my students to visit their own memory warehouses to see what experiences they have relied on for the emotional content of their stories. I want them to investigate the connections they soon discover between themselves and their characters.

By writing about these connections, students enter into a dialogue with their stories. They begin to think critically about themselves and their fiction. The essays they write demonstrate how they have been able to use their fiction as a way of thinking more deeply about themselves and their worlds. These essays also provide students with a better understanding of their characters and their stories. As long as the dialogue between the writers and their fiction is as open and as probing as possible, it usually leads them to some substantial discoveries. As my students converse with their own stories, they fuse the roles of participant and spectator, and, when they do, they gain insight into two texts: their stories, and themselves.

The essays this fusion produces are often powerful testaments to the learning that can take place when the fiction workshop honors the student as text as much as it does the fiction that student produces. Such knowledge is important for all writers, but particularly for less-talented writers since it is often these writers who also need to develop better critical thinking skills. They need to be able to look more closely at themselves and others in order to see ambiguities, conflicting truths, ironies. The ability to see issues clearly is a skill that will serve them well throughout their lives.

Students demonstrate this ability in the essays they write about their stories. One of my students, Jack, discovers something unexpected when he writes about his story and the experiences from his own life that have contributed to it. He realizes that a character he has presented as aloof and uncaring actually draws those qualities from himself. He originally thought that he was basing the character, Nichole, on his aunt, who had been unfaithful to his uncle. The story itself was very sympathetic to Mike, the character based on the uncle, and very judgmental of Nichole. In Jack's essay, he realizes that he has implicated himself in the story in a way he hasn't intended:

> The aspect of coldness in the relationship was based more on relationships I have had, as opposed to being part of the real relationship on which I was basing the story. I was involved in a few relationships in the past year in which I was very cold to the other people involved. I think that the distance between Mike and Nichole is very much from those relationships in my life. The relationship that I constructed within the story had more of my experience in it than I realized when I was writing it.

Later in the essay, he analyzes his own personality as held next to that of Nichole's in the story:

> Nichole's coldness, for the most part, comes from the coldness that I have shown to people I've been involved with in various circumstances. In both cases, the coldness was the result of over-aggressiveness on the other person's part, and my resulting inability to deal with that aggressiveness in a correct way.

Finally, he uses the character of Nichole to articulate an insight he has gained into himself: "In my life I struggle with giving myself to others, and I really see that in Nichole as well." Not only has he used his story to think critically about his own behaviors, he has also mustered some empathy for the character of Nichole, which helps him see her more truthfully and develop her with added dimension when he finally revises the story. The analytical discourse demonstrated in his essay—the fusing of "self" and "other"—displays his ability to think critically about himself *and* his story.

Another student, Mara, looks into the mirror of her story and sees something of the life she is living now, as well as the life she is intending to live. Britton claims that it is possible for us to be spectators of our futures as well as our pasts (102), and that is what Mara does when she writes about her fiction. She discovers a truth as she becomes both spectator and participant while examining the sources of the story. A premed student, she wrote a story about two friends (also pre-med students) and the suicide of one, a suicide she seems to have imposed on the material for its sensational effect, possibly so she might avoid facing the aspects of the story most centered in her own experience. That avoidance, though, is impossible for Mara to continue once she enters into a dialogue with the story. In the resulting essay, she examines some fears and dilemmas connected with her career choice. A single passage from her essay shows her trying to sort through these fears— the first time, she confesses later, that she has been able to articulate these concerns:

> I don't know what medical school, if I get accepted, will bring to my life. I wonder, however, what my ability will be to control my emotions when under pressure not to show them. I have done well so far in my experiences teaching Physiology; my students don't know my deep compassion and repulsion at the killing of these animals, especially when it was me who had to put them in that gas chamber so that they could dissect them for the experimental results we needed. No one knows the queasy feelings in my stomach when I read my parasitology book and see pictures of grotesquely enlarged livers and malshaped and insect-infested eyes, noses, mouths, and other body parts. I don't worry about the feelings so much as I worry whether I will continue to have these feelings. I don't know whether I will lose my compassion and ability to show emotion when it is appropriate or whether I will be so completely attached to some of my patients that their death or failure to recover will just continue to be burden after burden compiling on my already heavy shoulders. I certainly don't want to deal with this fact and upon getting into medical school, I will have to make amends to doing so or face the consequences Billy does in my story.

I should add here that Billy, in the revision of Mara's story, does not commit suicide. Instead, he struggles with alcohol abuse, a problem Mara herself constantly keeps in check. By engaging in an analytical dialogue with her story, she questions her present and its implications for her future. She also revises her story with an eye toward character development rather than manufactured plot effects.

Perhaps an approach to teaching fiction writing that allows students to succeed by demonstrating the ability to think critically about themselves and their worlds may seem to muddy the already murky process of evaluating work in creative writing classes. It may be true that the method requires an even more subjective grading eye, but still I find it rather simple to see my students' progress as critical thinkers. I also see their stories improve, a headway I'm not so sure many students would be able to make in workshops in which their only chances for success would depend on their talents, or lack thereof, as fiction writers.

Like Jack and Mara, many students in my workshops demonstrate little aptitude for writing fiction. Although it would be presumptuous of me to predict their futures, chances are I won't be seeing their stories in *The New Yorker,* or *Story,* or *The Georgia Review.* It's more likely they will make claims for themselves in fields other than fiction writing. But no matter their occupations, like Goldilocks, they will live lives filled with choices and decisions. They will have to make sense of issues and experiences, and, as they did in my fiction workshops, they will constantly move back and forth between the roles of participants and spectators. "We live at the level of our language," says Ellen Gilchrist (1987). "Whatever we can articulate we can imagine or understand or explore" (30). Fiction writing, like expository writing, can offer students opportunities to think with language. I've decided it's important for my workshops to help writers develop the critical thinking skills their lives will continue to require. To me, something about teaching these skills, especially to students who lack the talent they need to be top-notch fiction writers, seems "just right."

Works Cited

Berthoff, Ann. E. 1981. *The Making of Meaning.* Portsmouth, NH: Boynton/Cook.

Britton, James. 1970. *Language and Learning.* Coral Gables, Florida: University of Miami Press.

Gilchrist, Ellen. 1987. *Falling Through Space.* Boston: Little, Brown.

McNeil, Lynda D. 1989. "Logging the Interpretive Act: Dialogue in the Literature Classroom." *College Teaching* 37 (3): 86–90.

Shelnutt, Eve. 1989. "Transforming Experience into Fiction: An Alternative to the Workshop." In *Creative Writing in America: Theory and Pedagogy,* ed. Joseph Moxley, 151–67. Urbana: NCTE.

17

Responding to Creative Writing
Students-as-Teachers and the Executive Summary

Wendy Bishop
Florida State University

When I teach introductory poetry courses, we write into and out of forms in order to generate ideas and text. My students produce many poems, more than I can respond to personally. Yet my students crave such a response on every draft, despite my careful use of small and large peer response groups. And, even if I could respond to every draft, I often find that my overfull, overeducated response can appear too critical and overwhelm the exploratory impulse in student work. This situation is true of any introductory creative writing workshop, organized to explore a single genre or genres broadly. Students in these courses are learning to become better writers, but they also need to become better readers of professional and student texts. I believe they do this by learning to respond to their own work, carefully, making use of peer and teacher responses to take that work through revisions.

The response activities I share in this chapter developed out of my own need to explore the arena of "response to creative writing" in general. Unlike teachers and researchers in composition, creative writers have, in general, spent much more time on canon formation (creating anthologies) and discussions of technique and craft (creating guides that develop rules and prescriptions) than they have on the equally as important issues of response and evaluation. That doesn't surprise me, since responding to beginning texts is difficult, and evaluation of student writing is rarely a pleasurable activity for the dedicated writing teacher.

To address these concerns, I've asked creative writers to take a teacher's role vis-à-vis their texts, in order to:

1. Highlight some of what these students already know about their texts

2. Gain insights into the drafting choices they are making intentionally

3. Put myself into an ally's position, agreeing or disagreeing with or expanding upon what their already-internalized self-as-teacher can tell them

In addition, I've developed an executive summary and revision plan assignment to encourage students to take responsibility for workshop responses. This activity encourages them to make their revisions more mindfully.

Neither of these techniques is an instant panacea, turning beginners into expert practitioners. Still, considering response this way, as a dialogue, allows "learners" some of the free and unjudged space they need to risk real learning and allows me more time to become the student's teacher in the best sense of the word—one who offers invitations into the field.

Students-as-Teachers

Jennifer has just written a poem—an intentional cliché poem, after an in-class invention activity. Like the other members of the class, she brings five copies to her small group for comments the next day. Before groups form, I ask Jennifer and all the students in class to pretend they are the teacher, to sit down and comment on one copy of their own poem. This is the first publicly shared poem of the term. My students look at me in disbelief.

"What do you mean?"

"Like you will? We don't know how you'll grade."

I don't try to explain but encourage them: "I'm not talking about grading, but reading. Pretend you're a teacher. Write on the text, to the student—you."

Having collected these self-responses while the group members continue to offer each other revision advice, I am in a better response space than I was in former semesters. I don't have to guess from the text what my students know or don't know about contemporary poetry. If they use or abuse techniques, I don't have to imagine that practice-equals-person; instead I hear students-as-teachers offering me insights into what they do know whether it appears in the text or not.

In the right-hand margin of Figure 17–1, you'll read Jennifer's self-response. To the left of the poem, you'll find my written reactions: I respond to her responses and place an endnote just below the text.

Jennifer looks at repetition and has ideas for pruning the text. I am able to encourage this—agreeing with her impulse to cut—and telling her what I

Figure 17–1

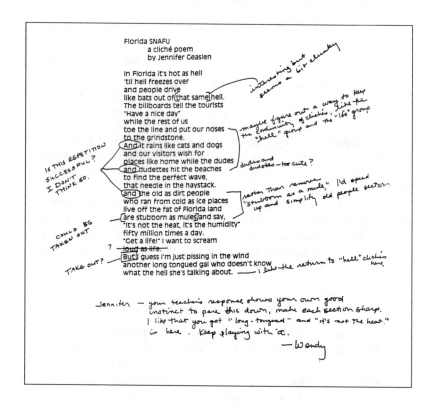

like. Then I find space to make two major suggestions. In doing this, I do not feel I am overwhelming her poem, rather I am responding in the spirit of her own "change-based" remarks. We are in a dialogue. Jennifer, who was new to writing poems, already had an internalized "teacher's voice" that she could call on to give her ideas for improving her work. She needed a method for accessing this voice. By responding to herself as a teacher, she found out what she already knew.

Matthew, whose poem appears in Figure 17–2, was an English major with a much stronger grounding in writing and poetry. In his case, asking him to be "teacher" revealed his investment in the text he had created. In fact, he wrote enough on his text, including an end comment, that my responses were thoroughly taken up with his. When I asked him to take our dialogue one step farther, writing me a note in response to my response, I learned that it would have done me little good to push for further revision of the poem draft since he felt it was "done," and he backed up this feeling with reasons that he was able to articulate. In the figure, the handwritten comments are Matthew's own. I've noted my responses at the end of the poem, including an indication of the line I responded to.

When Matthew comments on "dark sweet oblivion" as a neat image (a response I don't agree with—since I find it clichéd), I respond to his self-response with: "Doesn't seem the same as the rest of the poem, tonally, though." In saying this, I change my response from judgment (clichéd) to analysis (how the language differs in sections of the poem). When Matthew comments "not really answered, no change" to the last three lines of the poem, I push against his apparent acceptance of those lines and incorporate that push in a short endnote, my total response to his detailed self-analysis:

> Matthew, Good observation. Pivotal for the revision of this poem. Are you going to follow your own suggestions? —Wendy

Matthew's response to my response, for me, highlights the benefits of this student-as-teacher dialogue:

Figure 17–2

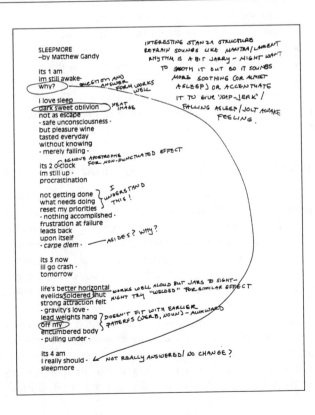

Well, I have made some changes (I'll submit a copy sometime soon). I agree "dark sweet oblivion" doesn't quite gel with the rest of the language of the piece, *but I like it so much, I'm keeping it as is.* I've made minor corrections (the asides make more sense as interior-monologue commentary). *However my intention was* for the questions to remain unanswered— the poem is at best a "temporary epiphany." It also is *not the strongest piece I've ever written* and it is not important enough to me to totally deconstruct it (which would likely take to make it substantially better). So, after these current corrections are reviewed, *I'm finished with it.* [emphasis mine]

Reading our dialogue, I (re)learn lessons that are all too easy to ignore from my "teacher-position" in the classroom. Matthew writes because he likes language, so telling him "dark sweet oblivion" is clichéd will be an ineffective act, uselessly challenging his taste and investment. Matthew also makes clear distinctions between his own stronger and weaker work and decides how much revision time is worth the effort. Matthew's remarks let me see that he had been involved to the point of making "corrections," but he knows "revision" will take more time than he's willing to give this poem. To push him would have been a poor use of my teaching time. In fact, he's shown me elements of his learning process that I would hope for from a serious course of study of poetry writing: he can estimate the worth of his own text and the usefulness of exploring further work on it. Together, we should proceed to other poems.

When we respond to poems in the context of a full-class workshop, I move to the use of an executive summary since I believe students like Matthew do need to take the time to learn from revision. They can choose which poem to set aside sometimes, but the course is also designed to ask them to push onward with revision at other times.

Writer's Executive Summary and Revision Plan

When a full-class response workshop backfires, it's discouraging. This occurs when students tell me that they received so many contradictory responses they didn't know where to begin revising. Sometimes writers say they heard one thing from the workshop and I distinctly remember the "message" of our total comments quite differently, or they overvalue my remarks and ignore useful peer comments. Surely, it is a stressful (though beneficial) moment for a writer when twelve to twenty-five peers and a teacher respond to a text.

To produce an executive summary and revision plan, I ask students to take peer responses home, to tabulate those responses, and to write an exploratory paragraph deciding how they plan to use (or ignore) workshop responses in their next draft. I've used this method in many variations—from compiling the responses myself, in order to learn what written comments really appeared on peer texts, to asking students to write executive summaries after small-group work and revision plans before they left class, in order not to forget what groups suggested. Currently, I orchestrate a full-group response session in an introductory class in this way:

1. All writers submit a poem with their own most important questions about the poem typed at the bottom. Their questions guide the workshop response.

2. Class members purchase a copy of class poems at a local copy shop, read and annotate the poems, and return to class prepared to discuss the text.

3. The poet reads the poem and we listen.

4. The poet chooses the first respondent. After this, we use a rotating chair model—the last speaker recognizes the next speaker.

5. I do not comment on the poem, instead I make a running transcript of the workshop comments, always finding that just as I'm bursting to comment, another class member will bring up the point I want to make.

6. After our allotted time is over, we return annotated copies of the poem to the poet. I give the poet my workshop transcript.

7. The author takes these comments home, writes up a summary with tabulations (how many respondents said what, in general) and a revision plan.

8. I collect a copy of the executive summary and revision plan. If I wish, I can check off those class comments I most agree with and encourage the poet to follow particular parts of his or her revision plan.

9. The poet revises.

10. I see the revision in the final portfolio unless we have a small-group response session devoted to looking at the changes the poet made.

Here is a sample of a revision plan. In this case, the class did not push the writer as far as it might have, but he chooses, through his self-analysis, to push himself. After tabulating responses, Jeff Matthews discusses revisions for his poem "The Wife of Bath":

> The vast majority of class comments on "Wife of Bath" were very positive. Many classmates found my images vivid and commented that they could actually "see" the person I was portraying.
>
> However, the class comments also directed my attention to several "trouble spots" in the poem. Several students had trouble with my use of "Mustang" in lines 5 and 8—they could not tell if I was referring to the

horse or to the car. In my revised version, I make it plain that I am comparing the "wife" to the car. A few classmates also saw the word "beriddled" in line 6 as being awkward. I hope "awash" in the revised version flows more effectively. Finally punctuation was called for to clear up confusion between the lines. I followed the advice.

On the other hand, several students had problems with lines, that, in my mind, were not trouble spots. The narrator's point of view seemed unclear to some people. This problem surfaced in lines 1 and 10. In line 1 there was confusion as to whom the "my" was referring. The "my" was referring to the narrator who was creating a portrait of the "wife." Just because the narrator does not refer to himself again in the poem, it does not mean that "my" was a typo or that his point of view is not present in the rest of the poem. Finally, many classmates felt that the last line did not fit with the rest of the poem and that it should be dropped. While I admit that it does not seem akin in nature to the other lines, I believe that it is a great line, nonetheless, and I refuse to delete it.

Jeff, like many students writing revision plans, has actually jumped in and written the revision and is narrating his plans, what he did and what he felt the results were. I don't mind when this happens, since planning and doing are so interwoven for most writers. And, as in Matthew Gandy's student-as-teacher response, Jeff has clearly indicated where he feels flexible and inflexible in the revision process. I find these discussions invaluable when a poet like Jeff comes for a conference about his poem. Instead of pushing on him to drop or change the last line, as I might have formerly, I can ask him to explore his investment in it; together we can talk about important issues like what—to this writer—constitutes a "great line" and why he feels his poems need to end with such a line even when the line "does not seem akin in nature to the other lines."

For me, broadening response options through student-as-teacher and executive summary activities performs two invaluable acts. Each activity encourages writer autonomy, authority, and ownership of a text and each puts the writer and me into a profitable dialogue about writing. At the same time, I find responding to creative texts more pleasurable since I'm in the position of agreeing or disagreeing or further exploring writers' stated positions rather than having to create those positions for them. No longer do I have to "invent" each writer, a heavy duty, indeed, for the writing teacher. Instead, I help the writers revise their developing personas and processes. I'm guessing there are many more ways to respond creatively to creative writing, and I'm eager to spend time finding them, for, as my students become better readers, I become a better—and happier—reader, too.

Contributors

Wendy Bishop's recent books include *Elements of Alternative Style: Essays on Writing and Revision* (Boynton/Cook, 1997) and *Teaching Lives: Essays and Stories* (Utah State, 1997). She coedited *Colors of a Different Horse: Rethinking Creative Writing Theory and Pedagogy* (NCTE, 1994) and *Genre and Writing: Issues, Arguments, Alternatives* (Boynton/Cook, 1997) with Hans Ostrom, and coauthored *Metro: A Guide to Writing Creatively* (Longman, forthcoming 1998) with Ostrom and Katherine Haake.

Patrick Bizzaro teaches creative writing at East Carolina University in Greenville, North Carolina, where he currently serves as Director of Graduate Studies. He is the author of *Dream Garden: The Poetic Vision of Fred Chappell* (LSU, 1997) and *The Harcourt Brace Guide to Writing in the Disciplines* (Harcourt, 1997), as well as numerous poems in magazines and articles in scholarly journals.

John Boe is a lecturer in English at the University of California at Davis, where he also directs the campus writing center. He is author of *Messiness is Next to Goddessness and Other Essays* (Chiron Press) and editor of *Writing on the Edge*. He performs frequently as a professional storyteller.

Alys Culhane is Assistant Professor of English at Coastal Carolina University in Conway, South Carolina. She has contributed articles to *Elements of Alternative Style* and *The Wisconsin English Journal*, and her journalism, fiction, poetry, and creative nonfiction have appeared in a variety of publications.

Since 1983 **Toby Fulwiler** has directed the writing program at the University of Vermont, where he teaches undergraduate and graduate courses in writing. He coedited *When Writing Teachers Teach Literature* (Boynton/Cook, 1996) with Art Young and is the author of *The Blair Handbook* (Boynton/Cook, 1997), *College Writing* (Boynton/Cook, 1997), *The Working Writer* (Prentice Hall, 1995), and *Teaching With Writing* (Boynton/Cook, 1987).

Sheryl I. Fontaine teaches at California State University, Fullerton, where she is also the coordinator of the writing center and the composition courses.

Muriel Harris is Professor of English and Director of the Writing Lab at Purdue University, where she edits the *Writing Lab Newsletter* and oversees the development of the writing lab's OWL (Online Writing Lab: http:// owl.english.purdue.edu. She has authored several books, including her brief grammar handbook, now in its third edition, *The Prentice Hall Reference*

Guide to Grammar and Usage (1997). Her numerous articles, book chapters, and conference presentations on writing center theory, practice, and pedagogy reflect her long-held and unshakeable conviction that one-on-one tutorial interaction is a superb environment in which to help students grow and develop as writers.

Will Hochman directs the writing center at the University of Southern Colorado. His book of poems, *Stranger Within,* was published by the Mellen Poetry Press.

George T. Karnezis is Associate Professor of English at North Central College in Naperville, Illinois, where he has taught introductory and advanced composition, along with graduate classes in public discourse. He directs North Central's writing center and is currently working on the development of cross-disciplinary writing courses.

Lee Martin is Assistant Professor of English at the University of North Texas and the fiction editor of *American Literary Review*. His collection of stories, *The Least You Need to Know* (Sarabande Books, 1997), was the winner of the Mary McCarthy Prize in Short Fiction.

Hans Ostrom is the author of *Three to Get Ready* (Cliffhanger, 1991), a novel, and has published poetry and fiction in a variety of magazines, including *Redbook, Ploughshares,* and *Poetry Northwest*. In 1994 he was a Fulbright Senior Lecturer at Uppsala University at Sweden, and he is currently Professor of English at the University of Puget Sound in Tacoma, Washington.

Francie Quaas is a composition instructor at California State University, Fullerton; Rancho Santiago College in Santa Ana, California; and Citrus College in Glendora, California.

Kate Ronald is Roger and Joyce L. Howe Professor of English and Business Administration at Miami University, Ohio. Her publications include articles in *Rhetoric Review* and *The Journal of Advanced Composition*; with Hephzibah Roskelly, she is coeditor of *Farther Along: Transforming Dichotomies* (Boynton/Cook 1990) and *Reason to Believe: Romanticism, Pragmatism, and the Possibility of Teaching.*

Hephzibah Roskelly teaches at the University of North Carolina-Greensboro, where she directs the composition program and teaches courses in rhetoric and composition and American literature. Her master's thesis was a collection of short stories entitled *Woman With Child*. She recently finished collaborating with Kate Ronald on *Reason to Believe* and is currently collaborating on a novel.

David Starkey has published several books of poetry and several hundred poems in literary magazines. His articles on teaching writing and literature appear in a number of journals and in *Colors of a Different Horse: Rethinking*

Creative Writing Theory and Pedagogy (NCTE). With Richard Guzman, he is coeditor of the forthcoming *Smokestacks and Skyscrapers: An Anthology of Chicago Literature* (Loyola, 1998).

Michael Steinberg teaches writing at Michigan State University. His most recent book, *Those Who Do, Can: Teachers Writing, Writers Teaching* (with Robert L. Root, Jr.), was published in 1997 by NCTE. Currently he is completing a collection of memoirs and personal essays, and coediting (also with Robert Root) *The Fourth Genre: Contemporary Writers of/on Creative Nonfiction*.

John Paul Tassoni is Assistant Professor of English at Miami University, Middletown. His work in pedagogy has appeared in *Social Issues in the English Classroom* (NCTE, 1992), *Ecofeminist Literary Criticism* (Illinois), and *Teaching English in the Two Year College*. With Gail Tayko, he edited *Sharing Pedagogies: Students and Teachers Write About Dialogic Practices* (Boynton/Cook, 1997).

Art Young is Campell Chair in Technical Communication, Professor of English and Professor of Engineering at Clemson University. He coordinates Clemson's communication-across-the-curriculum program, an initiative to integrate written, oral, visual, and electronic communications into courses throughout the curriculum. His most recent coedited books are *When Writing Teachers Teach Literature: Bringing Writing to Reading* (Boynton/Cook, 1995) and *Critical Theory and the Teaching of Literature* (NCTE, 1996). He has served as a consultant in writing across the curriculum to more than fifty colleges and universities in the United States and Europe.